# PAYSAGES ET INTÉRIEURS

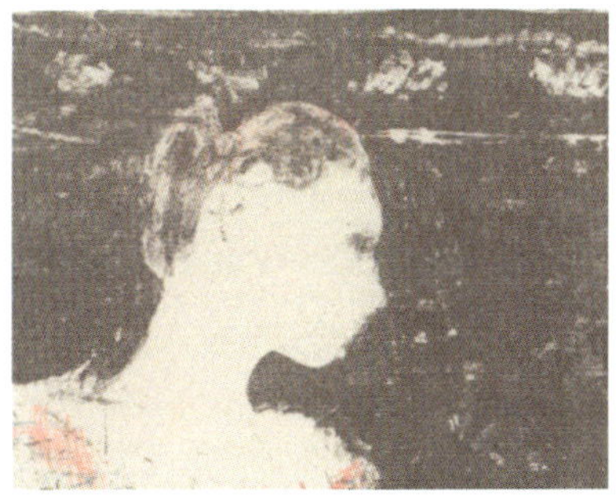

# LANDSCAPES AND INTERIORS

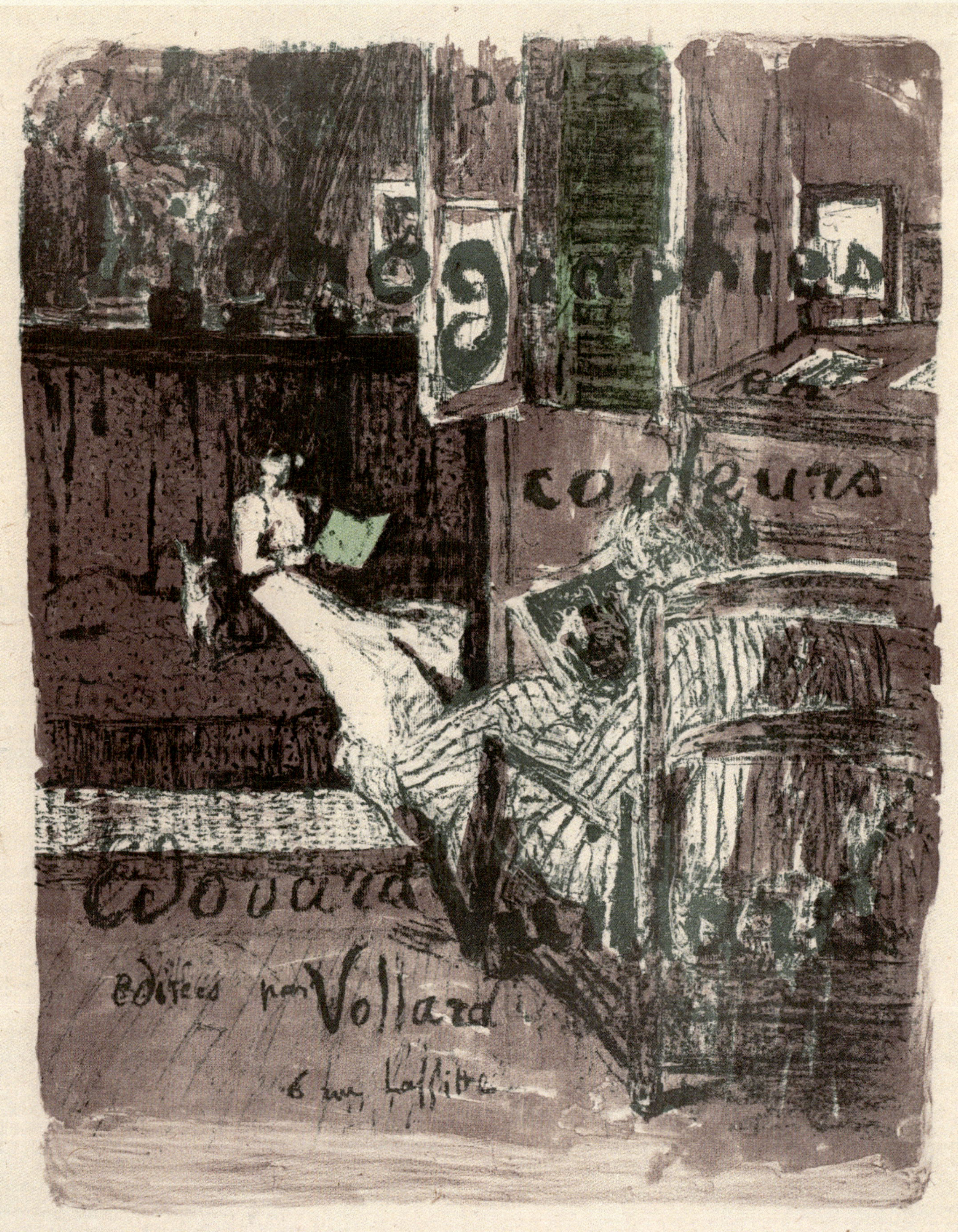

Deux
graphie en
couleurs
Bonnard
Editées par Vollard
6 rue Laffitte

# Paysages et intérieurs

## *Landscapes and Interiors*

### Édouard Vuillard

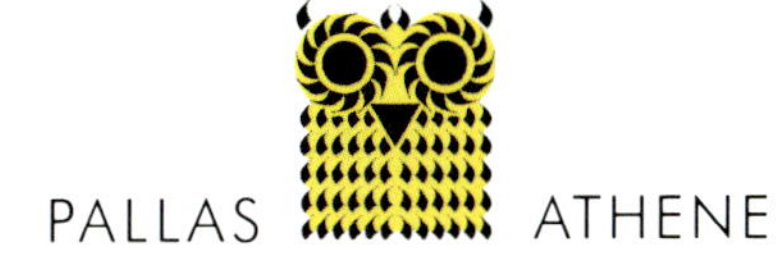

I.

La partie de dames
*The Game of Checkers*


330 x 257 mm

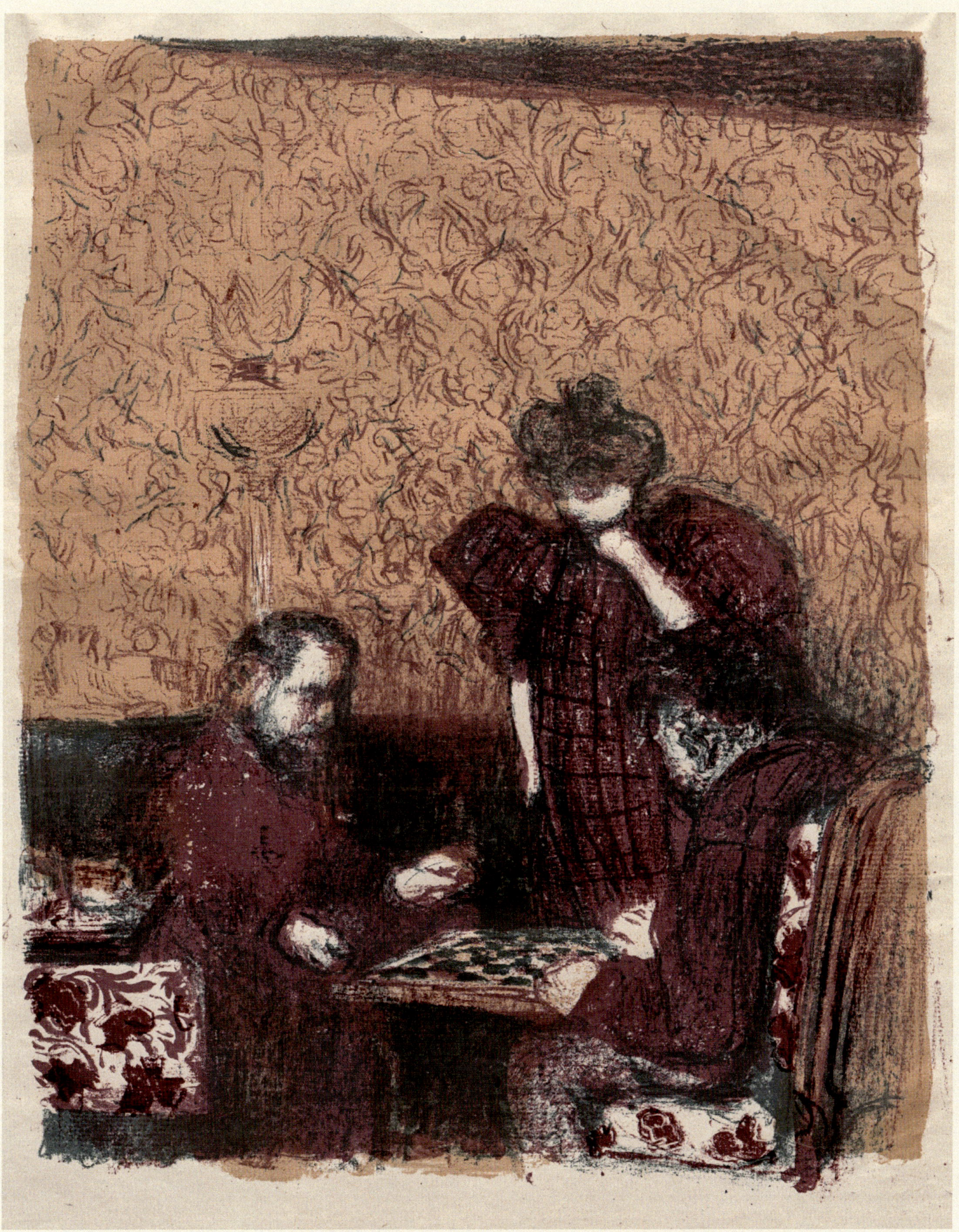

2.

L'Avenue

*The Avenue*

311 x 414 mm

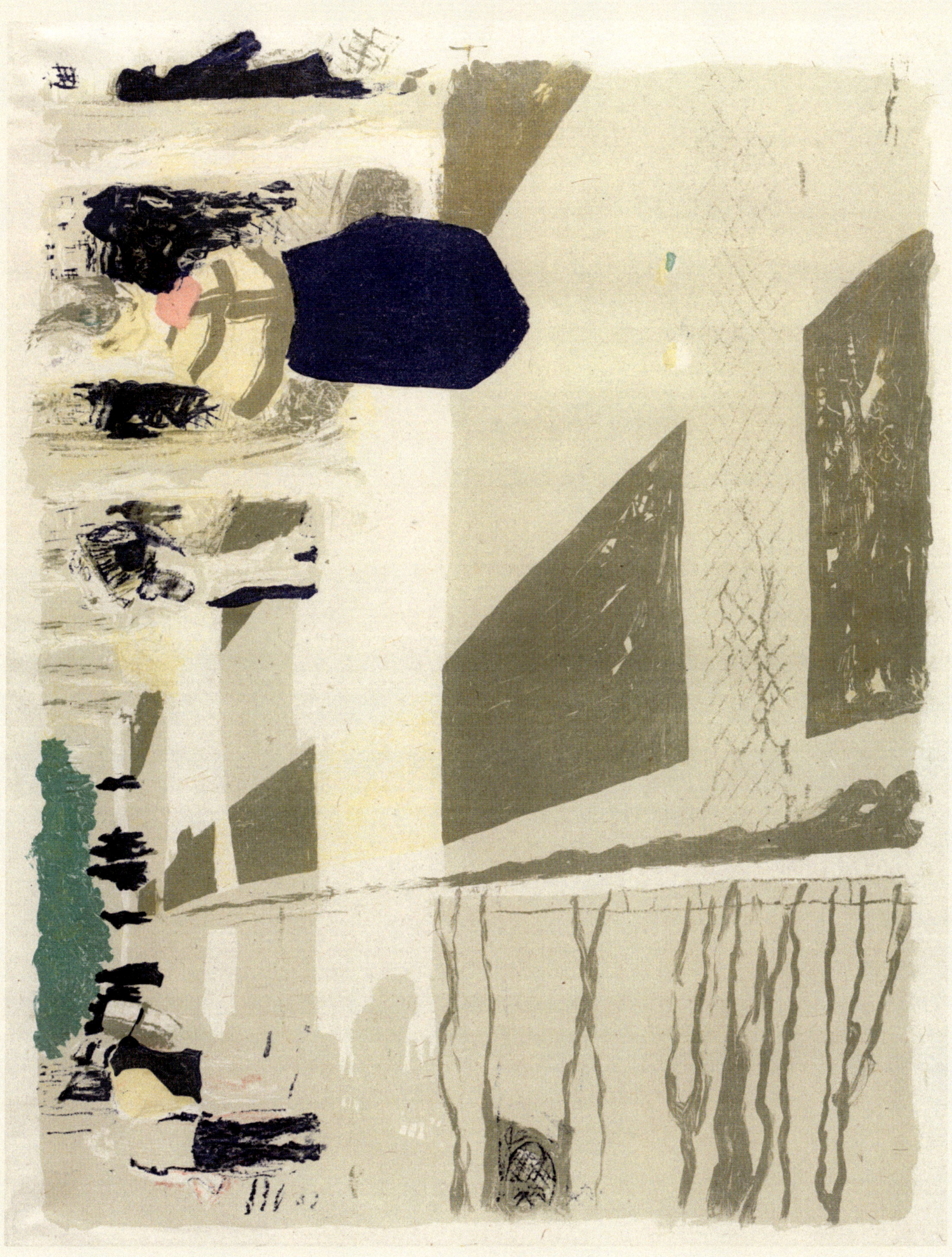

3.
À travers champs
*Across the Fields*

260 x 345 mm

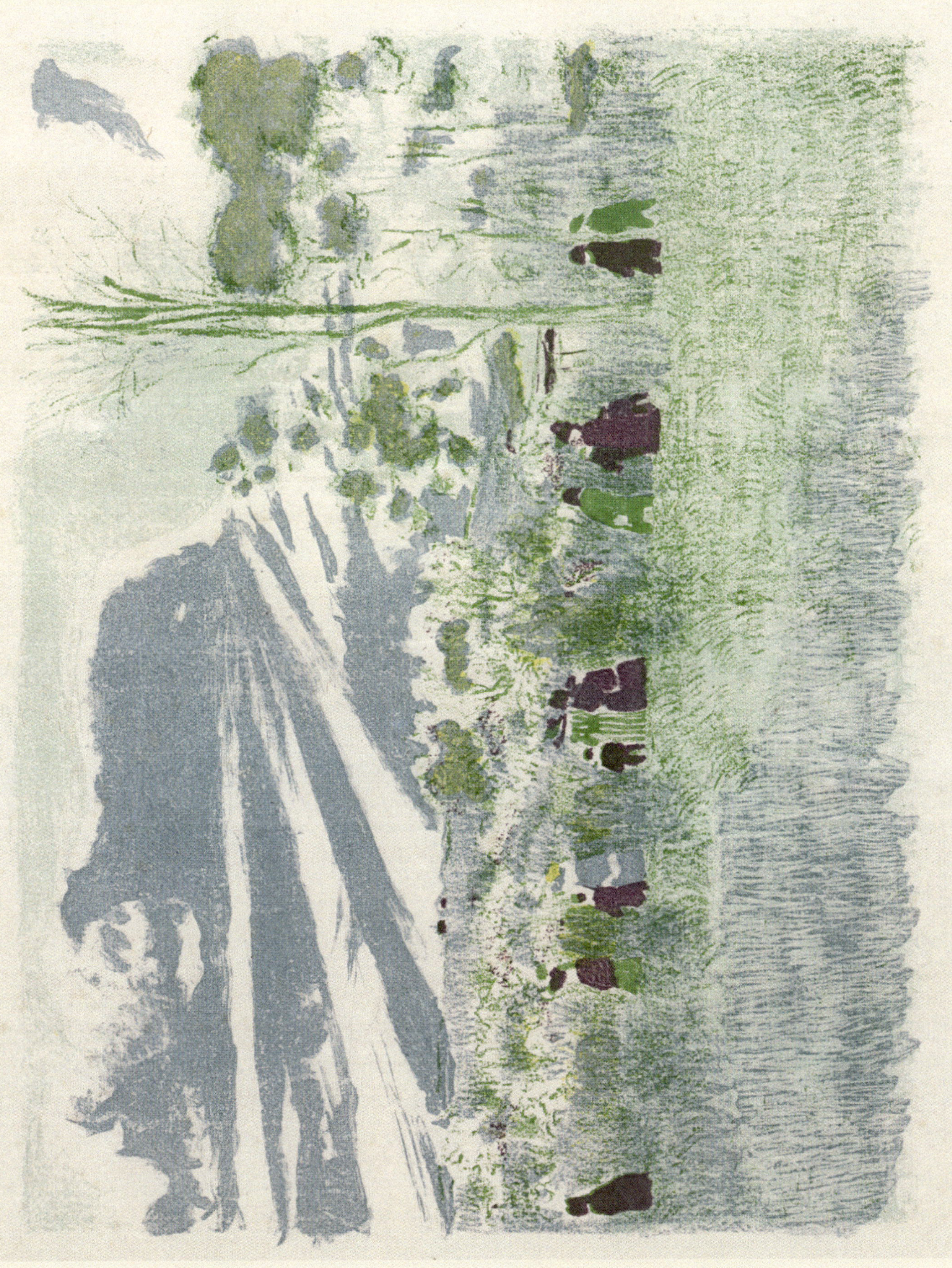

4.
Intérieur à la suspension
*Interior with Ceiling Lamp*

356 x 282 mm

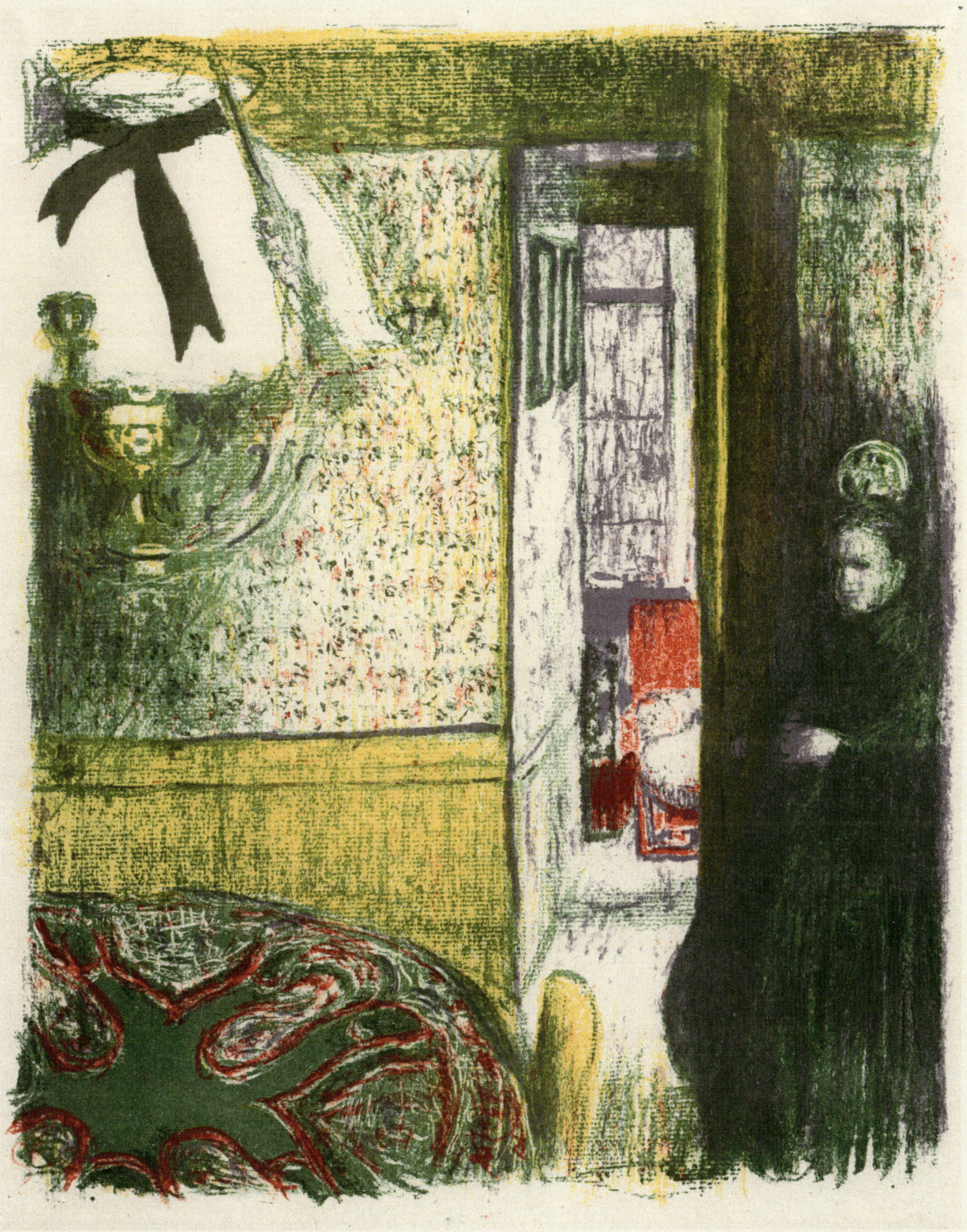

5.
Intérieur aux tentures roses I
*Interior with Pink Wallpaper I*

354 x 278 mm

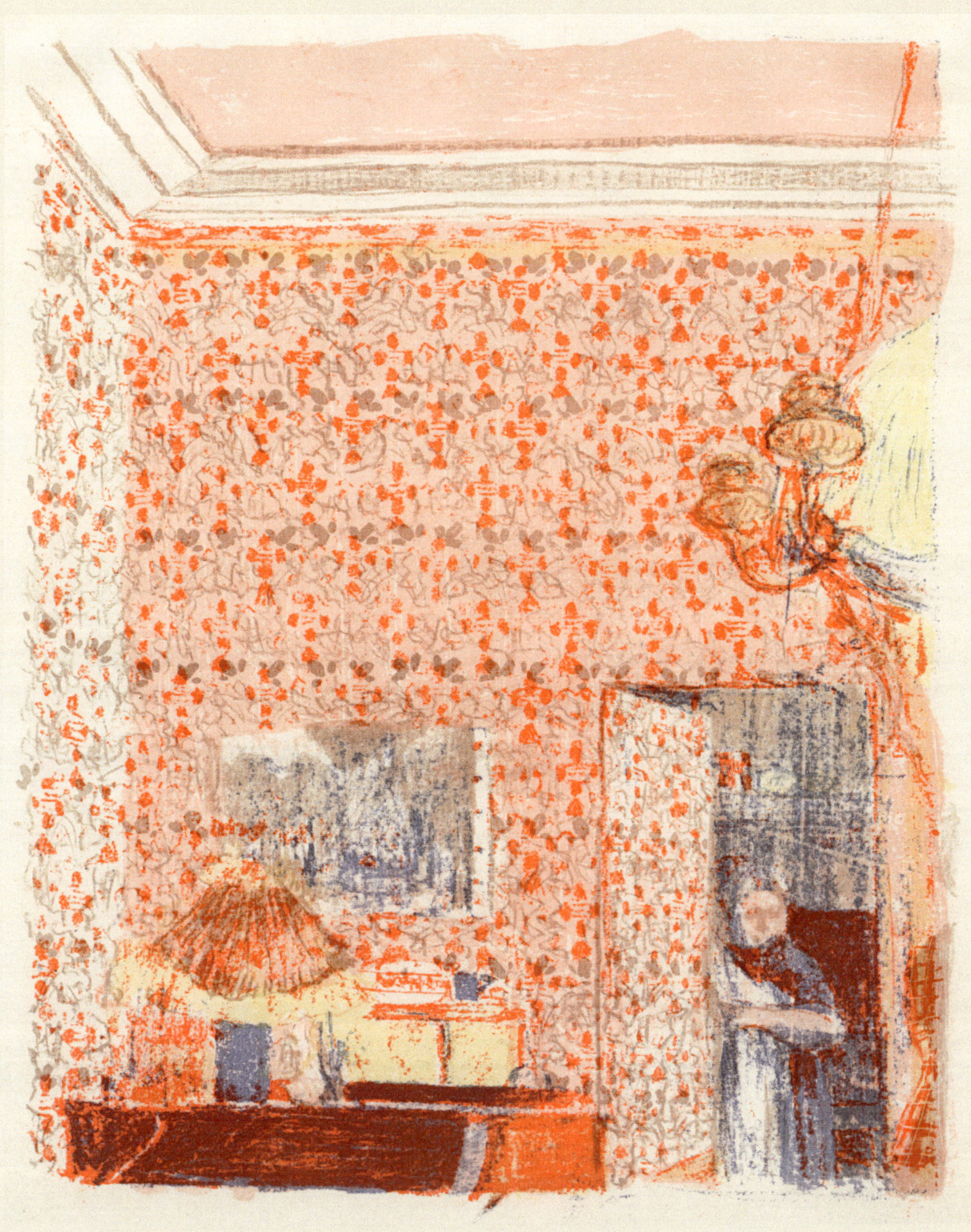

6.
Intérieur aux tentures roses II
*Interior with Pink Wallpaper II*

346 x 282 mm

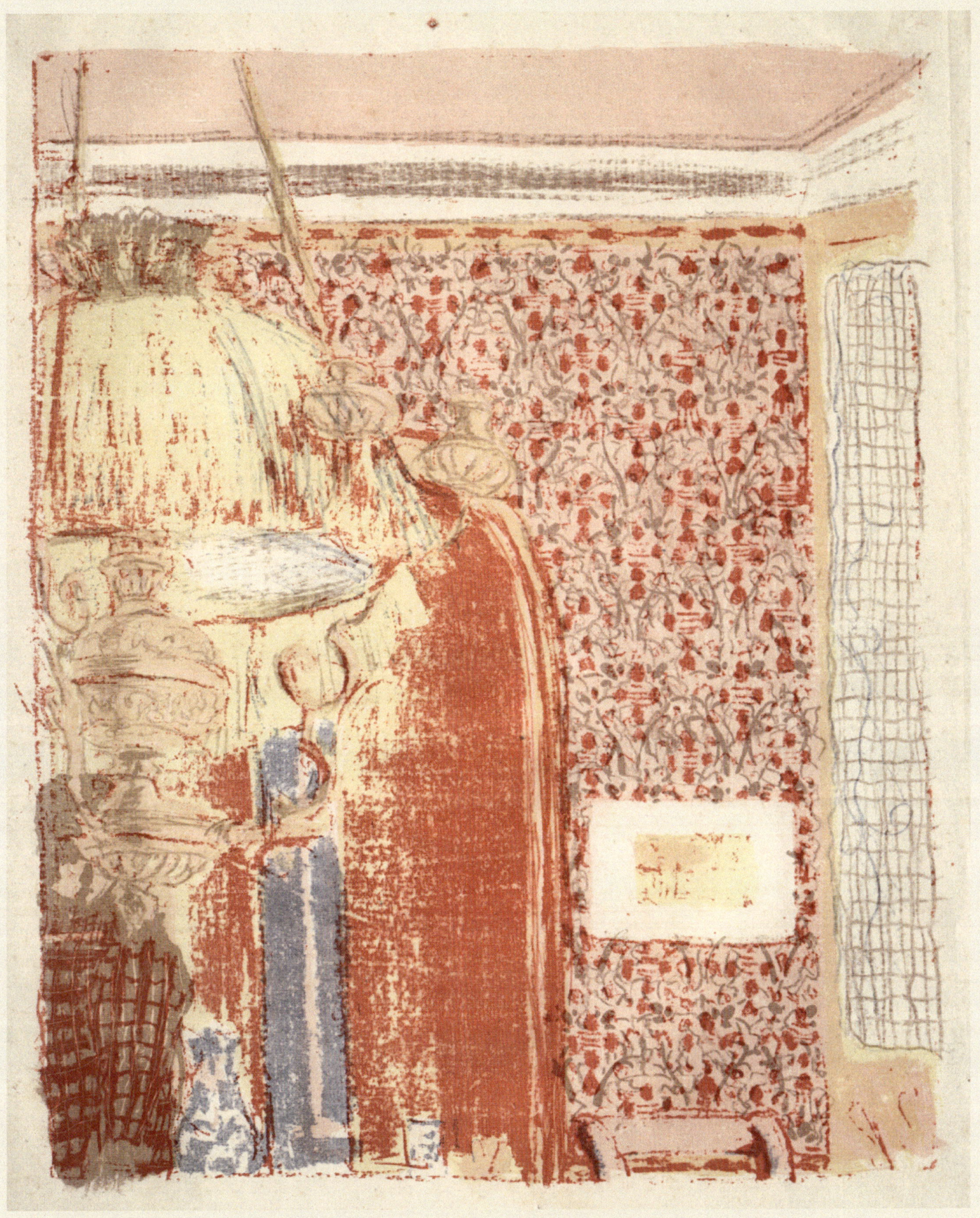

7.

Intérieur aux tentures roses III
*Interior with Pink Wallpaper III*

342 x 273 mm

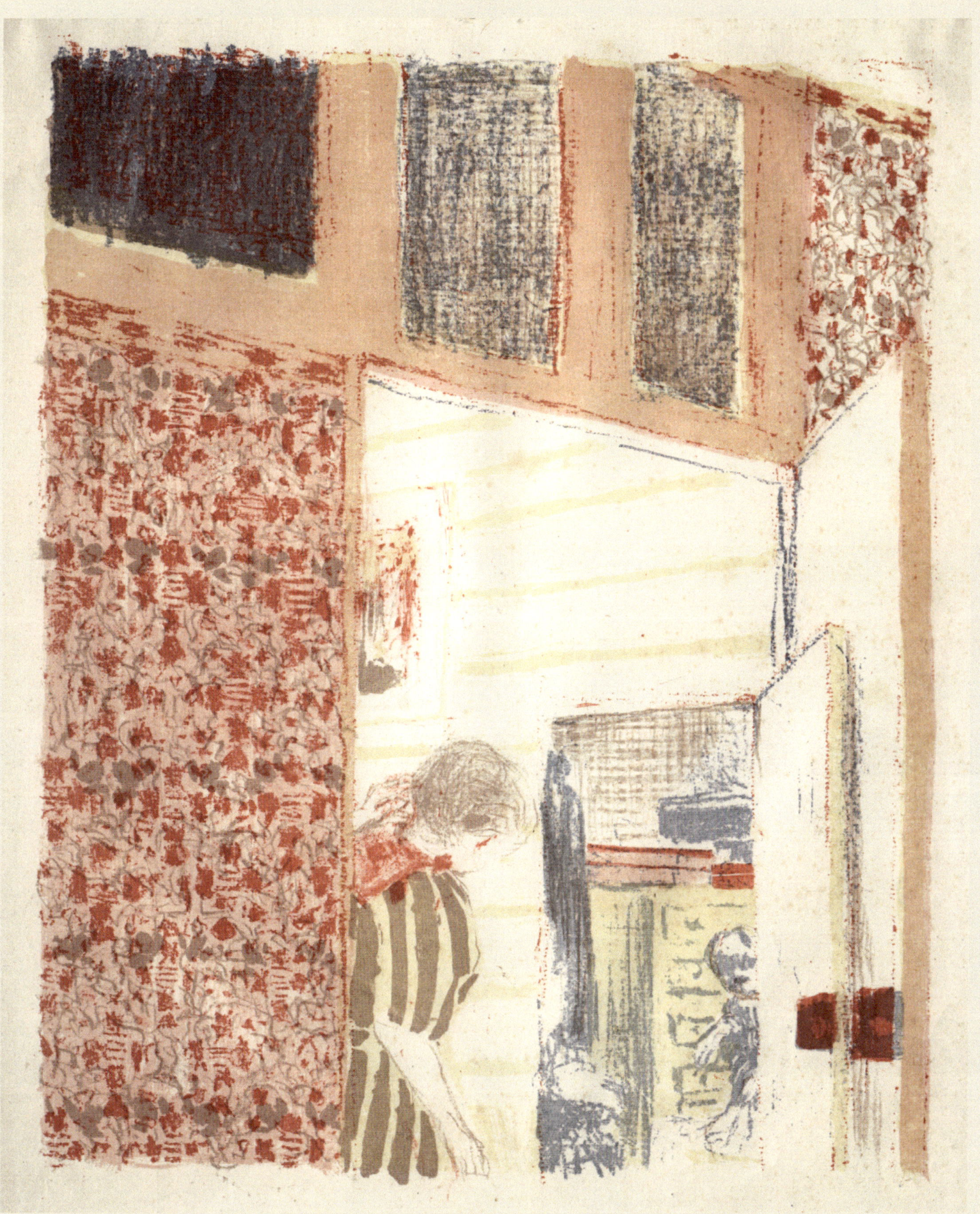

8.

L'Âtre

*The Hearth*

343 x 277 mm

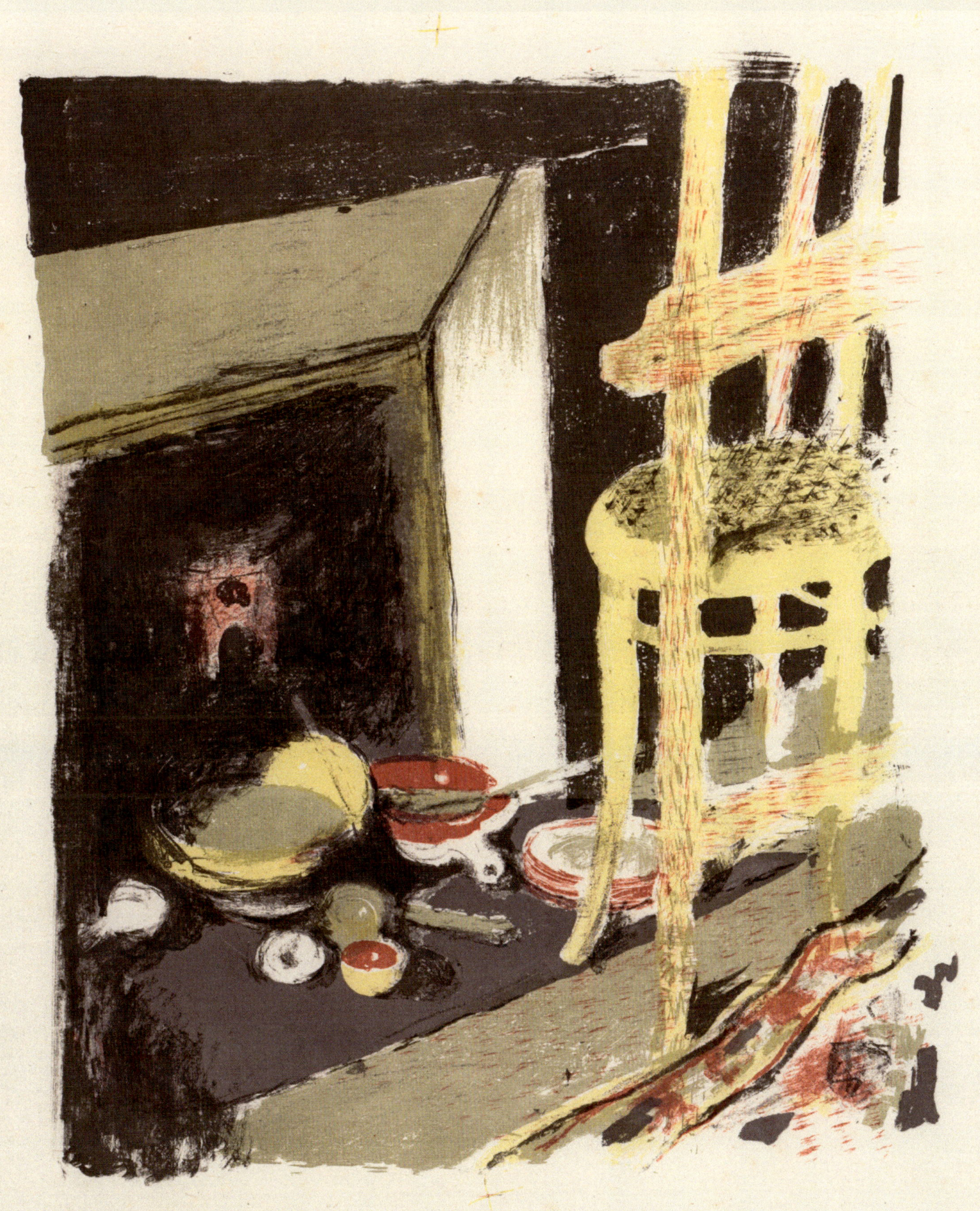

9.
Sur le pont de l'Europe
*On the Pont de l'Europe*

343 x 277 mm

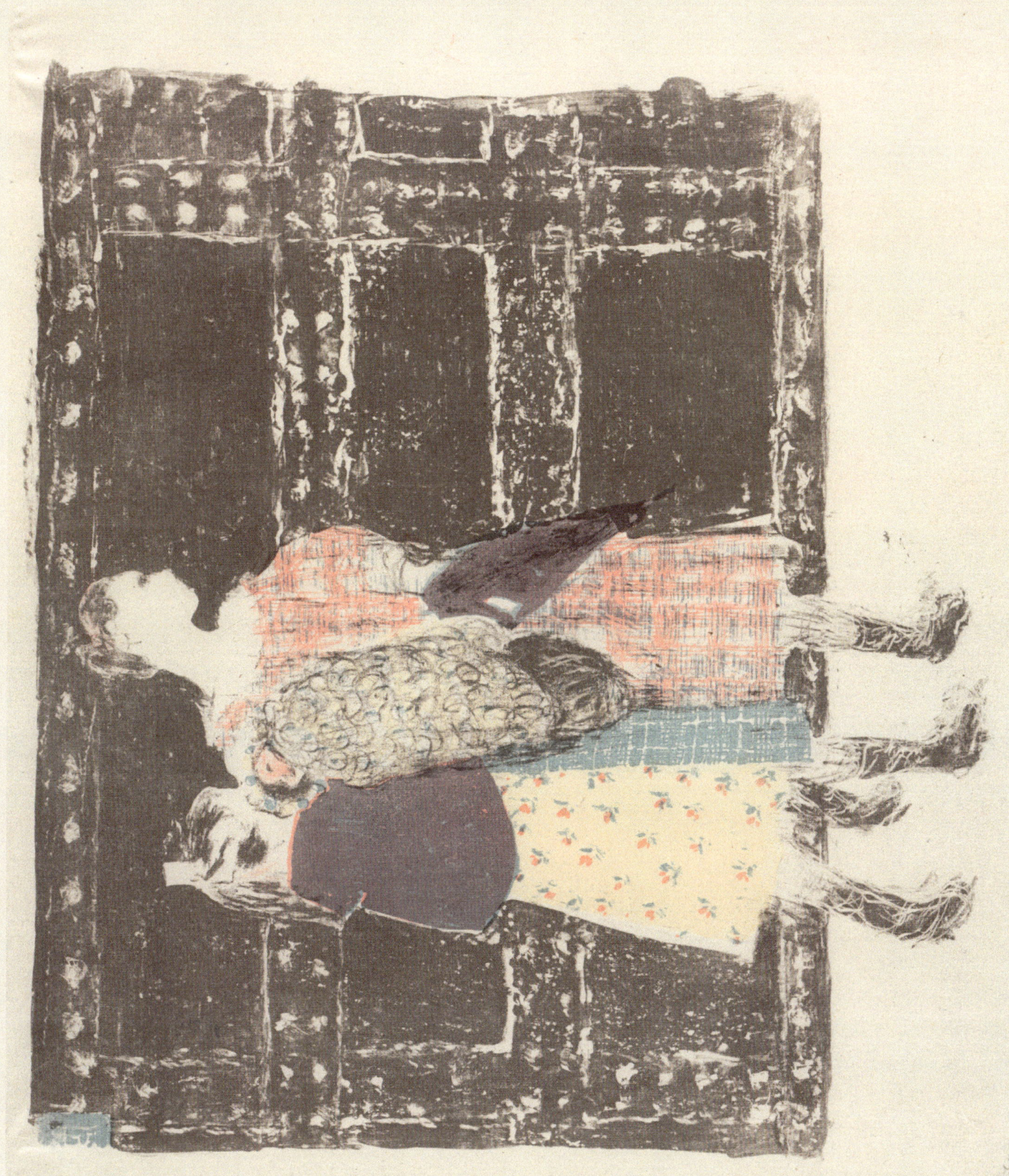

10.
La Pâtisserie
*The Pastry Shop*

351 x 275 mm

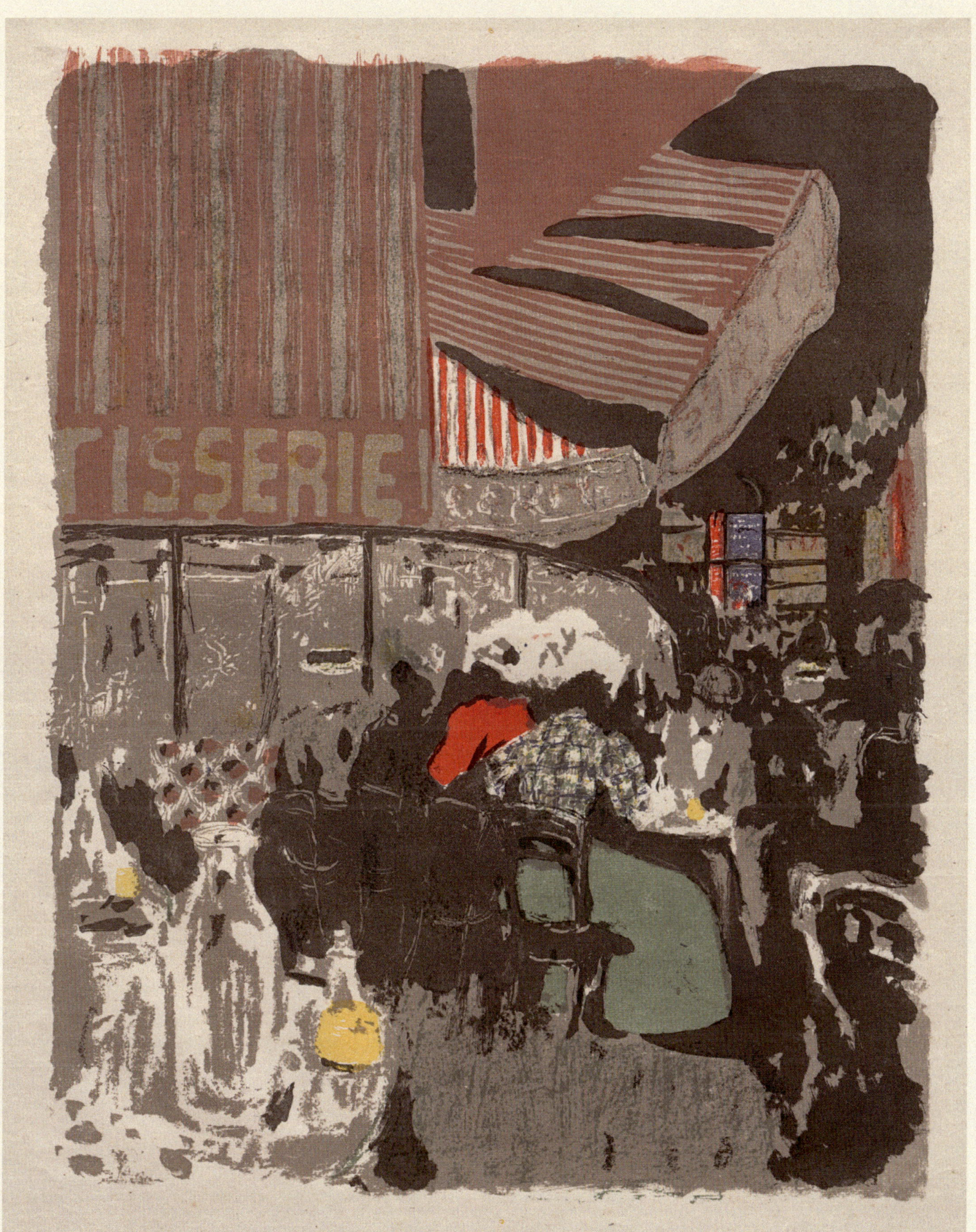
TISSERIE

II.

La Cuisinière (la mère de l'artiste)
*The Cook (the artist's mother)*

350 x 277 mm

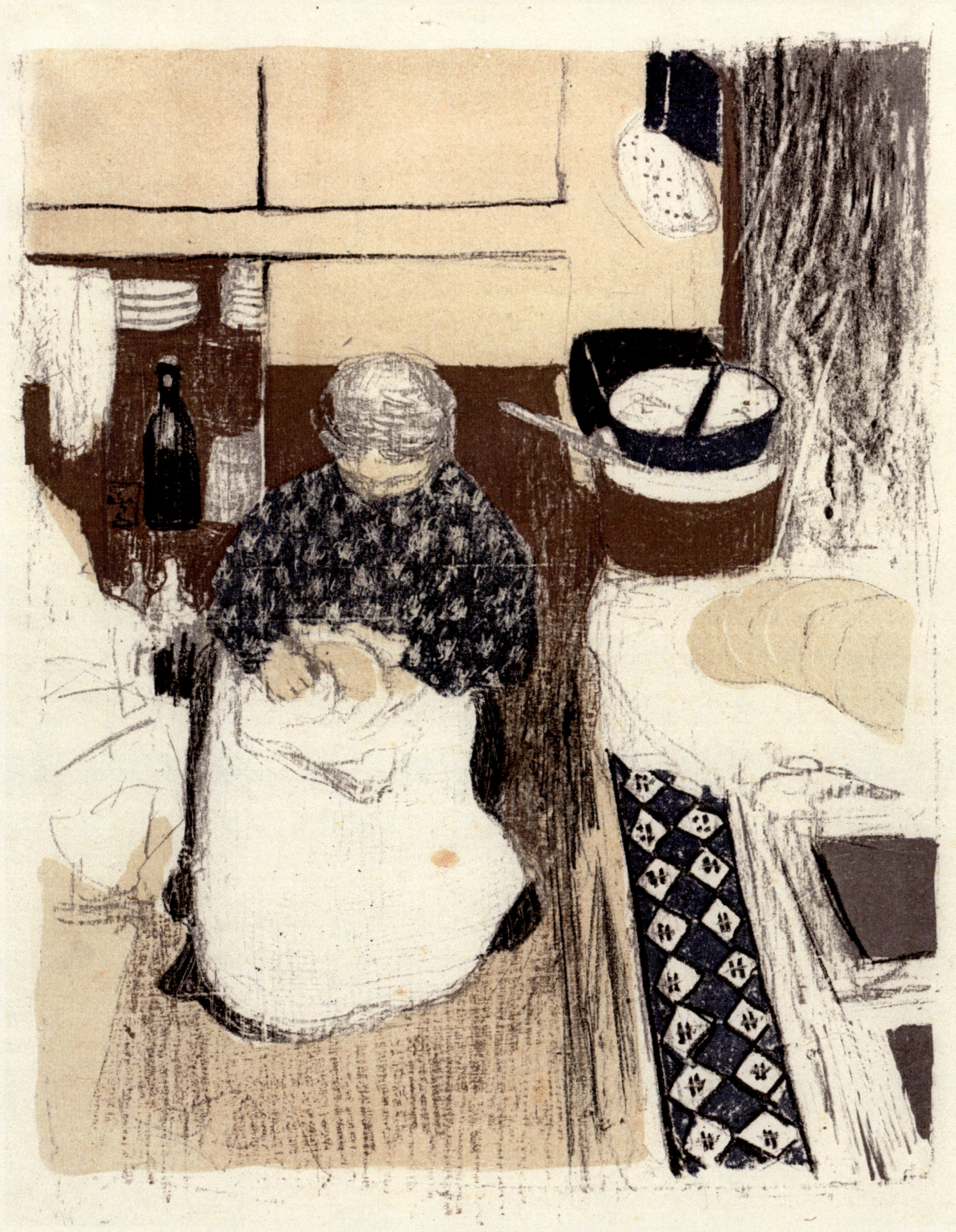

12.
Les deux belles-sœurs
*The Two Sisters-in-Law*

368 x 294 mm

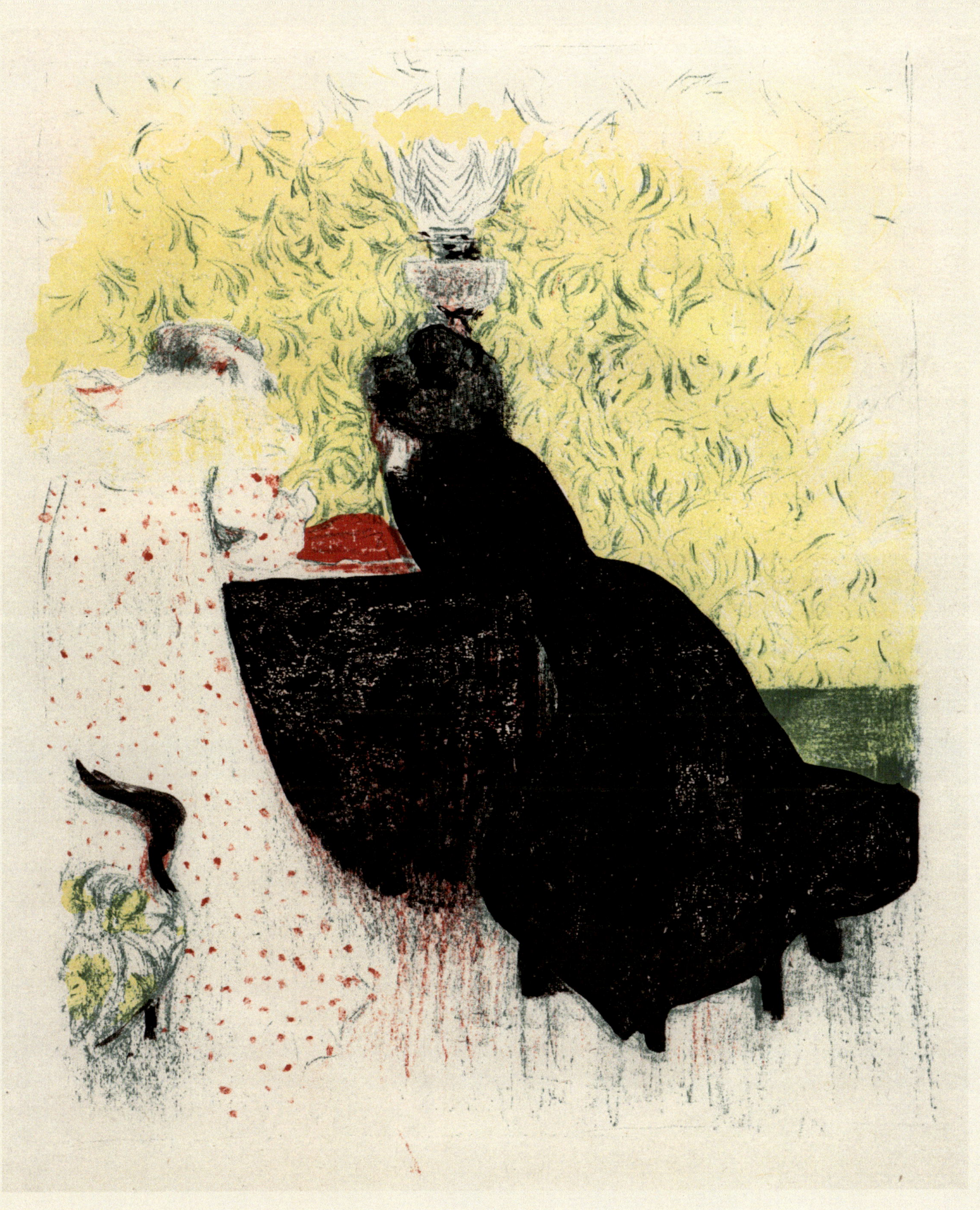

PAYSAGES ET INTÉRIEURS/
LANDSCAPES AND INTERIORS
Suite de 12 planches et une couverture,
imprimée par Auguste Clot. Éditée à
Paris par Ambroise Vollard en 1899,
et tirée à 100 exemplaires./
*Suite of 12 plates and a cover, printed
by Auguste Clot. Published in Paris by
Ambroise Vollard in 1899, in an edition
of 100 copies.*

Cette édition/*This edition*
© Pallas Athene (Publishers) Ltd,
London, 2026

Pallas Athene (Publishers) Ltd,
2 Birch Close, London N19 5XD

**www.pallasathene.co.uk**

ISBN 978 1 84368 299 8 (édition française)
ISBN 978 1 84368 298 1 (English edition)

Imprimé en Angleterre par Blissetts/
*Printed in England by Blissetts*

3

# PAYSAGES ET INTÉRIEURS

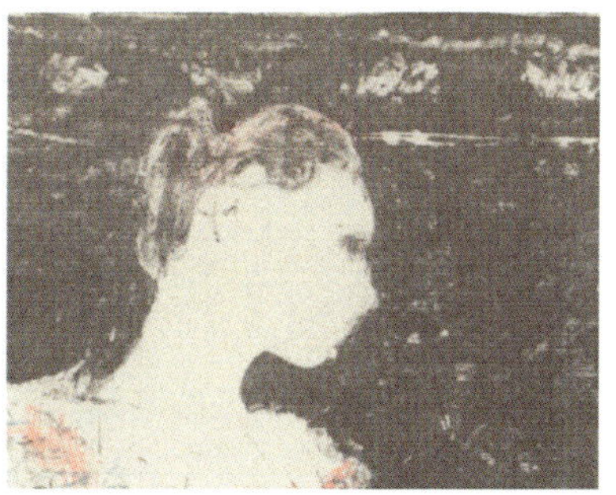

# LANDSCAPES AND INTERIORS

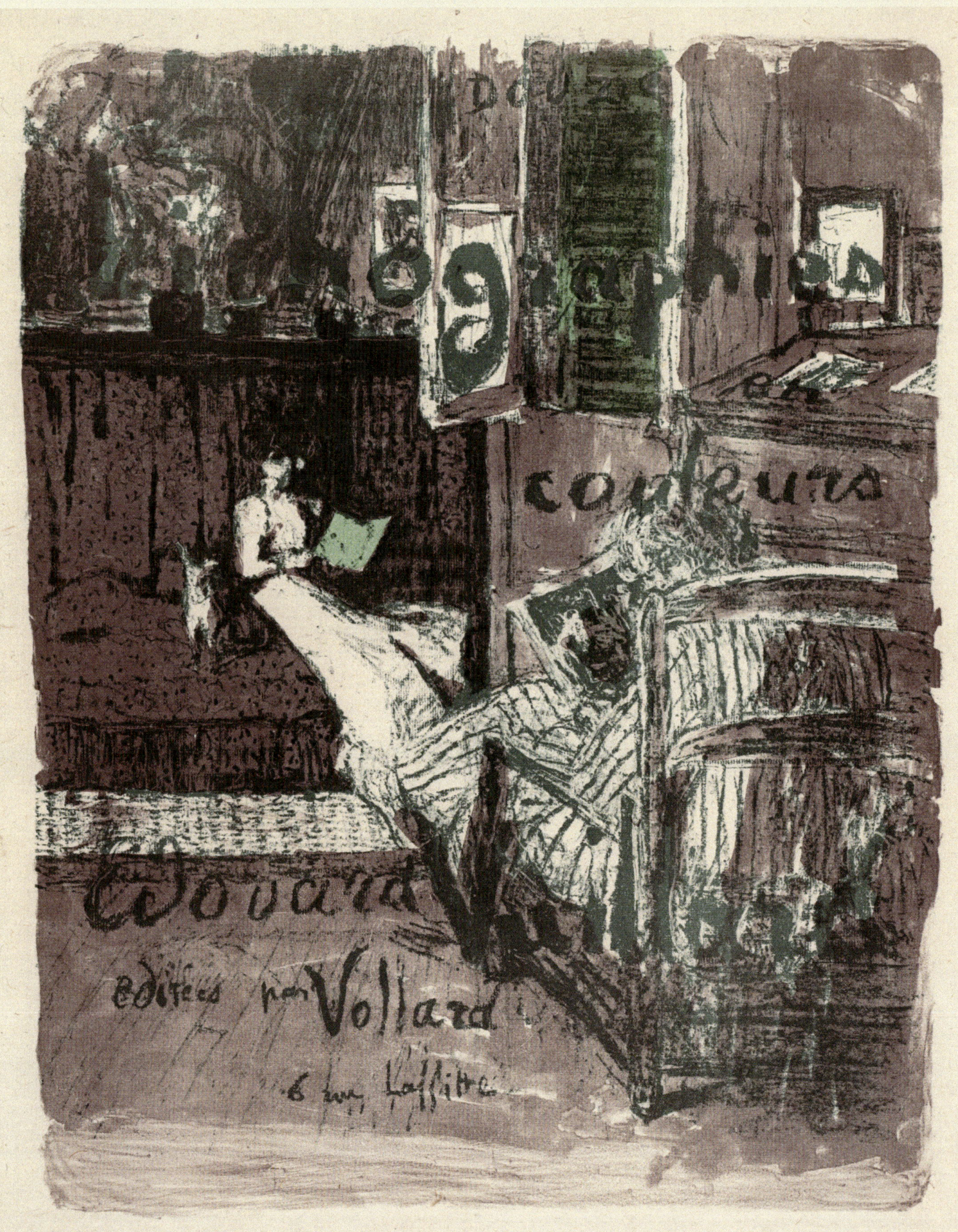
Douze
lithographies
en
couleurs
Vuillard
Editées par Vollard
6 rue Laffitte

# Paysages et intérieurs

# *Landscapes and Interiors*

## Édouard Vuillard

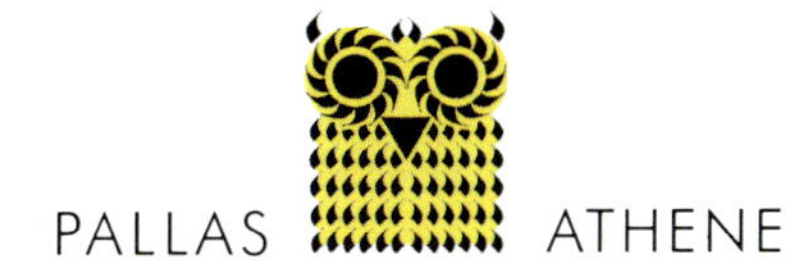

Pallas Athene

I.

La partie de dames
*The Game of Checkers*

330 x 257 mm

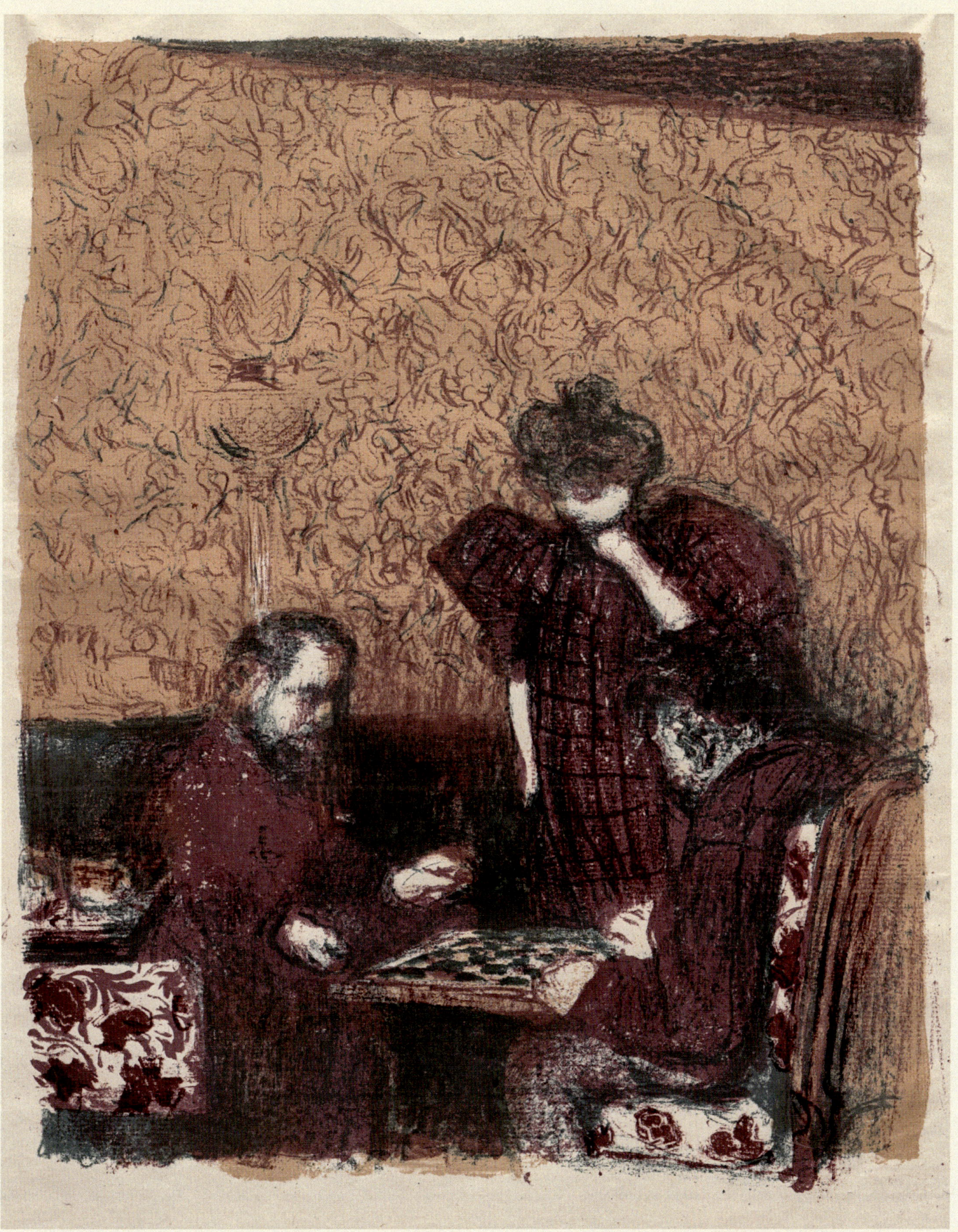

2.

L'Avenue

*The Avenue*

311 x 414 mm

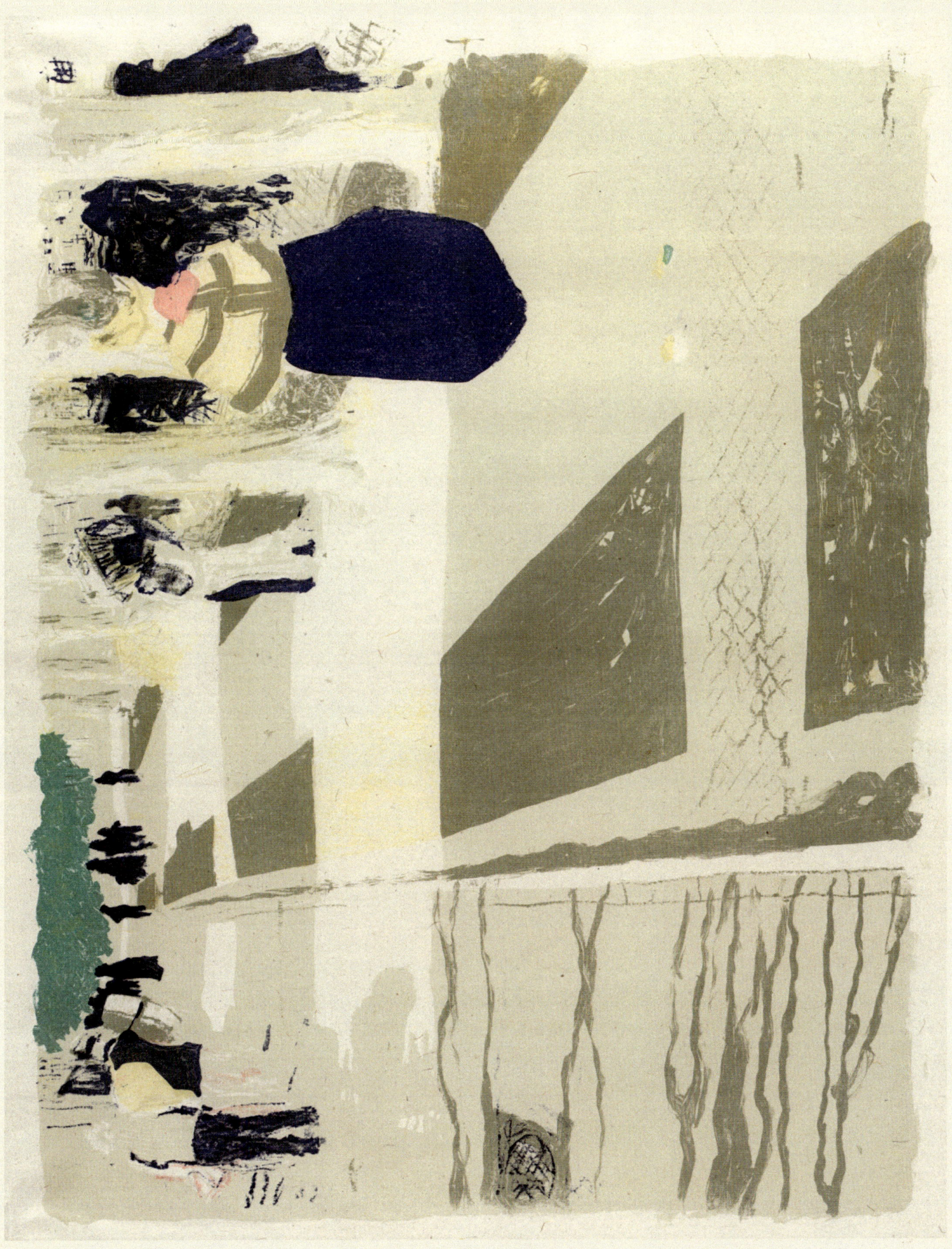

3.
À travers champs
*Across the Fields*

260 x 345 mm

4.
Intérieur à la suspension
*Interior with Ceiling Lamp*

356 x 282 mm

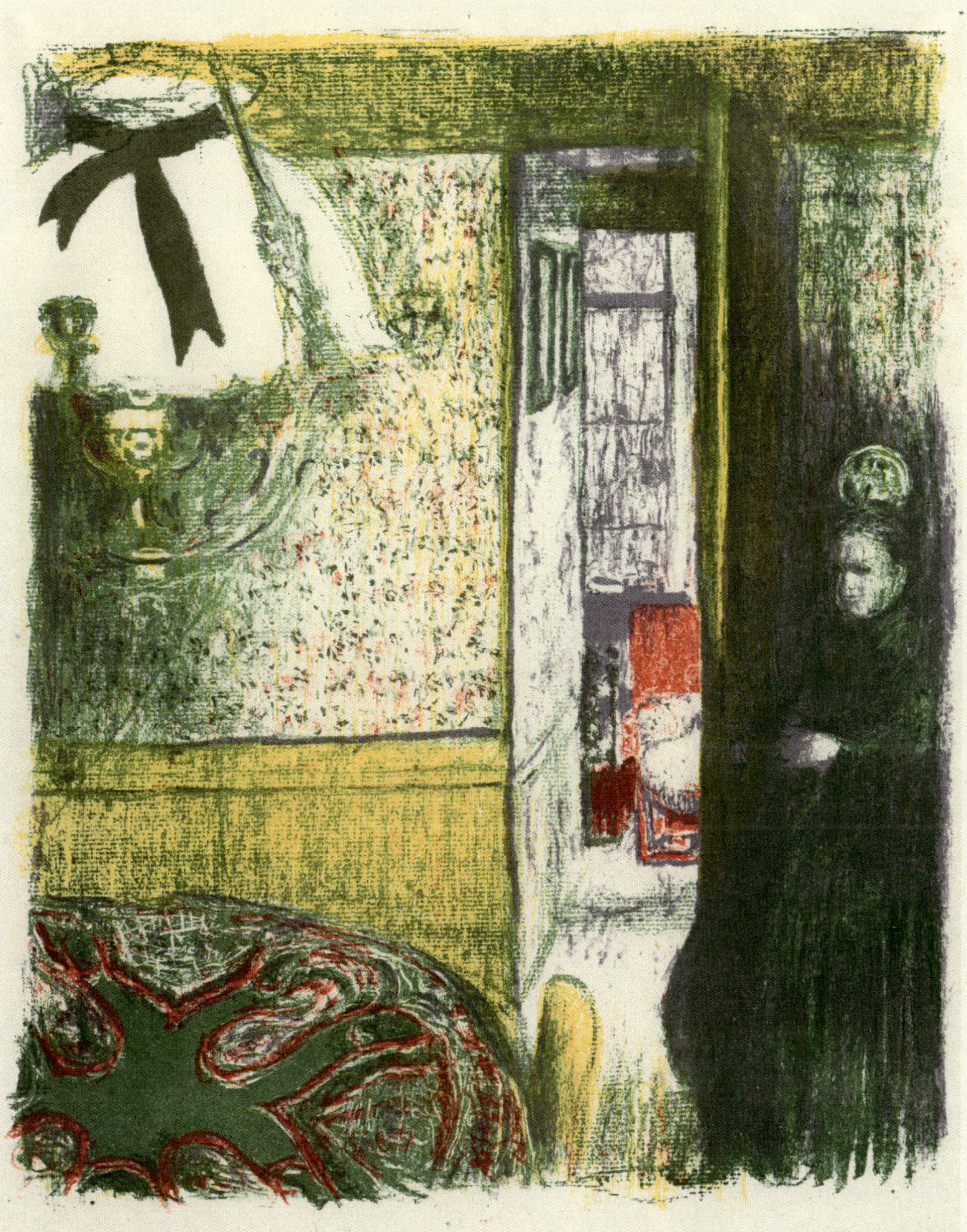

5.
Intérieur aux tentures roses I
*Interior with Pink Wallpaper I*

354 x 278 mm

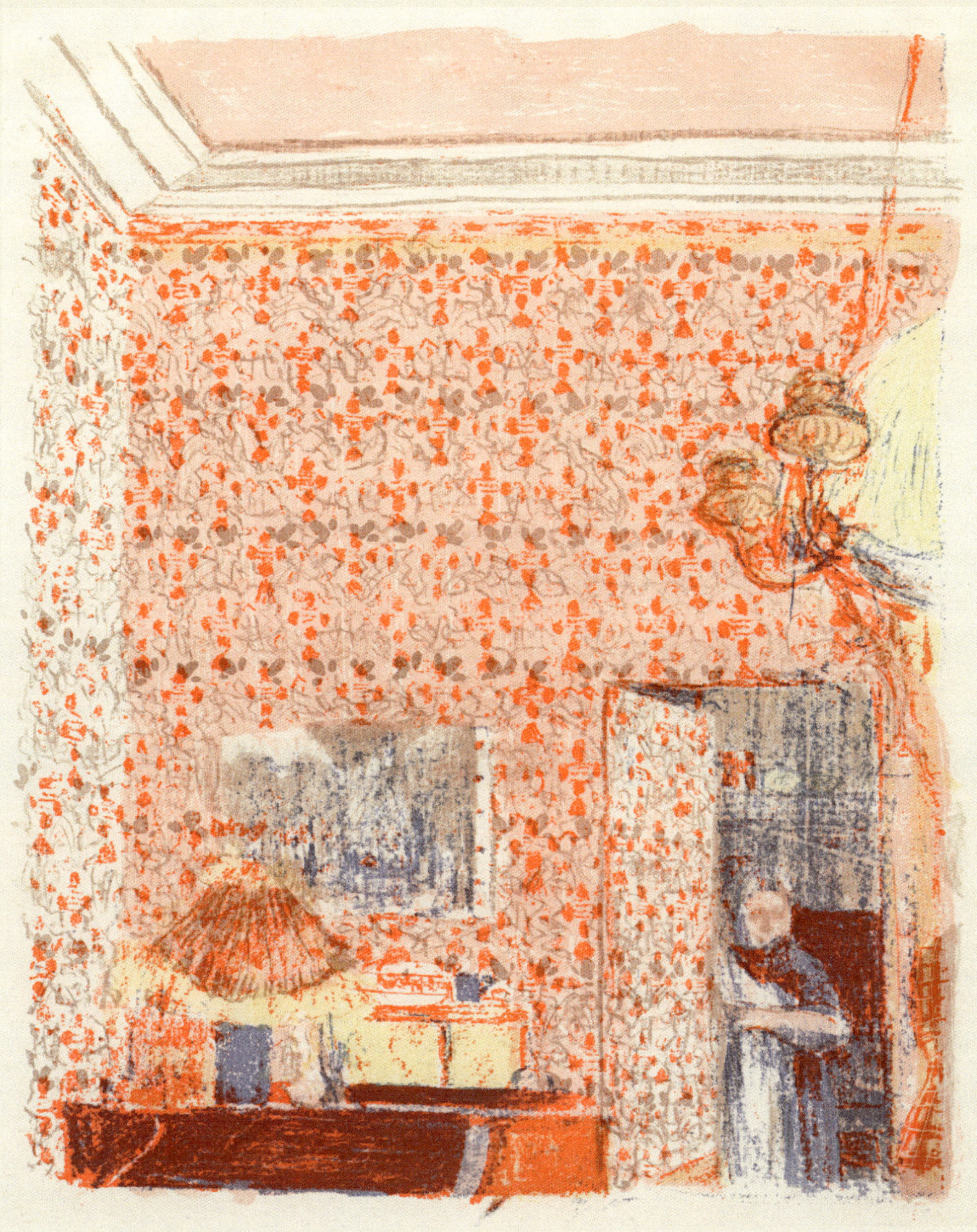

6.

Intérieur aux tentures roses II

*Interior with Pink Wallpaper II*

346 x 282 mm

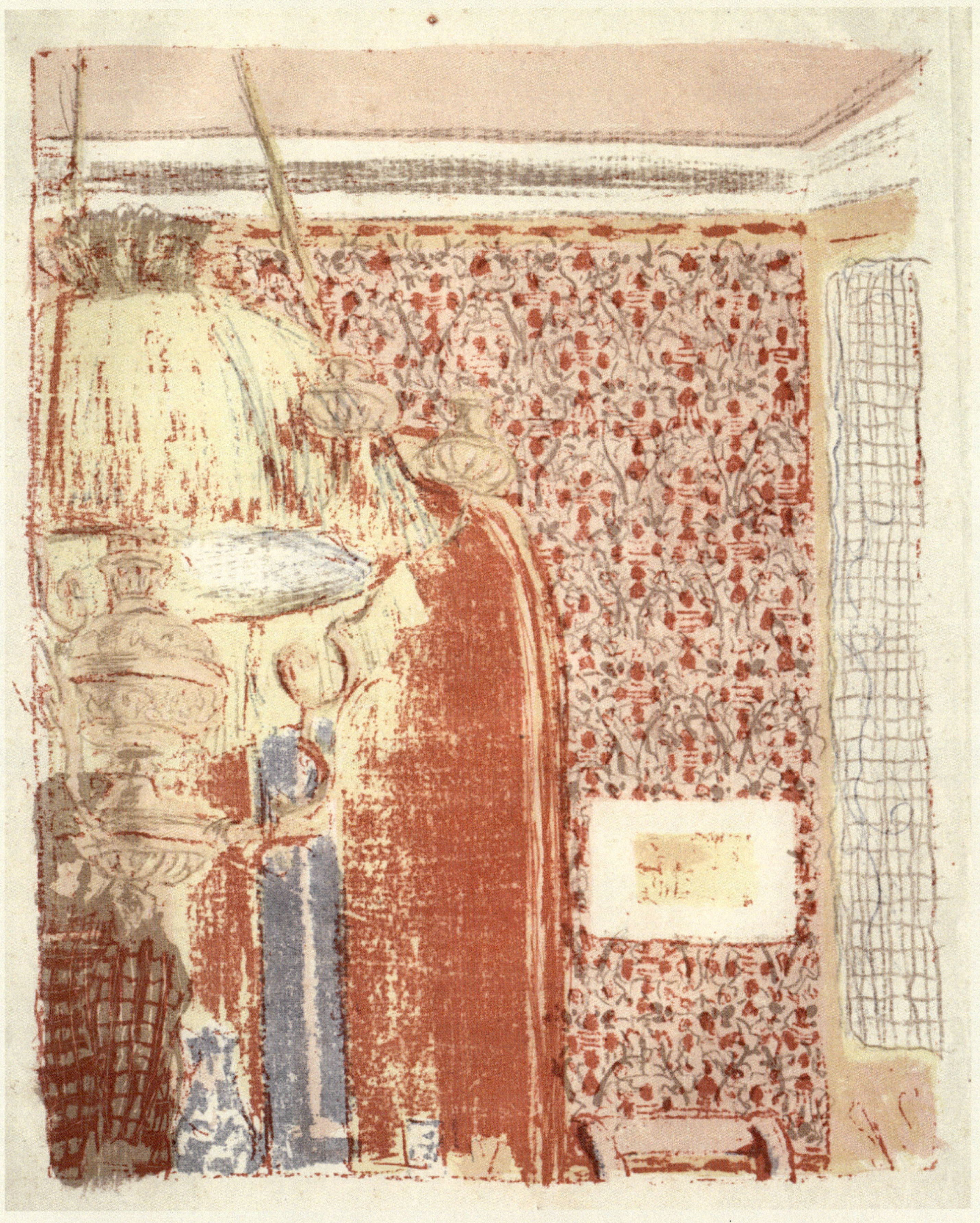

7.
Intérieur aux tentures roses III
*Interior with Pink Wallpaper III*

342 x 273 mm

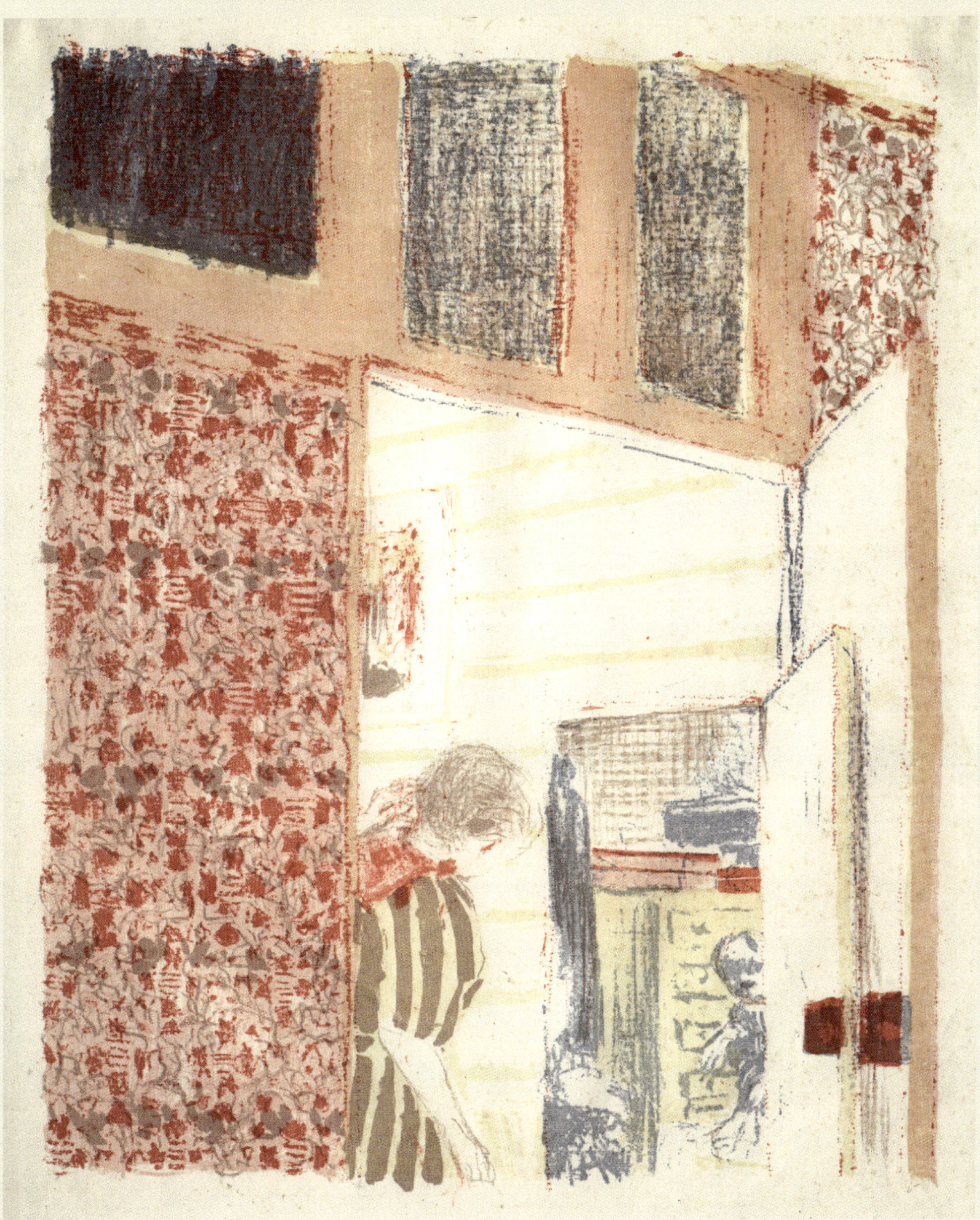

8.

L'Âtre

*The Hearth*

343 x 277 mm

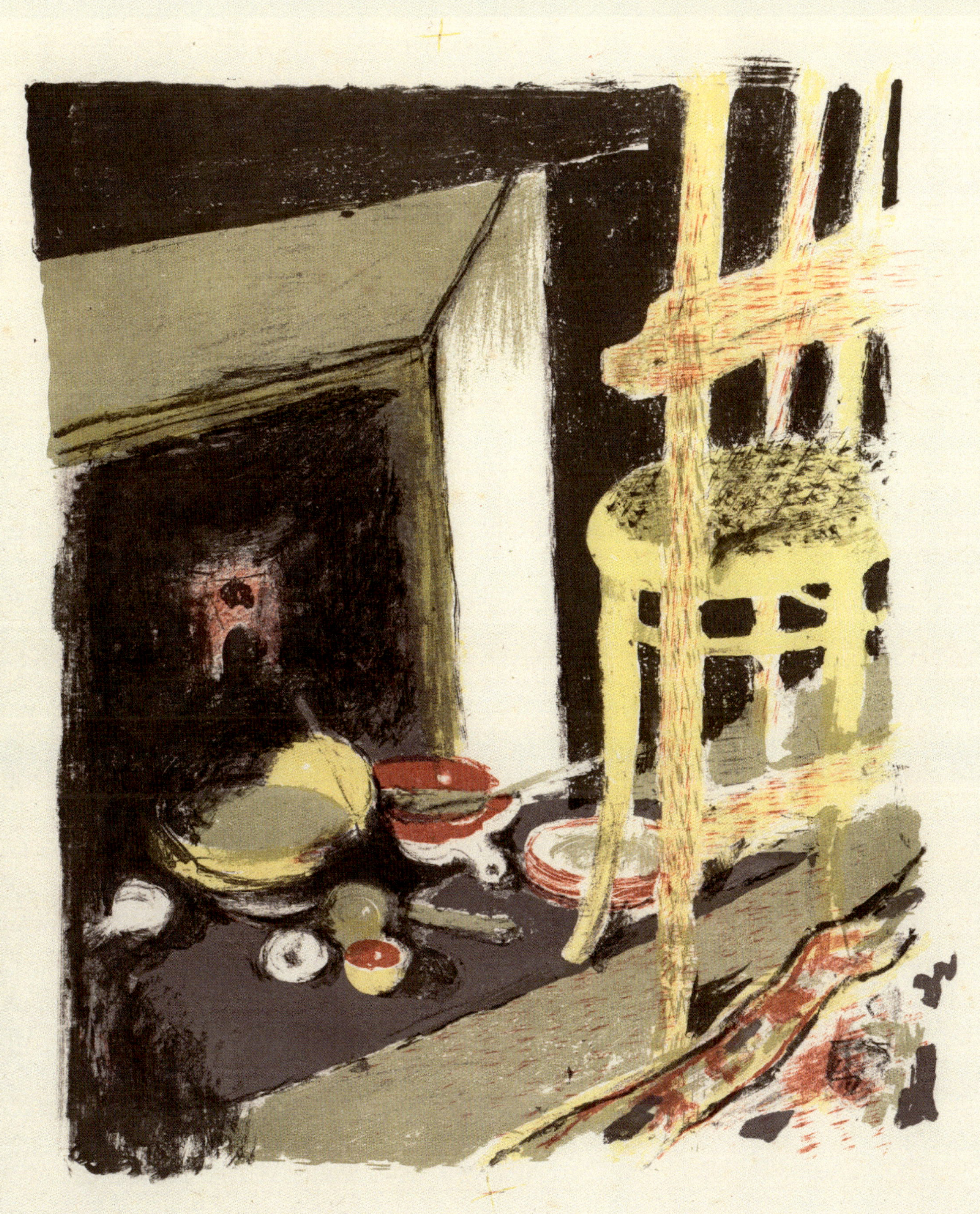

9.
Sur le pont de l'Europe
*On the Pont de l'Europe*

343 x 277 mm

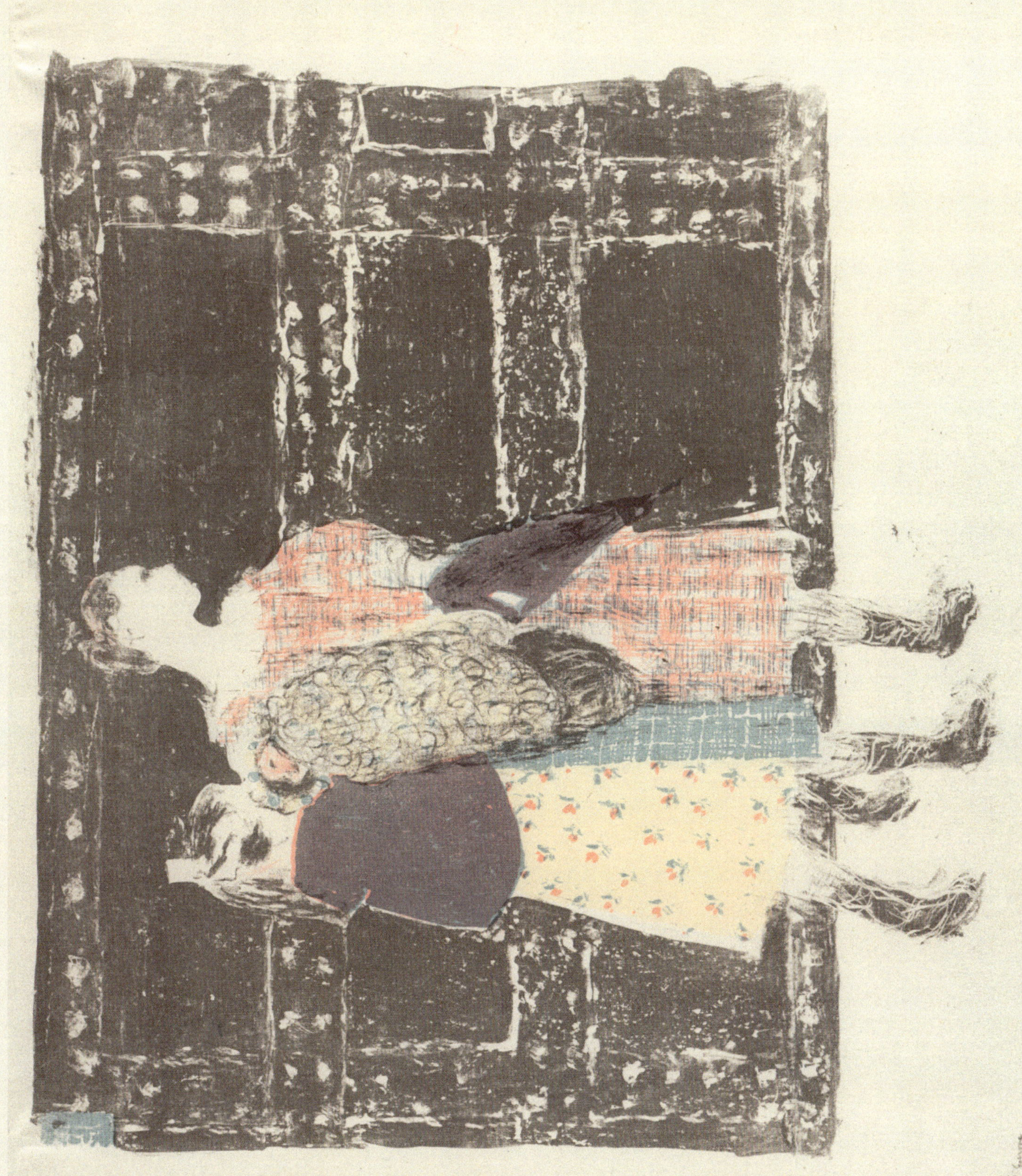

10.

La Pâtisserie
*The Pastry Shop*

351 x 275 mm

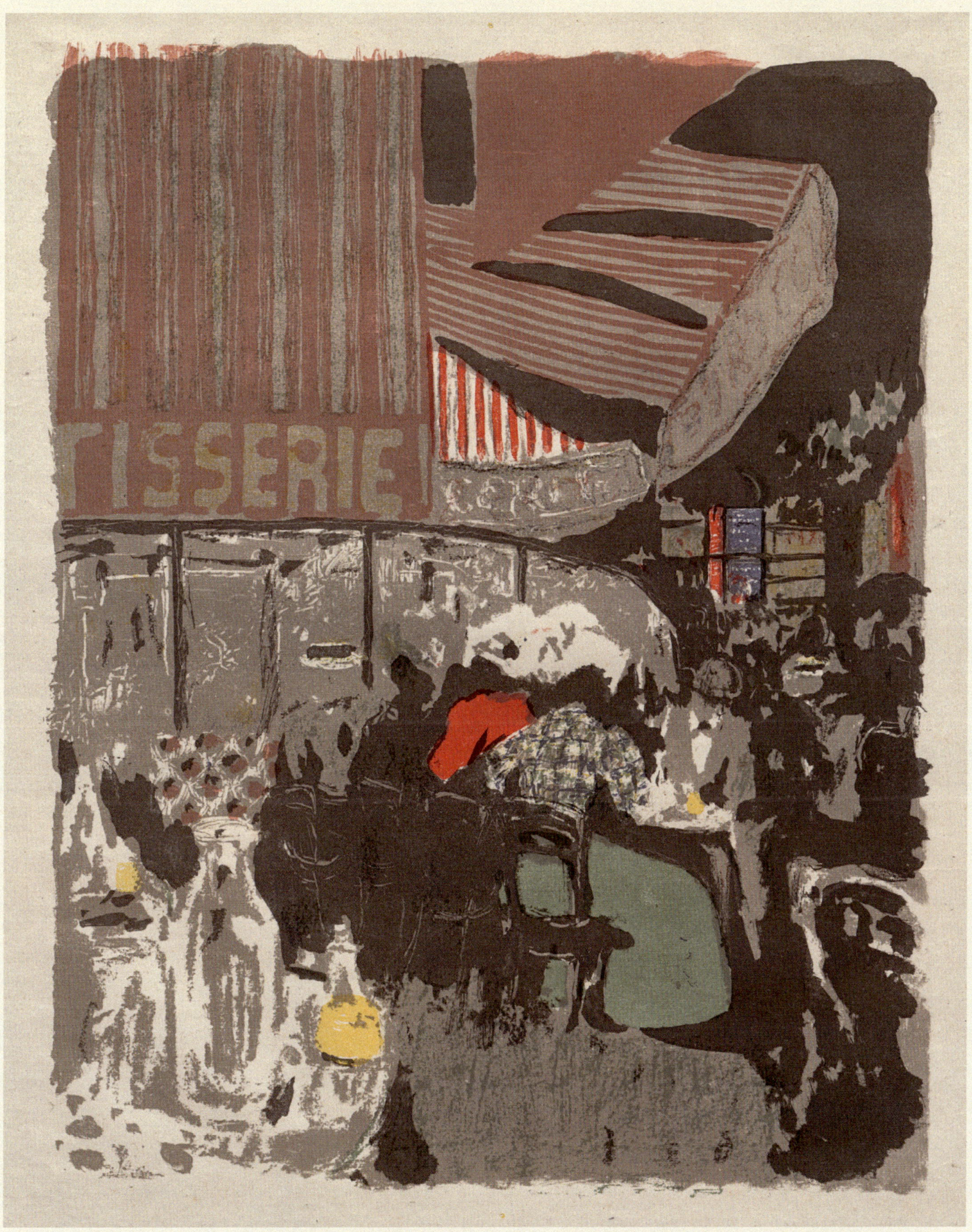
TISSERIE

11.

La Cuisinière (la mère de l'artiste)
*The Cook (the artist's mother)*

350 x 277 mm

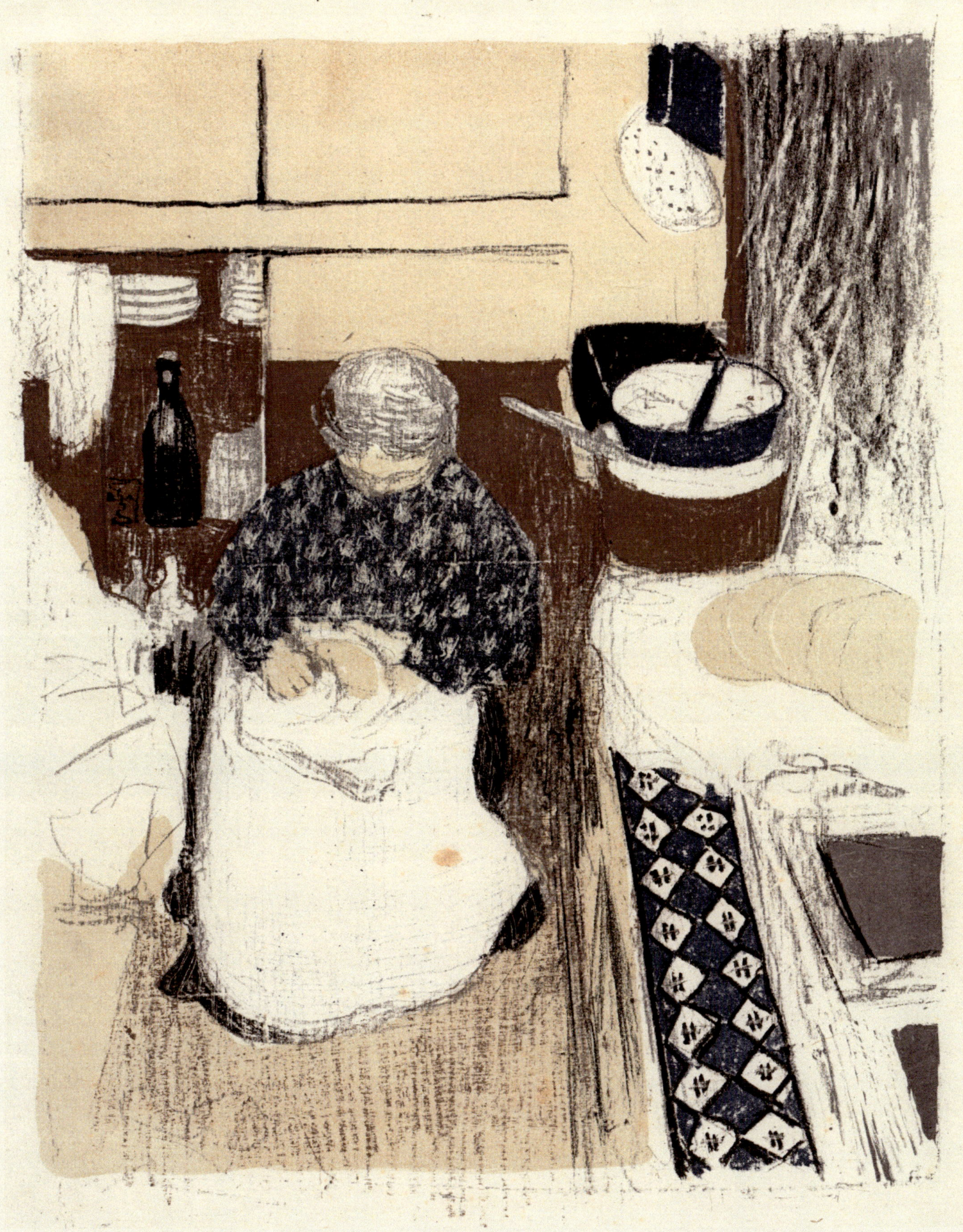

12.
Les deux belles-sœurs
*The Two Sisters-in-Law*

368 x 294 mm

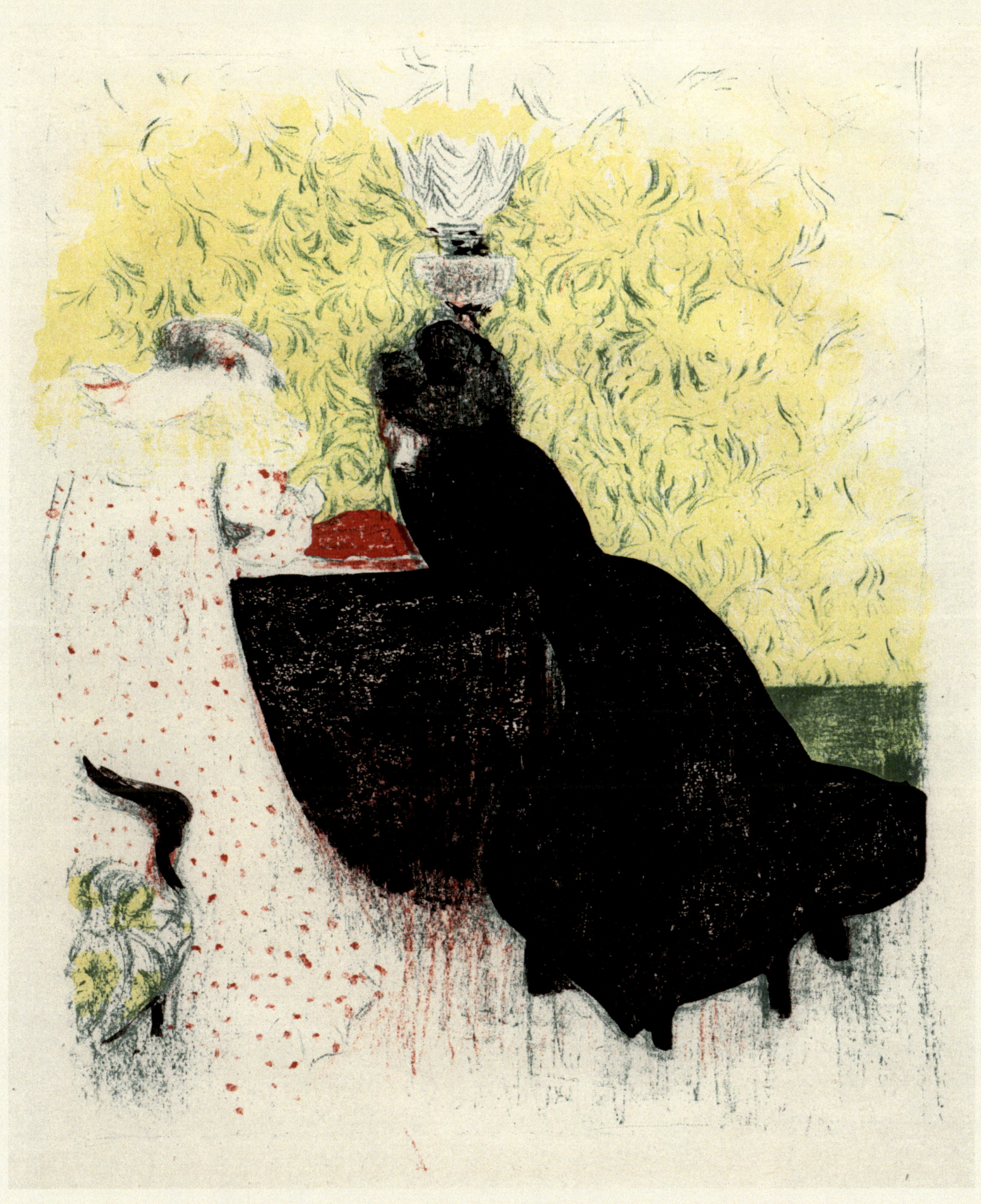

PAYSAGES ET INTÉRIEURS/
LANDSCAPES AND INTERIORS
Suite de 12 planches et une couverture,
imprimée par Auguste Clot. Éditée à
Paris par Ambroise Vollard en 1899,
et tirée à 100 exemplaires./
*Suite of 12 plates and a cover, printed
by Auguste Clot. Published in Paris by
Ambroise Vollard in 1899, in an edition
of 100 copies.*

Cette édition/*This edition*
© Pallas Athene (Publishers) Ltd,
London, 2026

Pallas Athene (Publishers) Ltd,
2 Birch Close, London N19 5XD

**www.pallasathene.co.uk**

ISBN 978 1 84368 299 8 (édition française)
ISBN 978 1 84368 298 1 (English edition)

Imprimé en Angleterre par Blissetts/
*Printed in England by Blissetts*

3

PAYSAGES
ET INTÉRIEURS

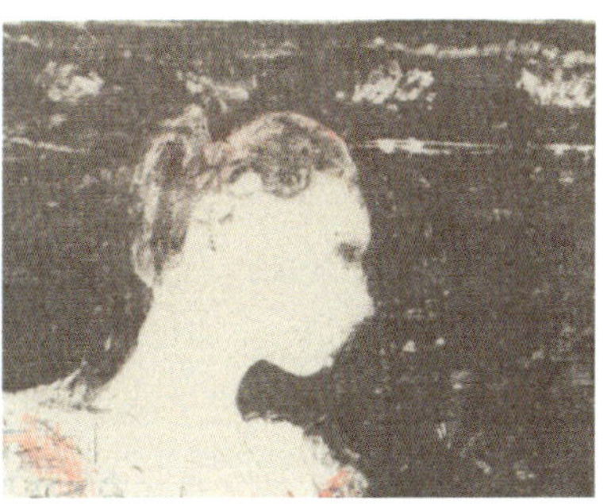

LANDSCAPES AND
INTERIORS

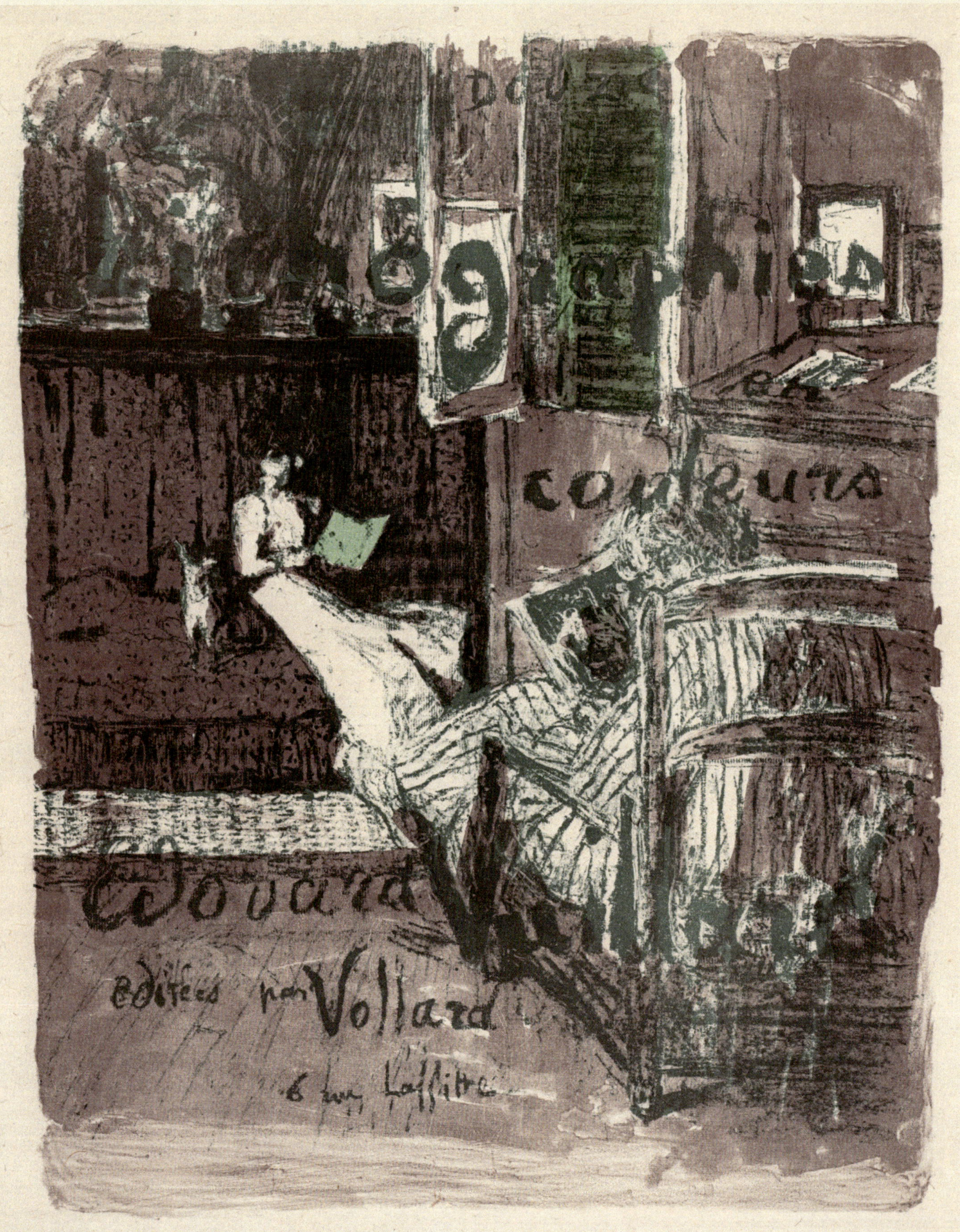

Douze
lithographies
en
couleurs
Vuillard
Éditées par Vollard
6 rue Laffitte

# Paysages et intérieurs

# *Landscapes and Interiors*

## Édouard Vuillard

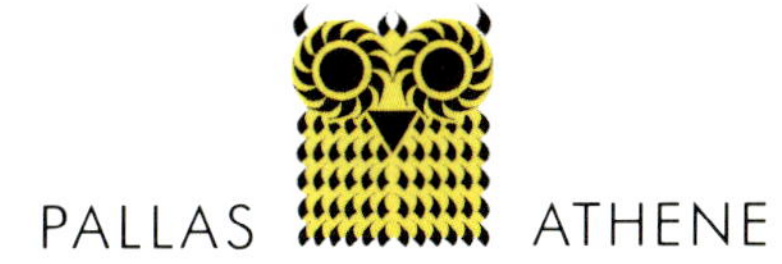

I.

La partie de dames
*The Game of Checkers*

330 x 257 mm

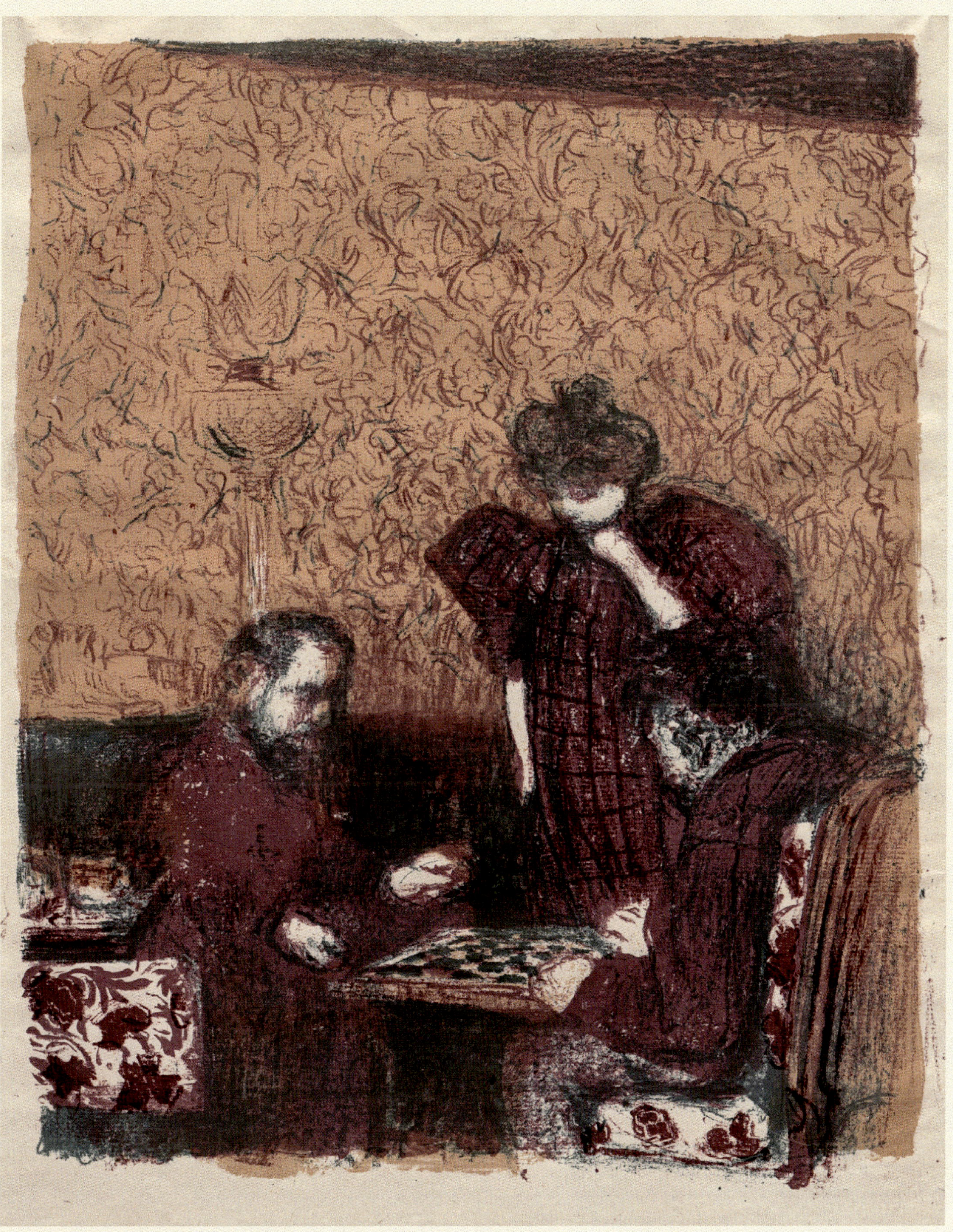

2.

L'Avenue

*The Avenue*

311 x 414 mm

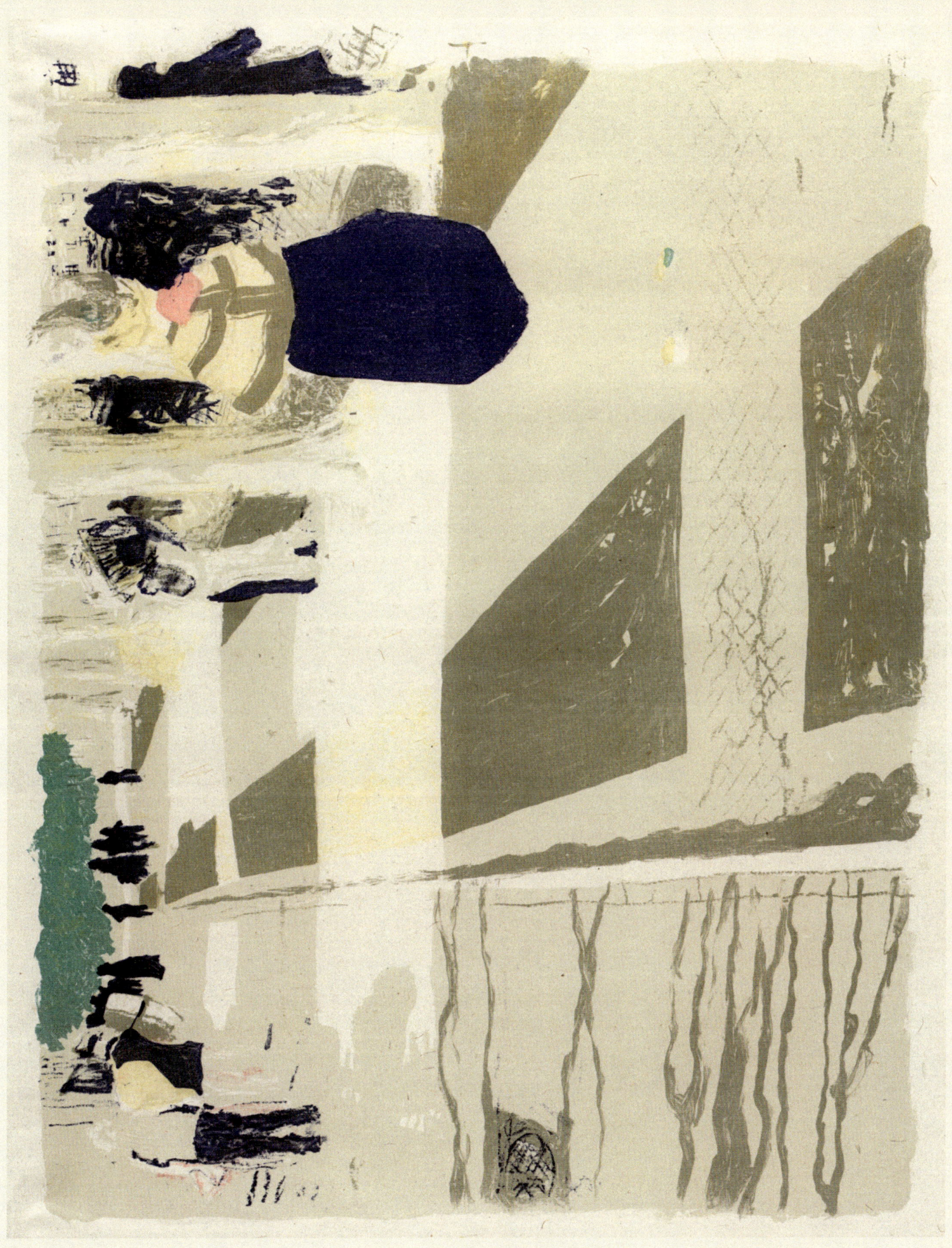

3.
À travers champs
*Across the Fields*

260 x 345 mm

4.
Intérieur à la suspension
*Interior with Ceiling Lamp*

356 x 282 mm

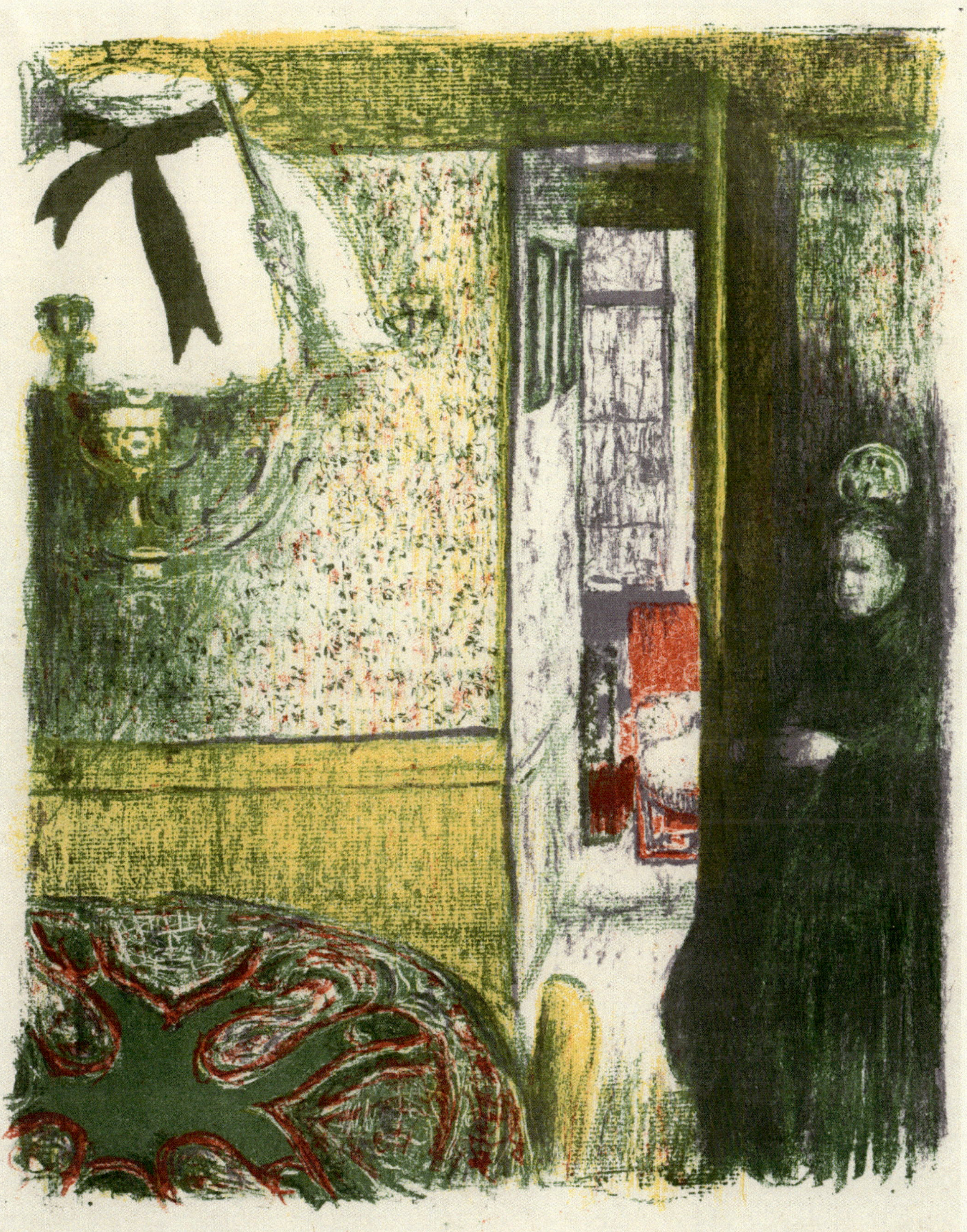

5.
Intérieur aux tentures roses I
*Interior with Pink Wallpaper I*

354 x 278 mm

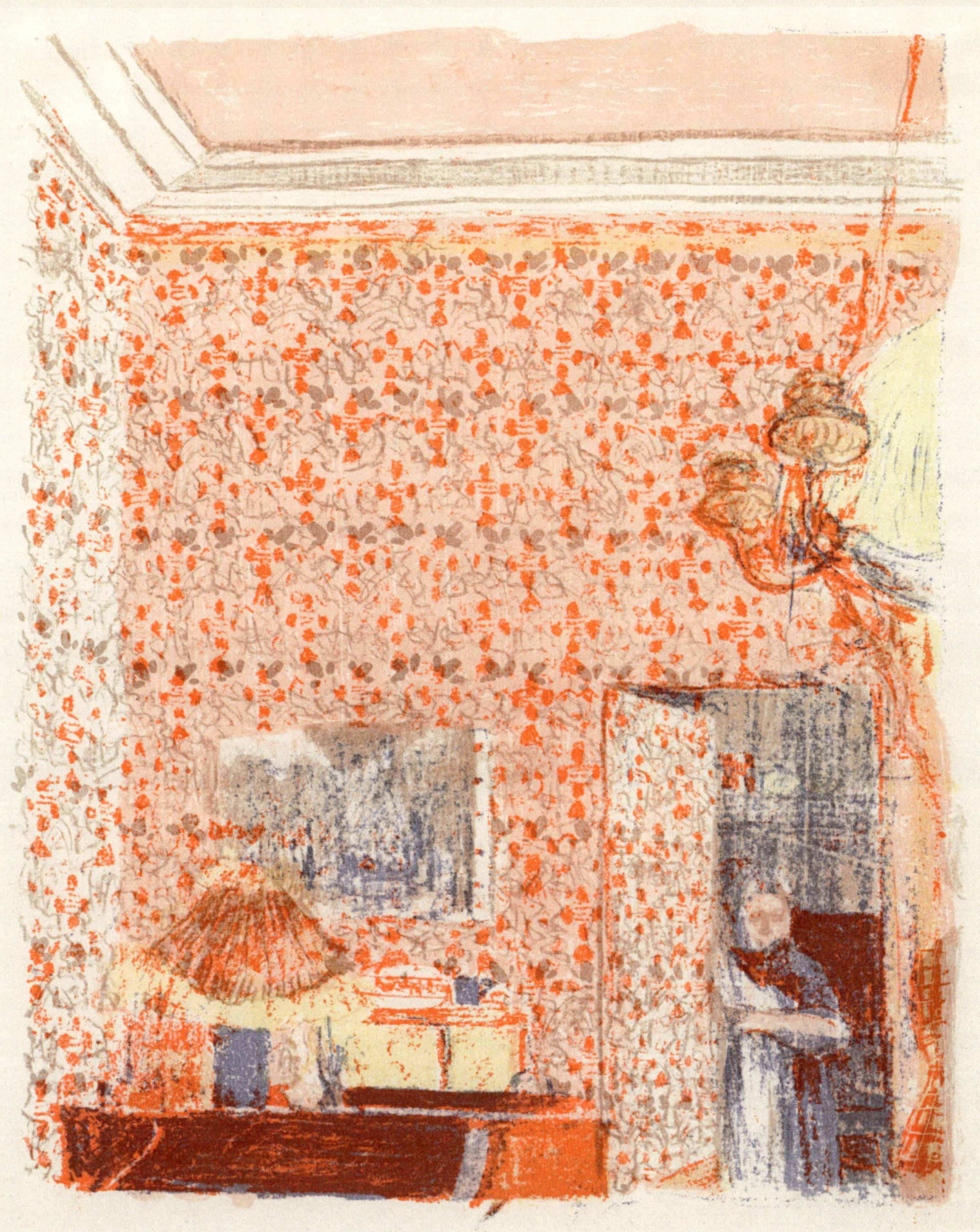

6.
Intérieur aux tentures roses II
*Interior with Pink Wallpaper II*

346 x 282 mm

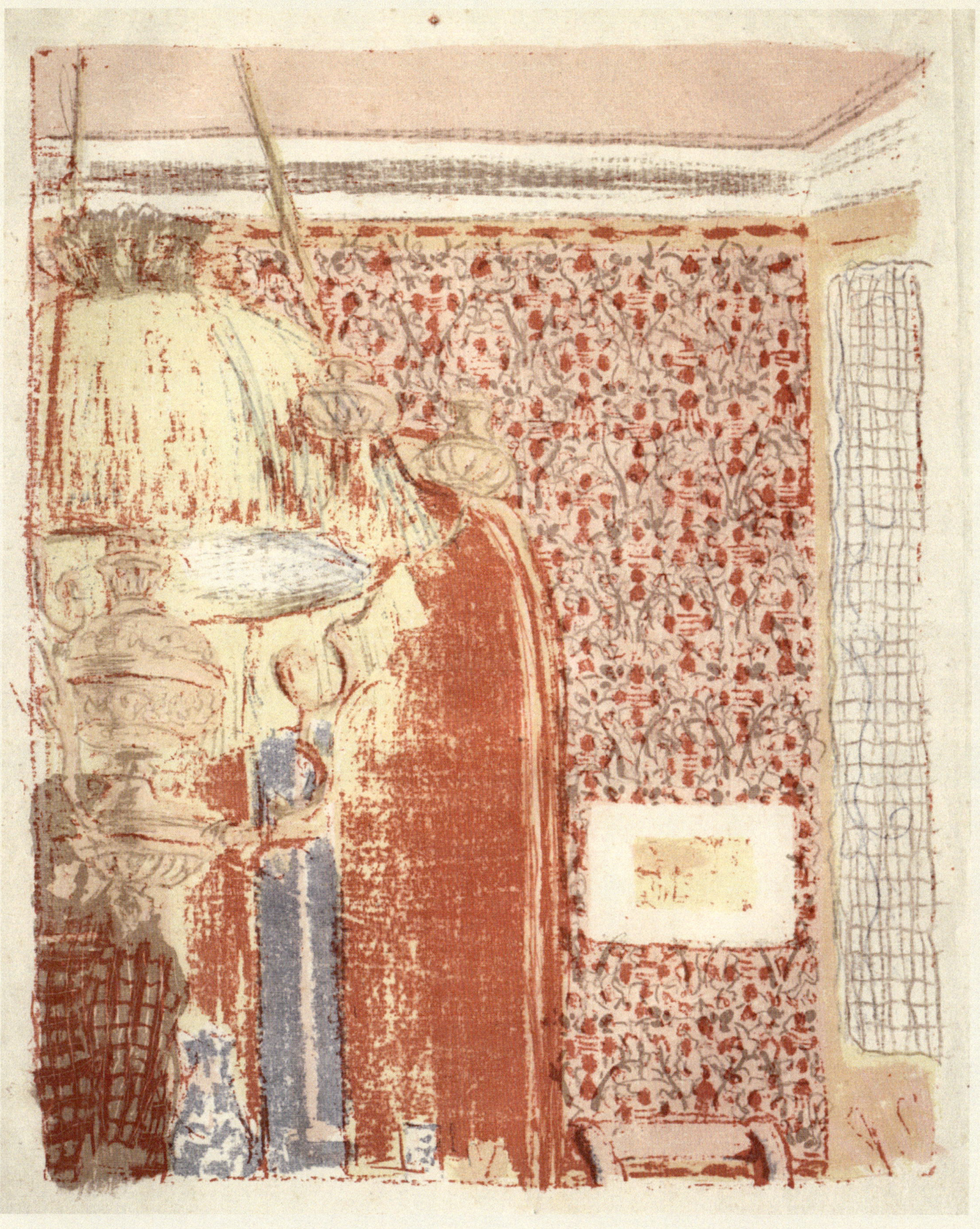

7.
Intérieur aux tentures roses III
*Interior with Pink Wallpaper III*

342 x 273 mm

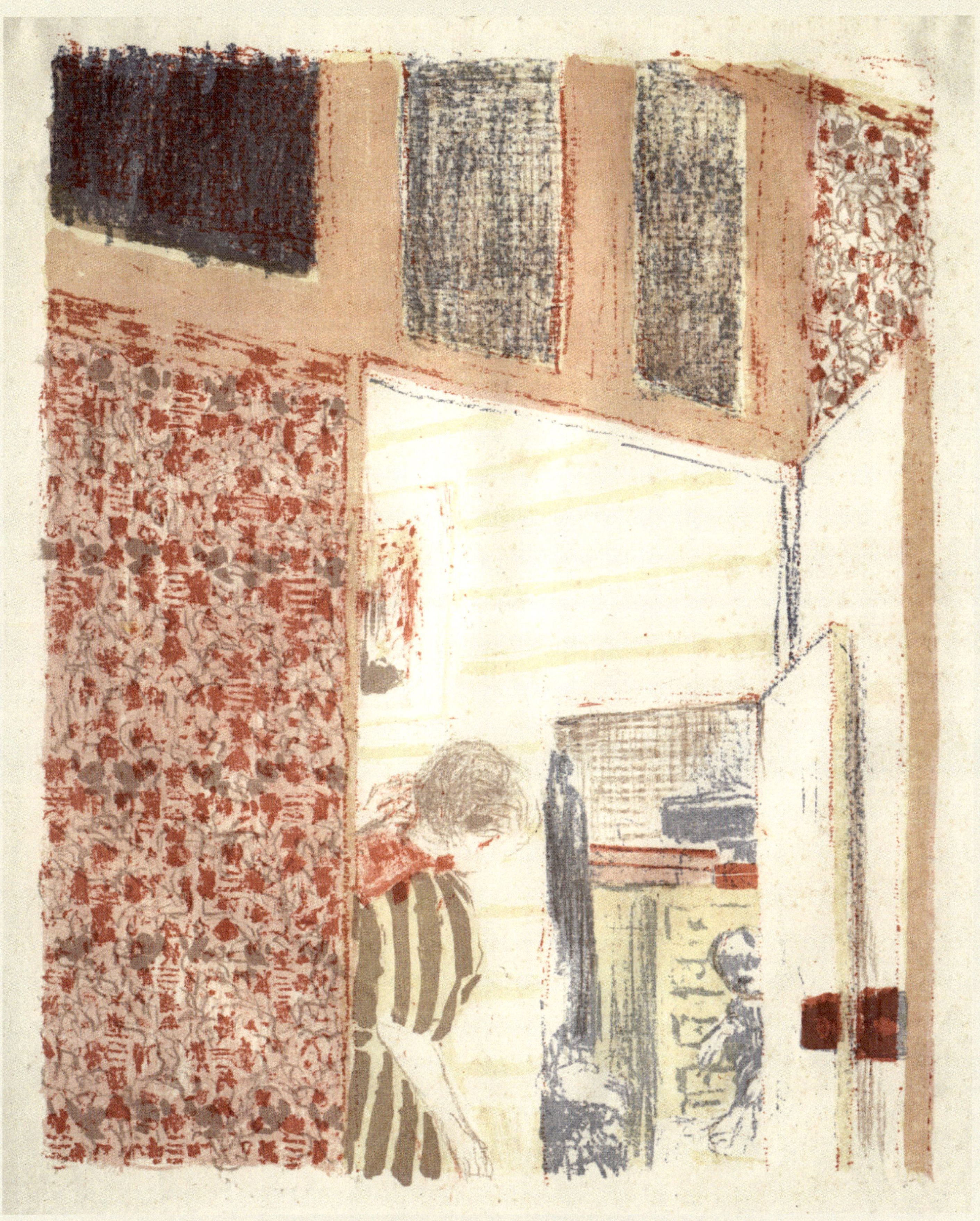

8.

L'Âtre

*The Hearth*

343 x 277 mm

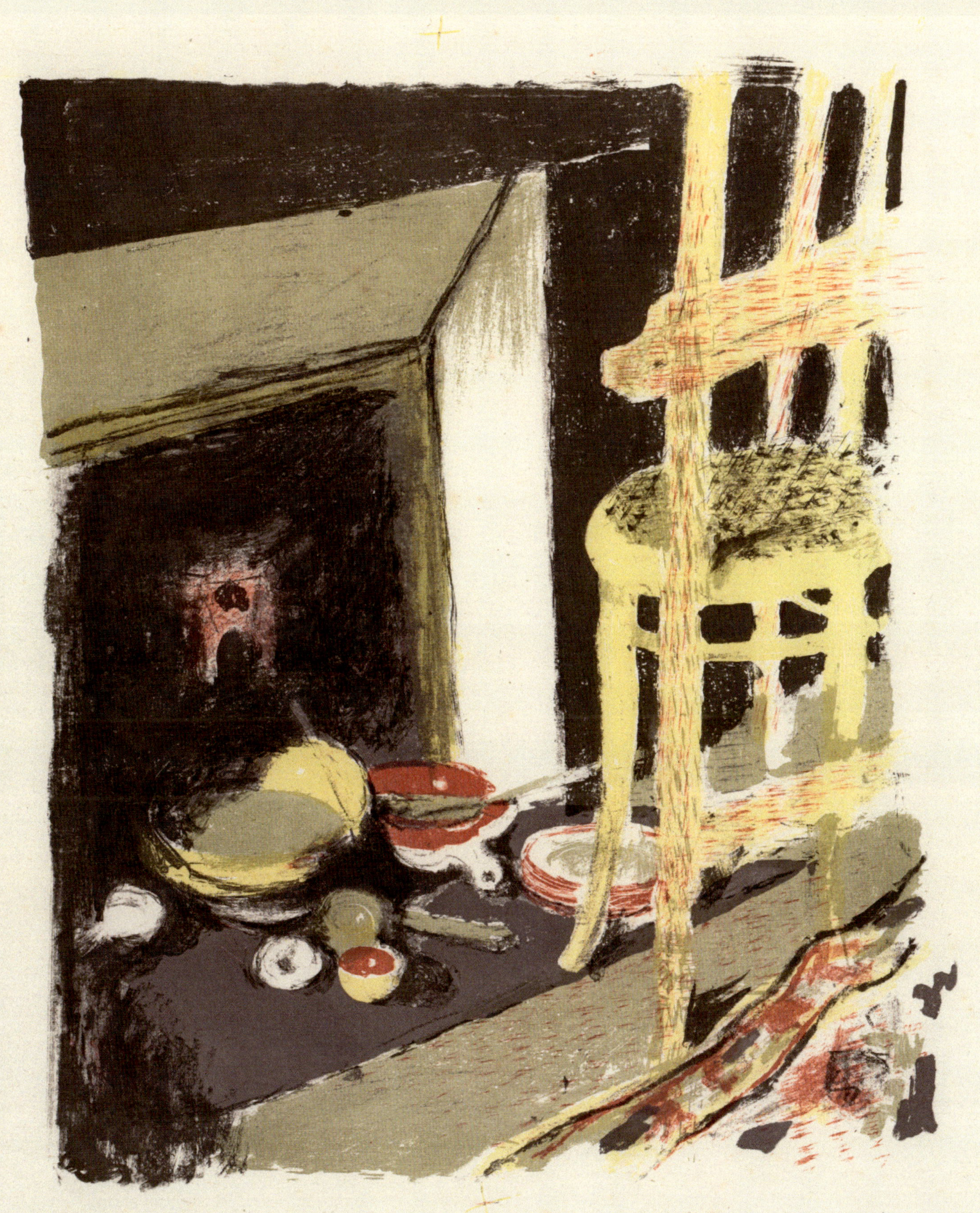

9.

Sur le pont de l'Europe

*On the Pont de l'Europe*

343 x 277 mm

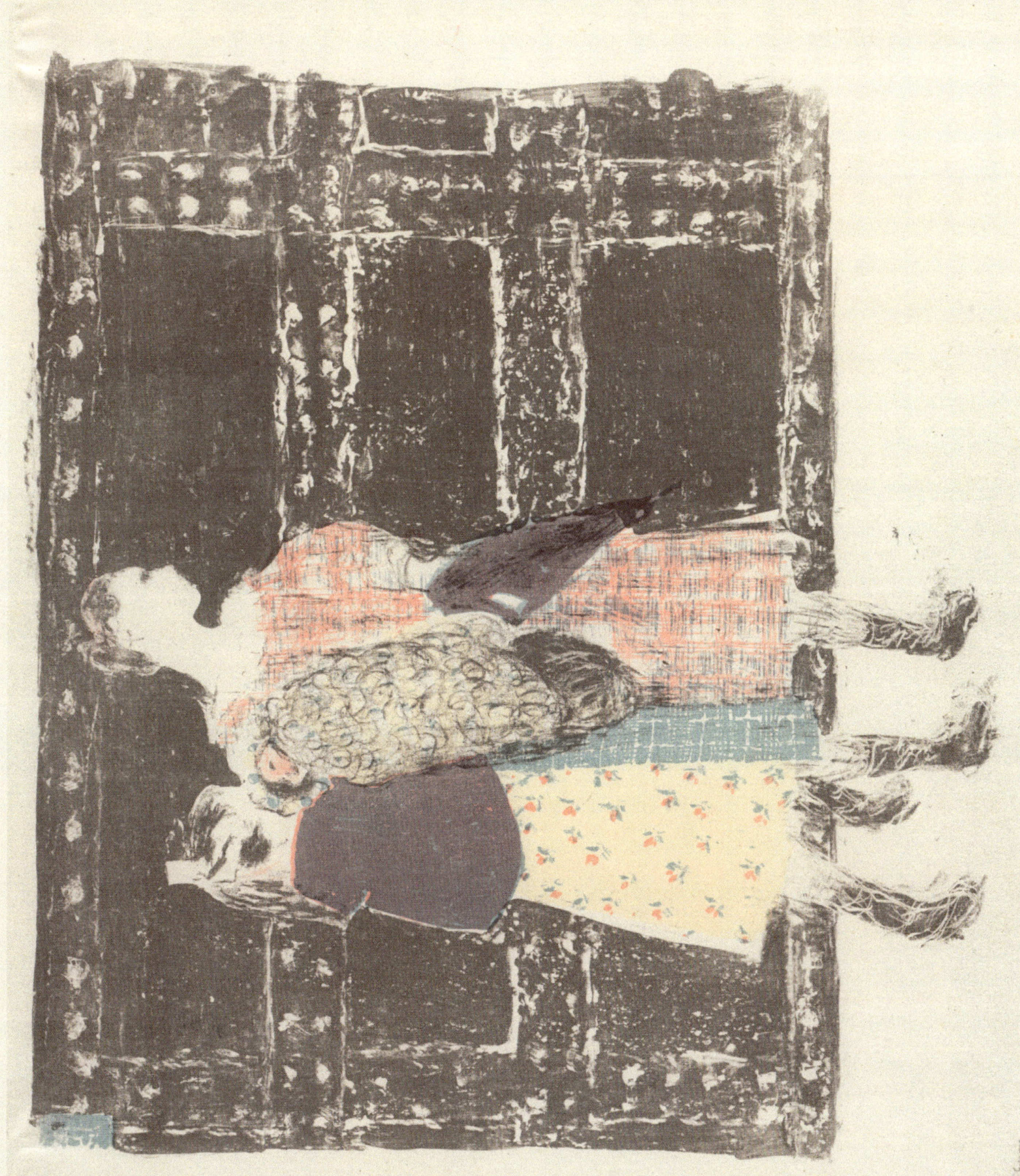

10.

La Pâtisserie
*The Pastry Shop*

351 x 275 mm

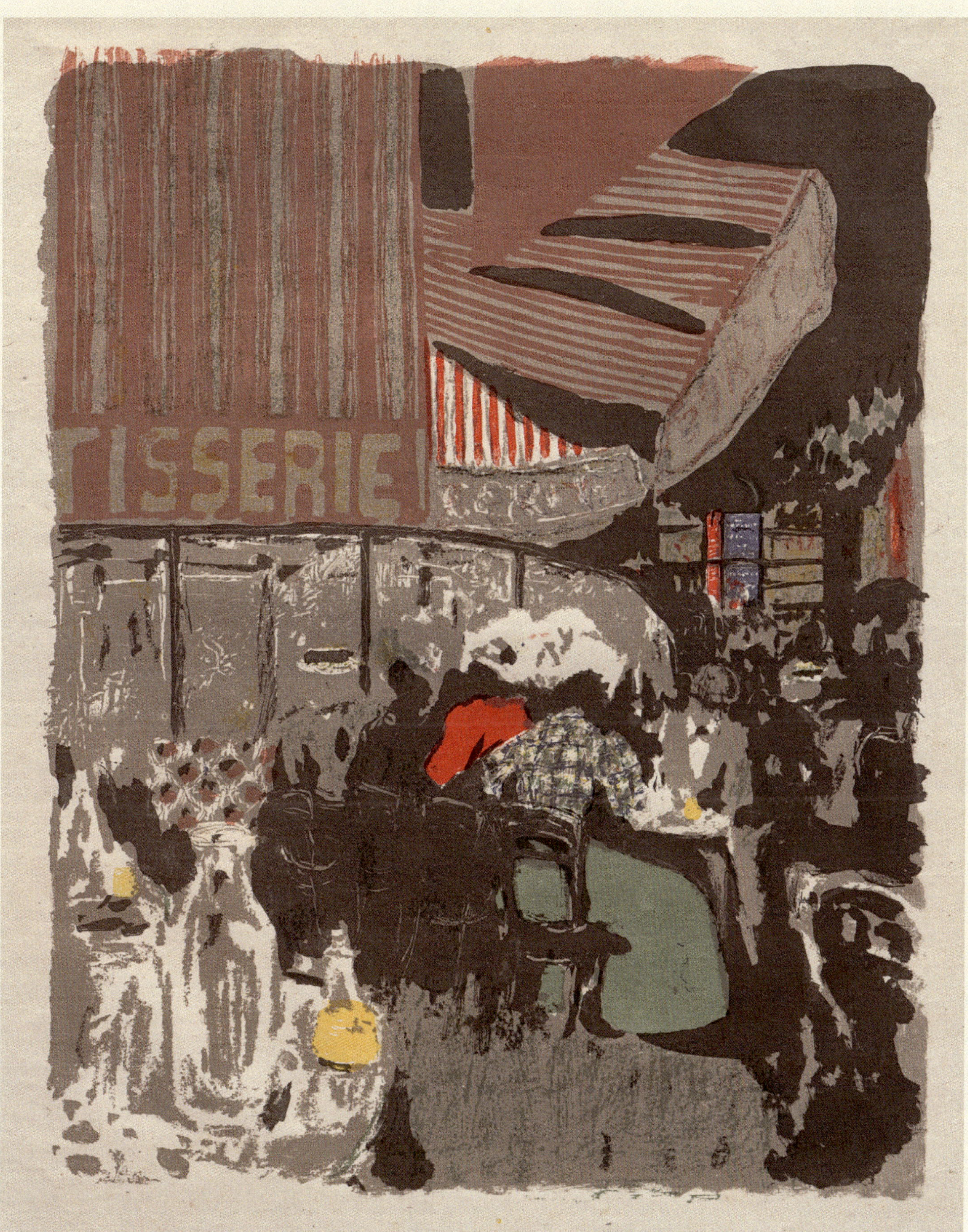
TISSERIE

11.
La Cuisinière (la mère de l'artiste)
*The Cook (the artist's mother)*

350 x 277 mm

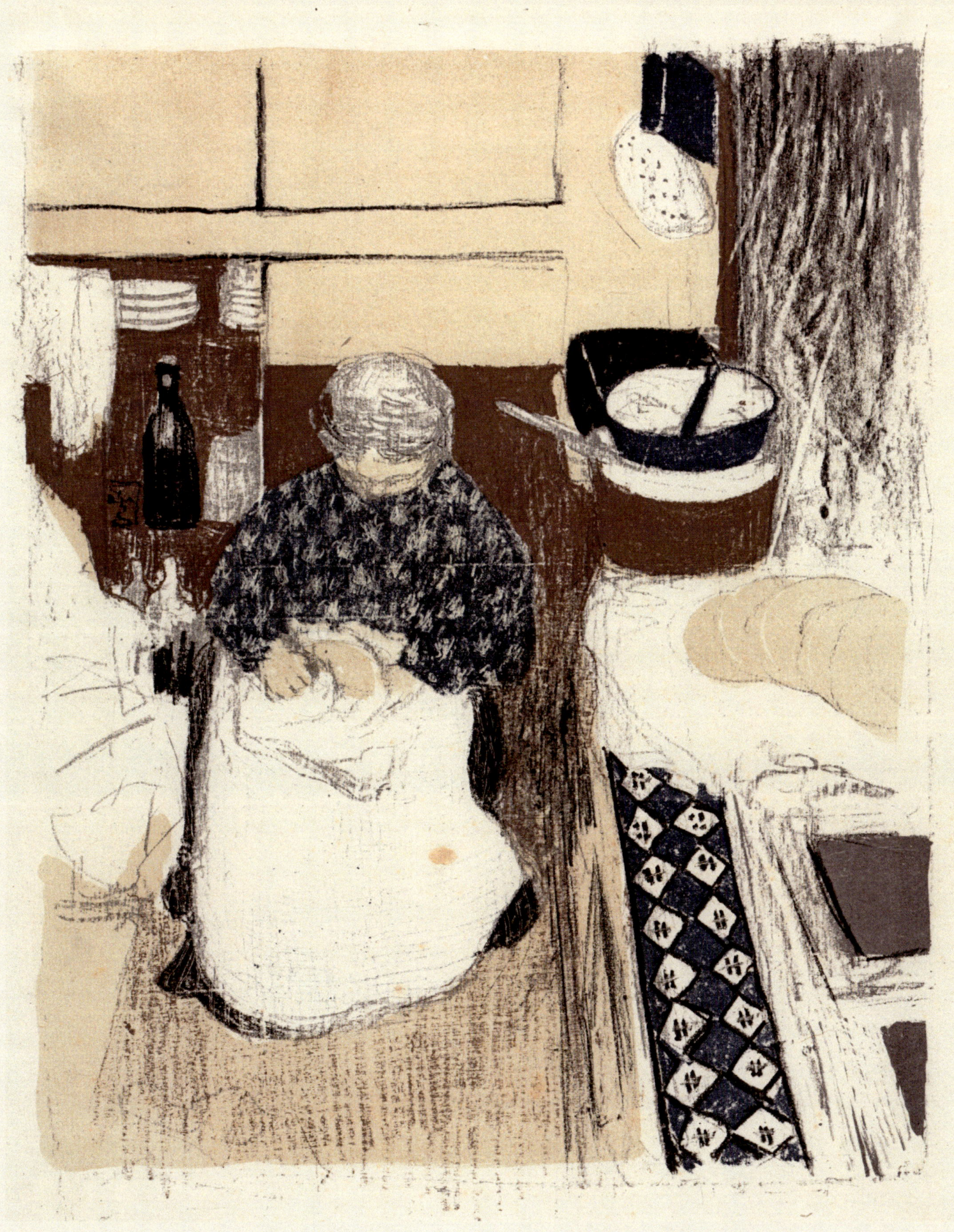

12.
Les deux belles-sœurs
*The Two Sisters-in-Law*

368 x 294 mm

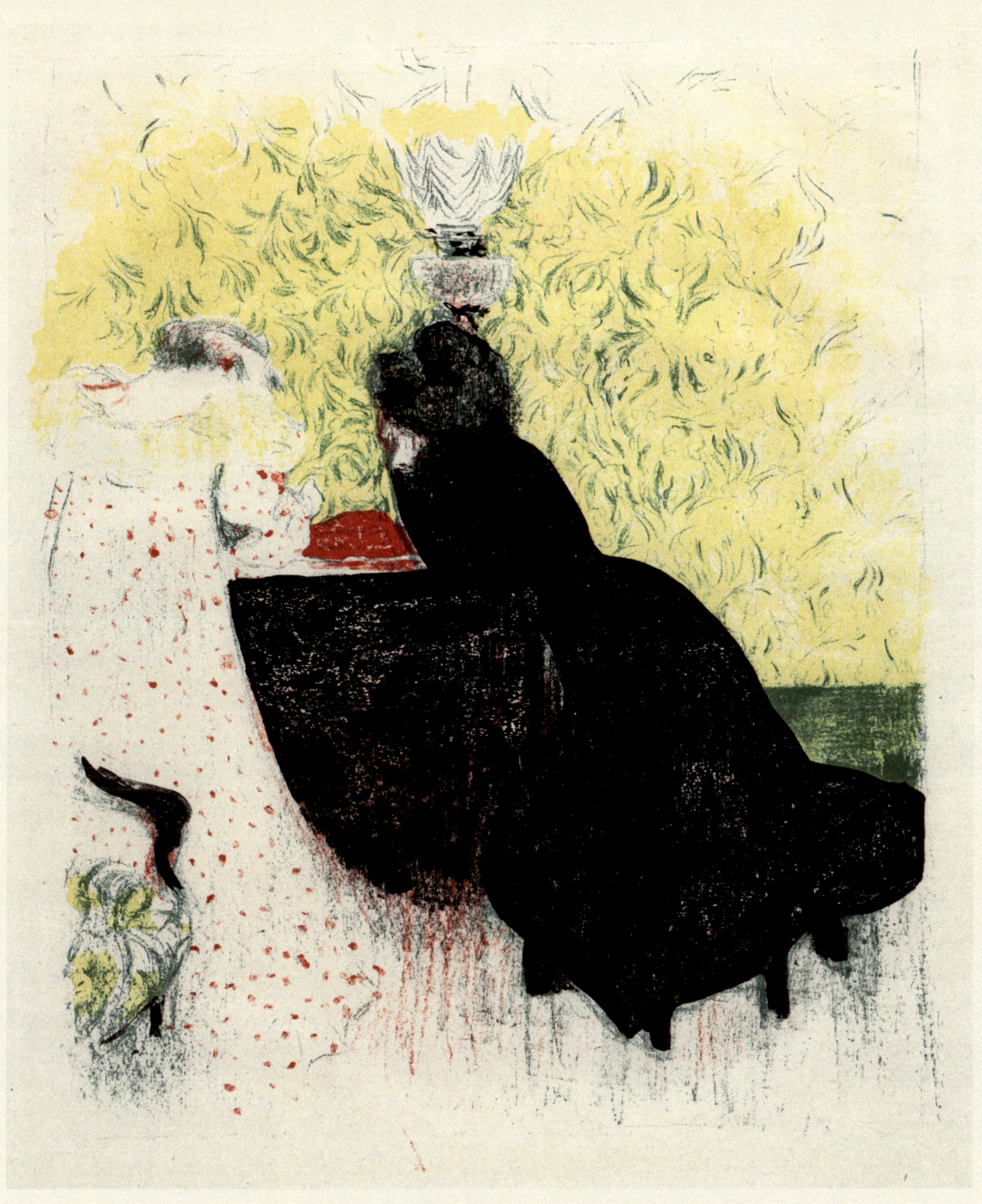

PAYSAGES ET INTÉRIEURS/
LANDSCAPES AND INTERIORS
Suite de 12 planches et une couverture,
imprimée par Auguste Clot. Éditée à
Paris par Ambroise Vollard en 1899,
et tirée à 100 exemplaires./
*Suite of 12 plates and a cover, printed
by Auguste Clot. Published in Paris by
Ambroise Vollard in 1899, in an edition
of 100 copies.*

Cette édition/*This edition*
© Pallas Athene (Publishers) Ltd,
London, 2026

Pallas Athene (Publishers) Ltd,
2 Birch Close, London N19 5XD

**www.pallasathene.co.uk**

ISBN 978 1 84368 299 8 (édition française)
ISBN 978 1 84368 298 1 (English edition)

Imprimé en Angleterre par Blissetts/
*Printed in England by Blissetts*

3

# PAYSAGES
# ET INTÉRIEURS

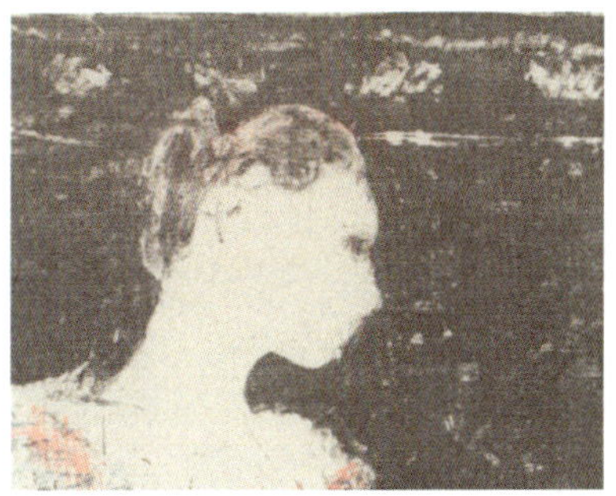

# LANDSCAPES AND
# INTERIORS

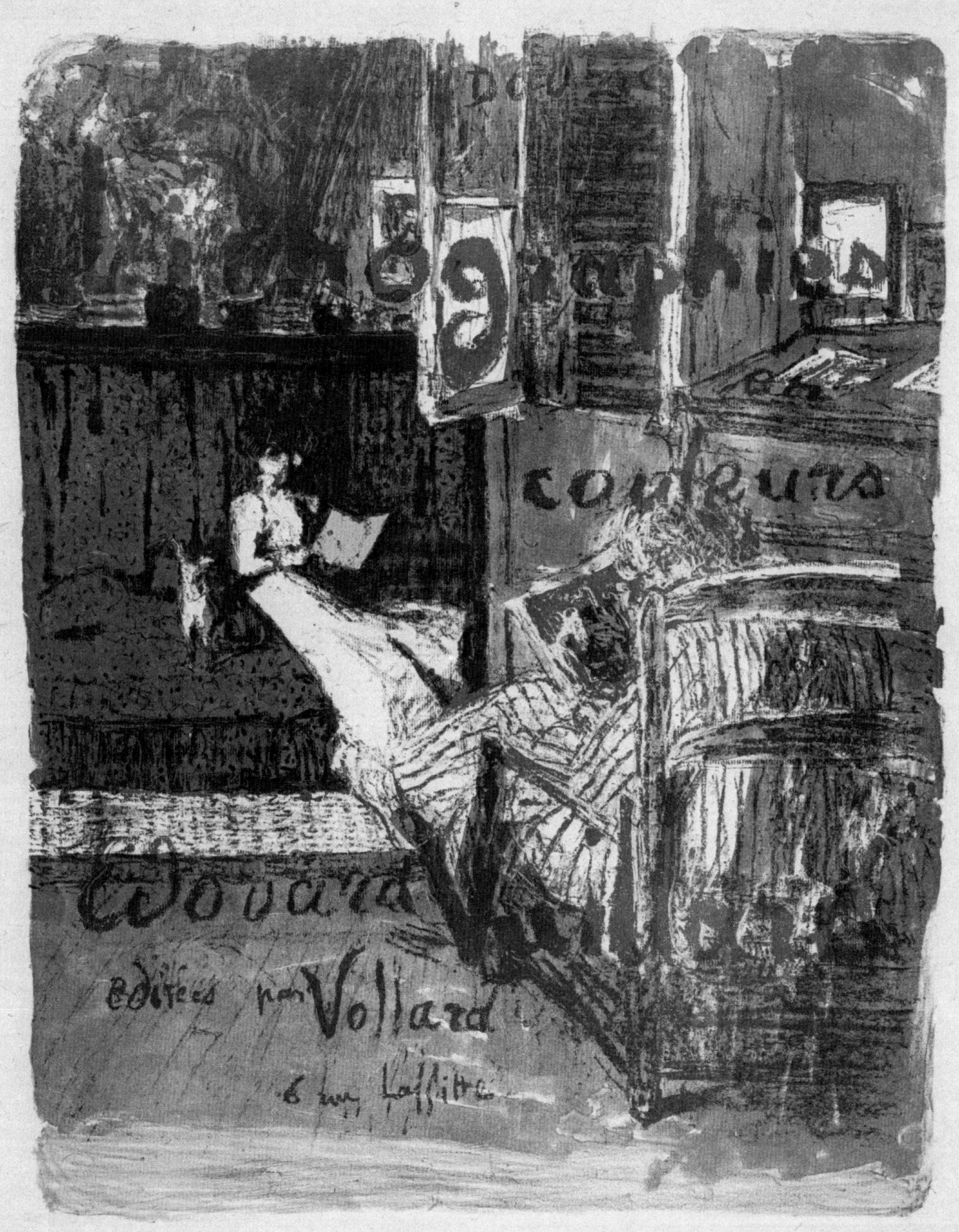
Lithographies
en
couleurs
Éditées par Vollard
Rue Laffitte

# Paysages et intérieurs

# *Landscapes and Interiors*

## Édouard Vuillard

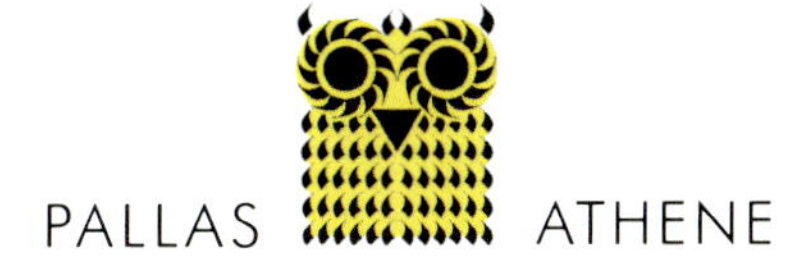

1.
La partie de dames
*The Game of Checkers*

330 x 257 mm

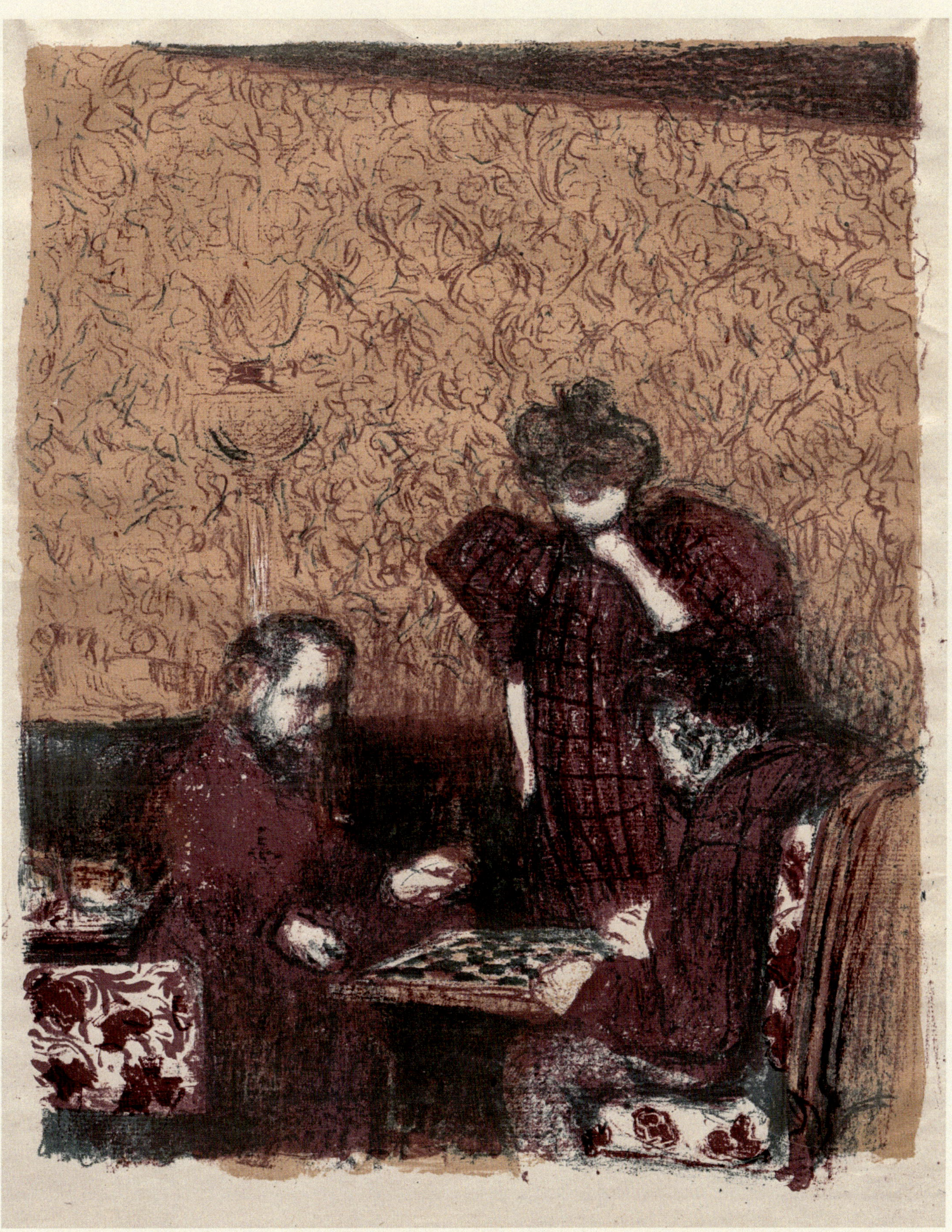

2.

L'Avenue

*The Avenue*

311 x 414 mm

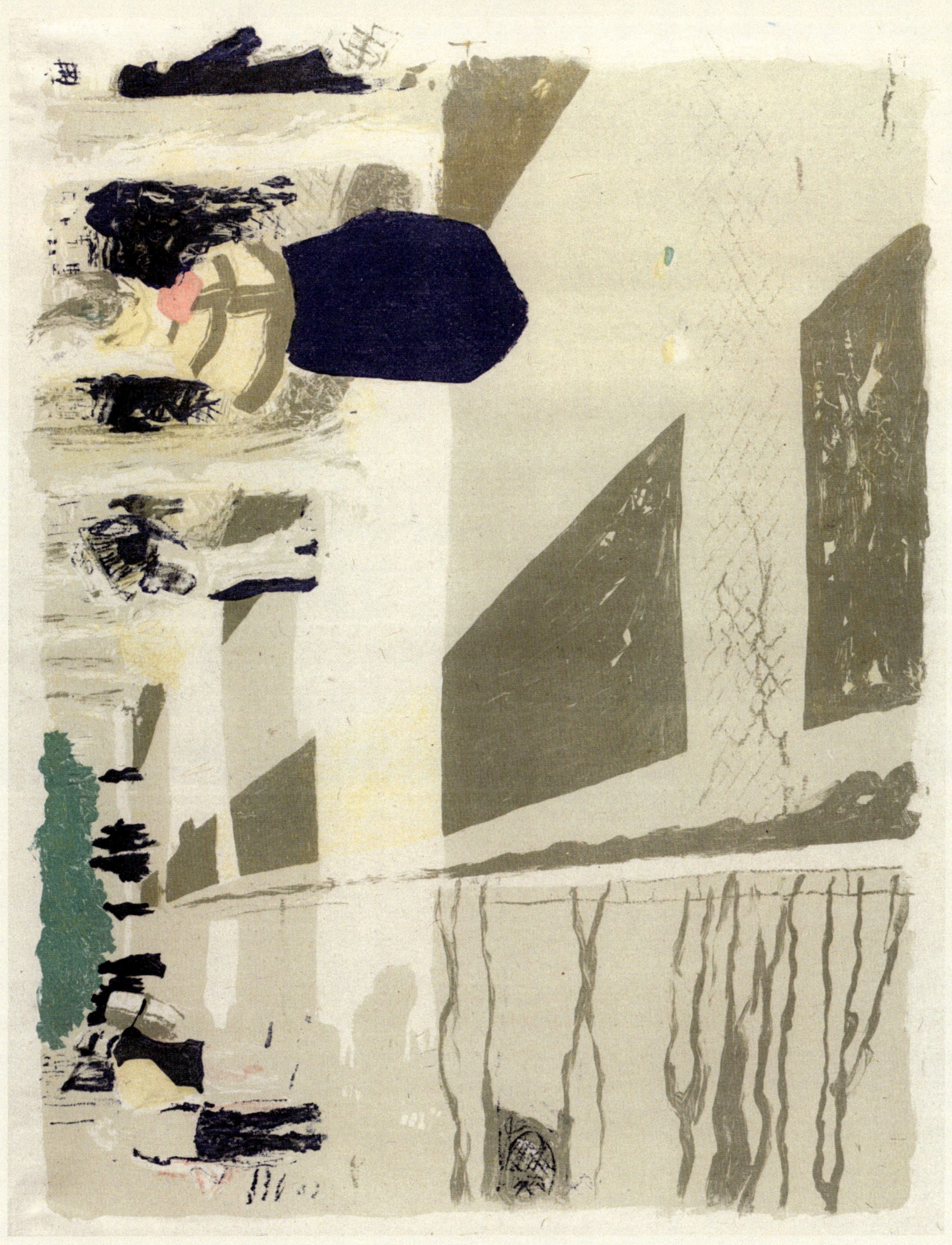

3.
À travers champs
*Across the Fields*

260 x 345 mm

4.
Intérieur à la suspension
*Interior with Ceiling Lamp*

356 x 282 mm

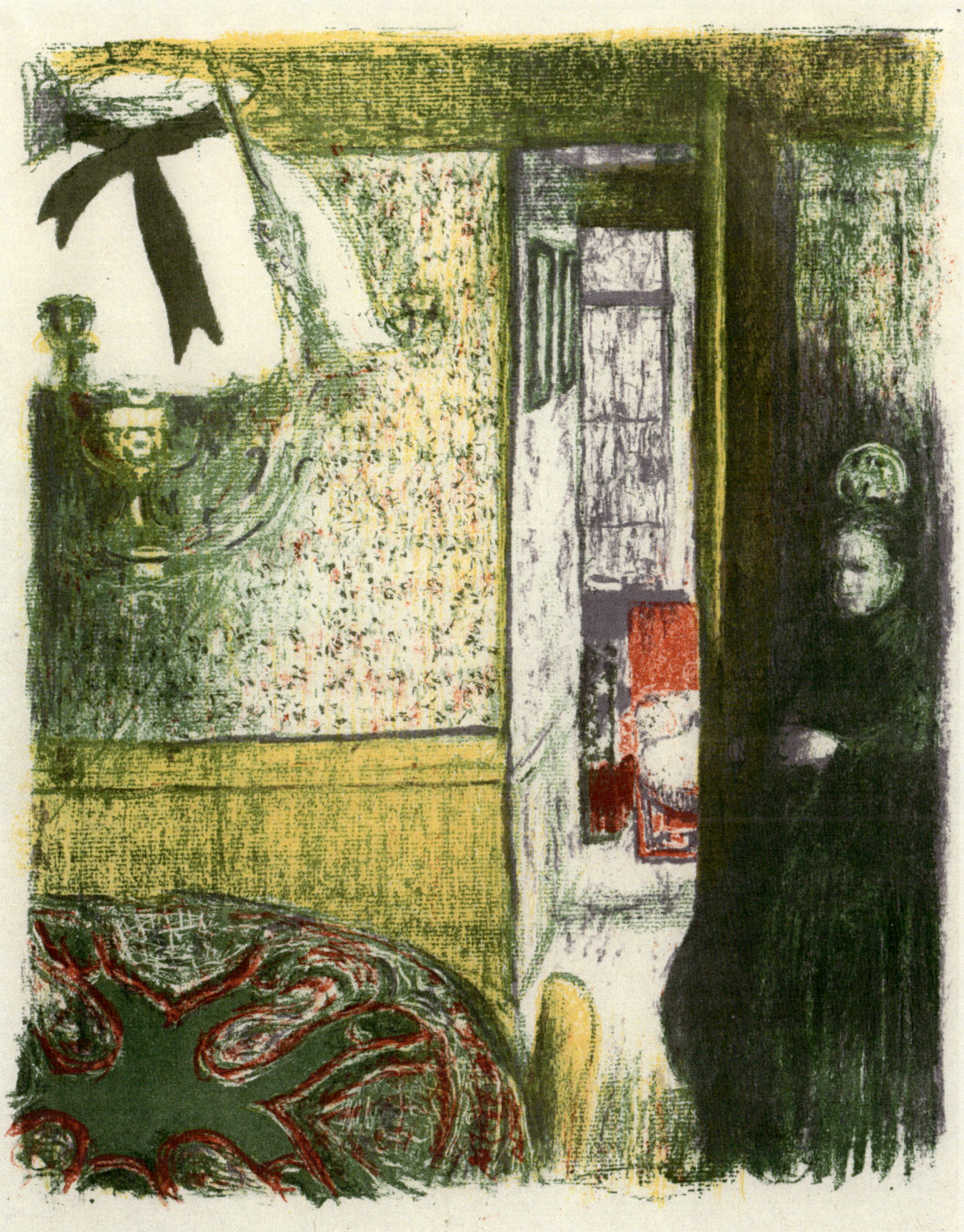

5.
Intérieur aux tentures roses I
*Interior with Pink Wallpaper I*

354 x 278 mm

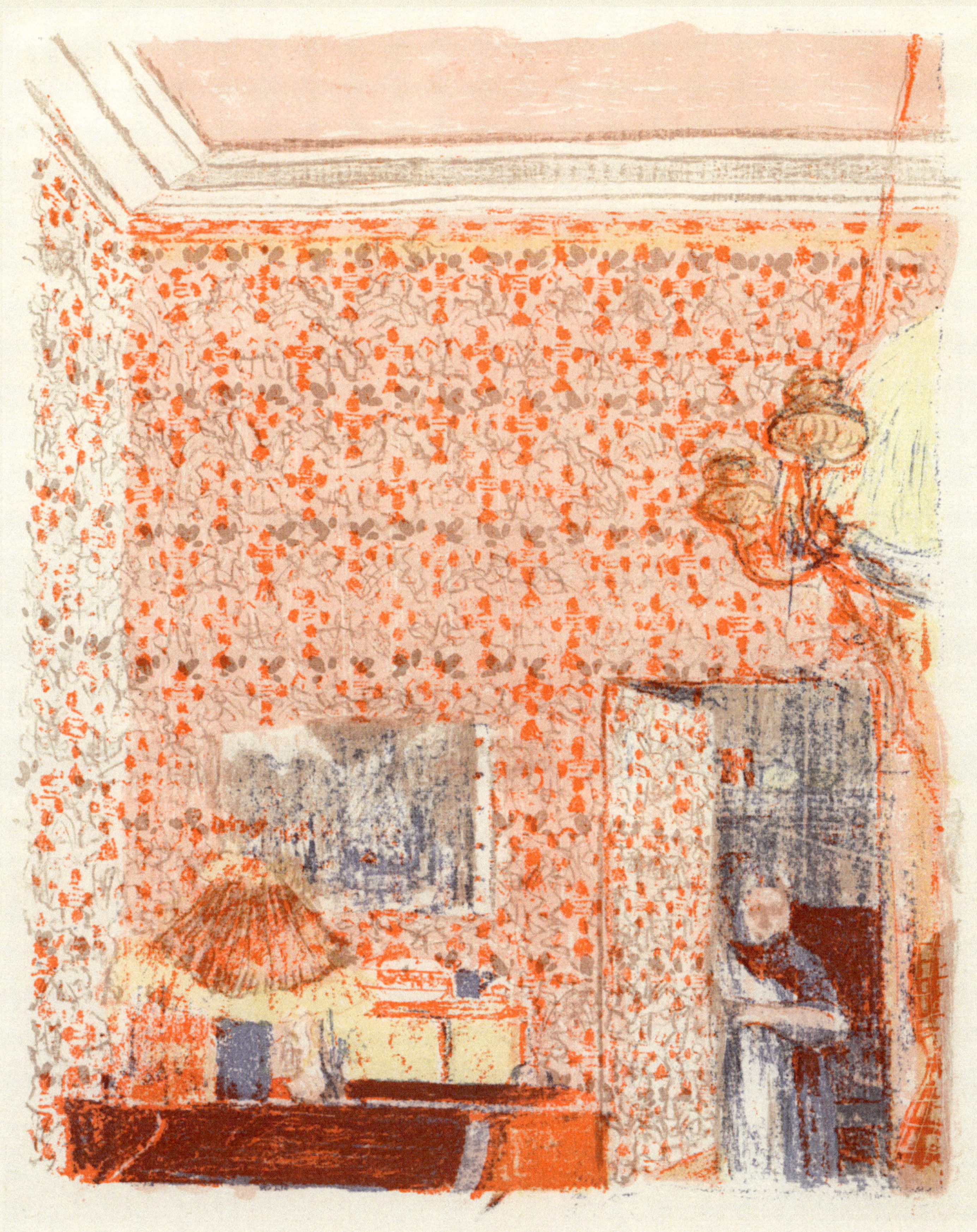

6.
Intérieur aux tentures roses II
*Interior with Pink Wallpaper II*

346 x 282 mm

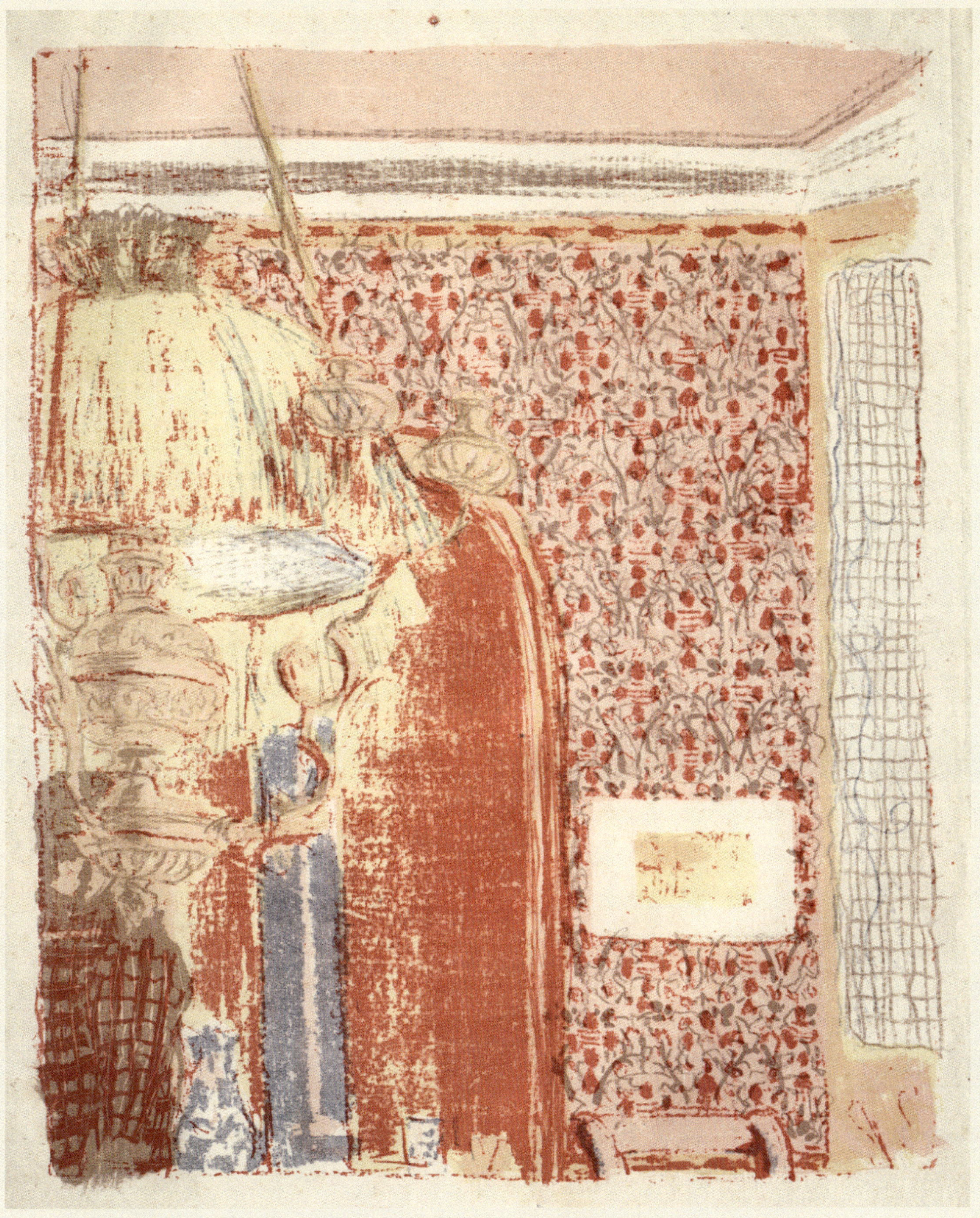

7.
Intérieur aux tentures roses III
*Interior with Pink Wallpaper III*

342 x 273 mm

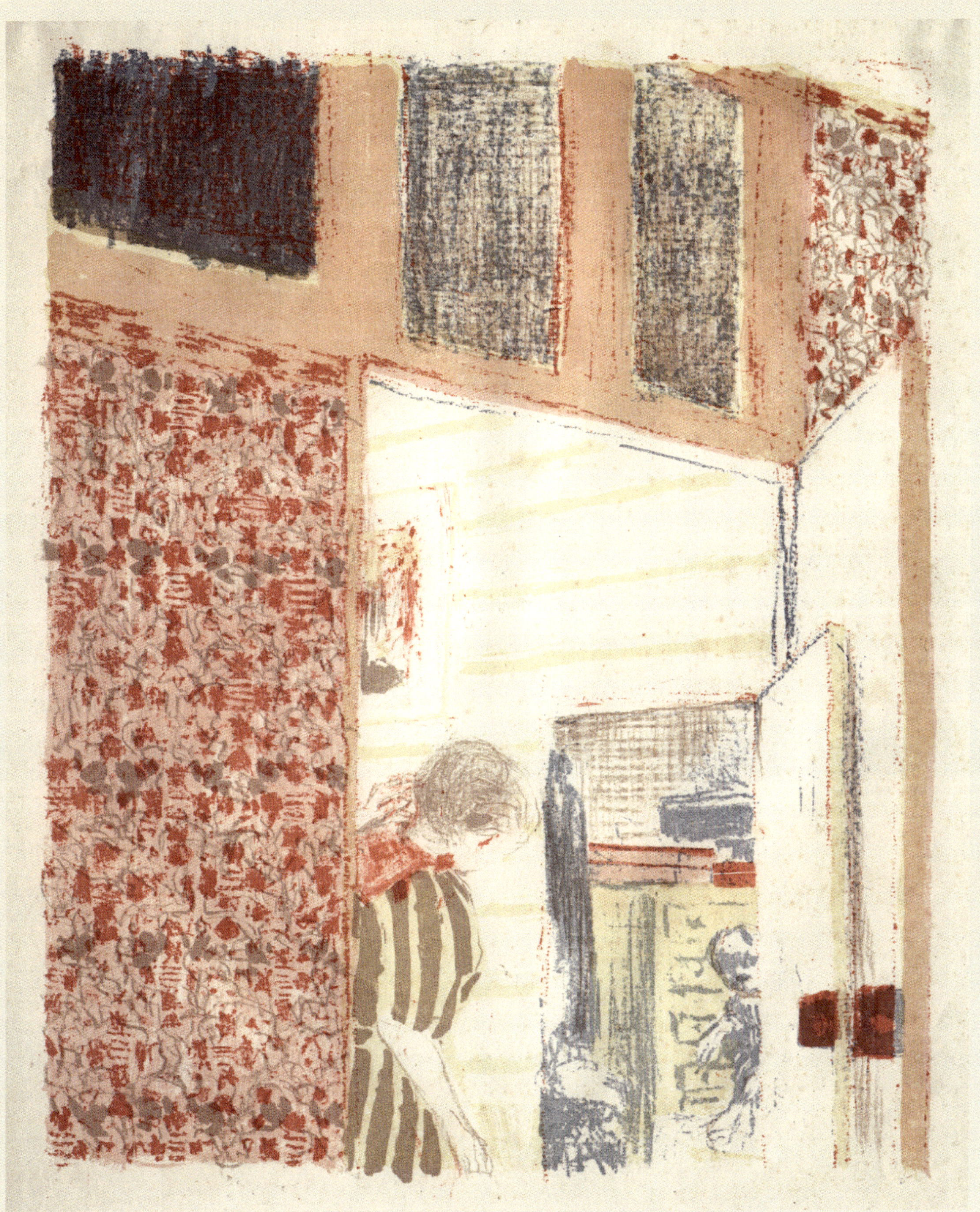

8.

L'Âtre

*The Hearth*

343 x 277 mm

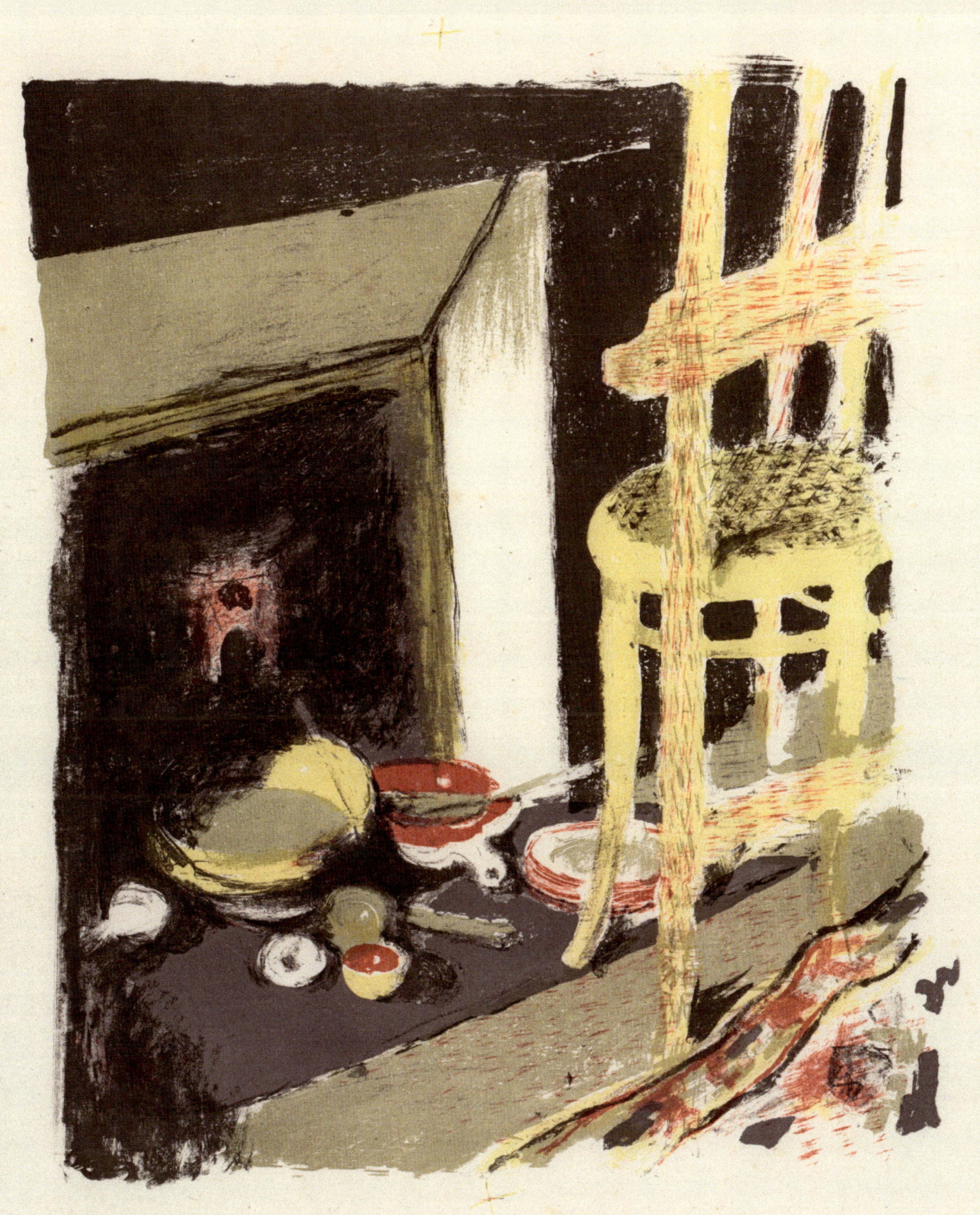

9.
Sur le pont de l'Europe
*On the Pont de l'Europe*

343 x 277 mm

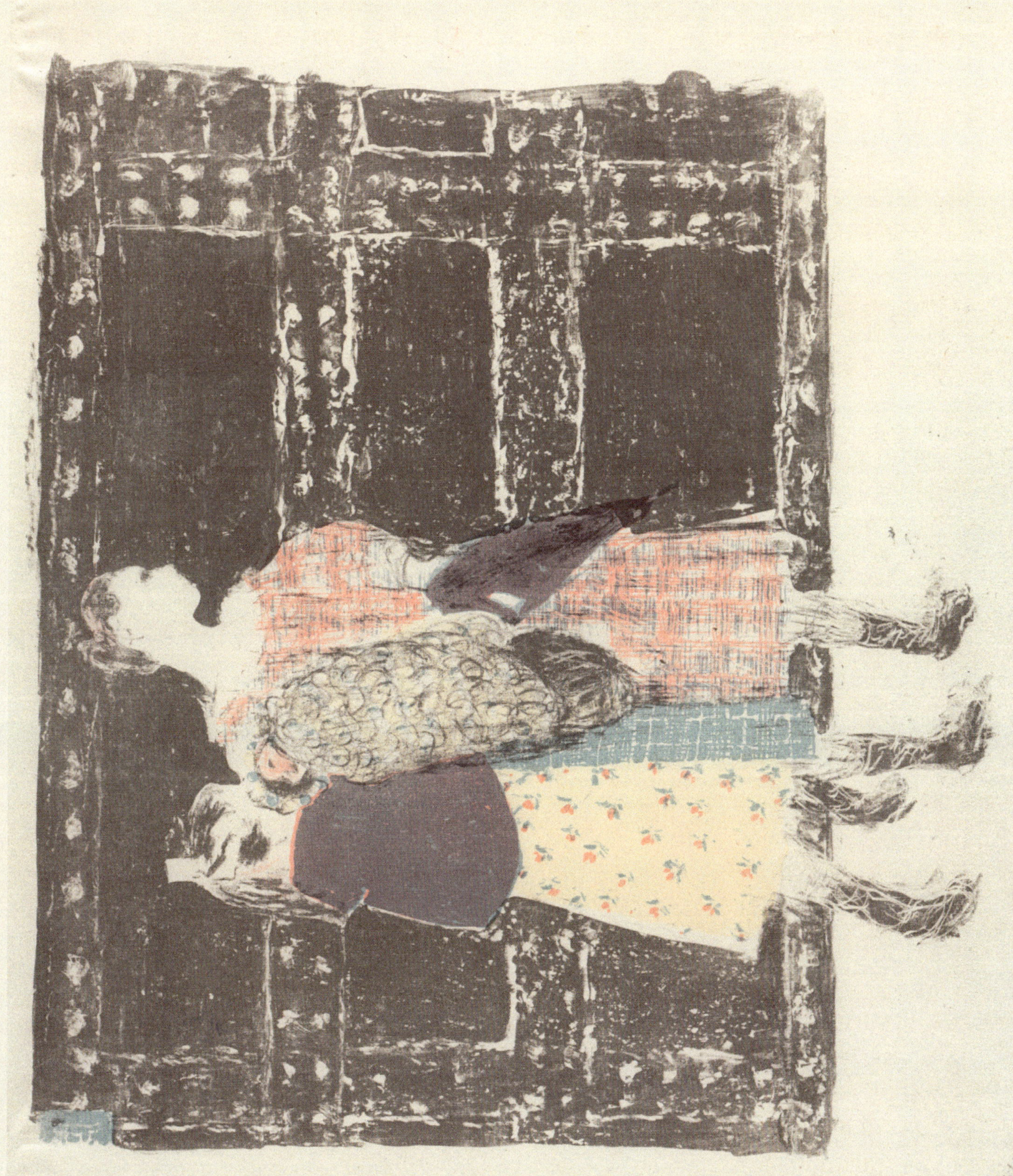

10.
La Pâtisserie
*The Pastry Shop*

351 x 275 mm

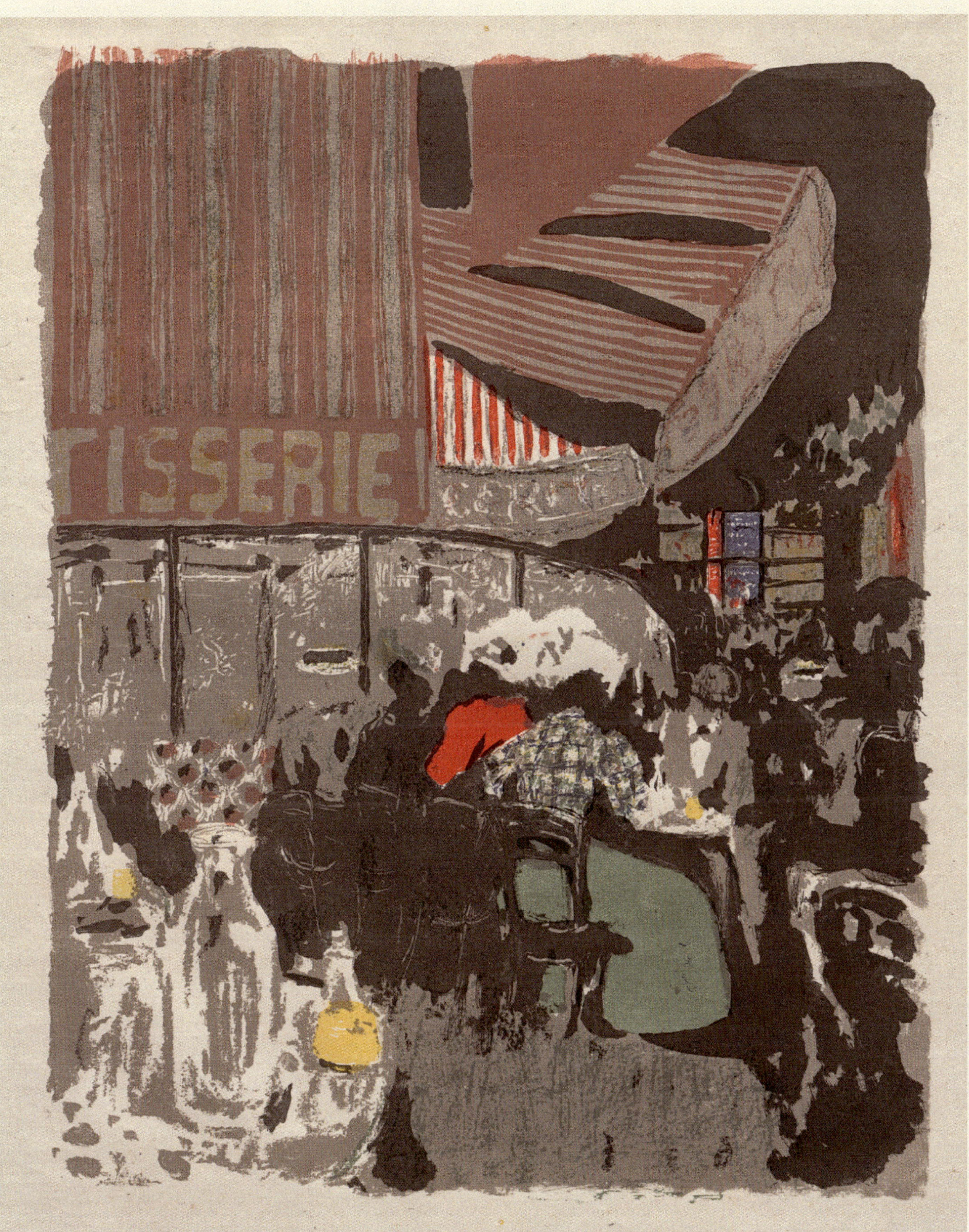
TISSERIE

11.
La Cuisinière (la mère de l'artiste)
*The Cook (the artist's mother)*

350 x 277 mm

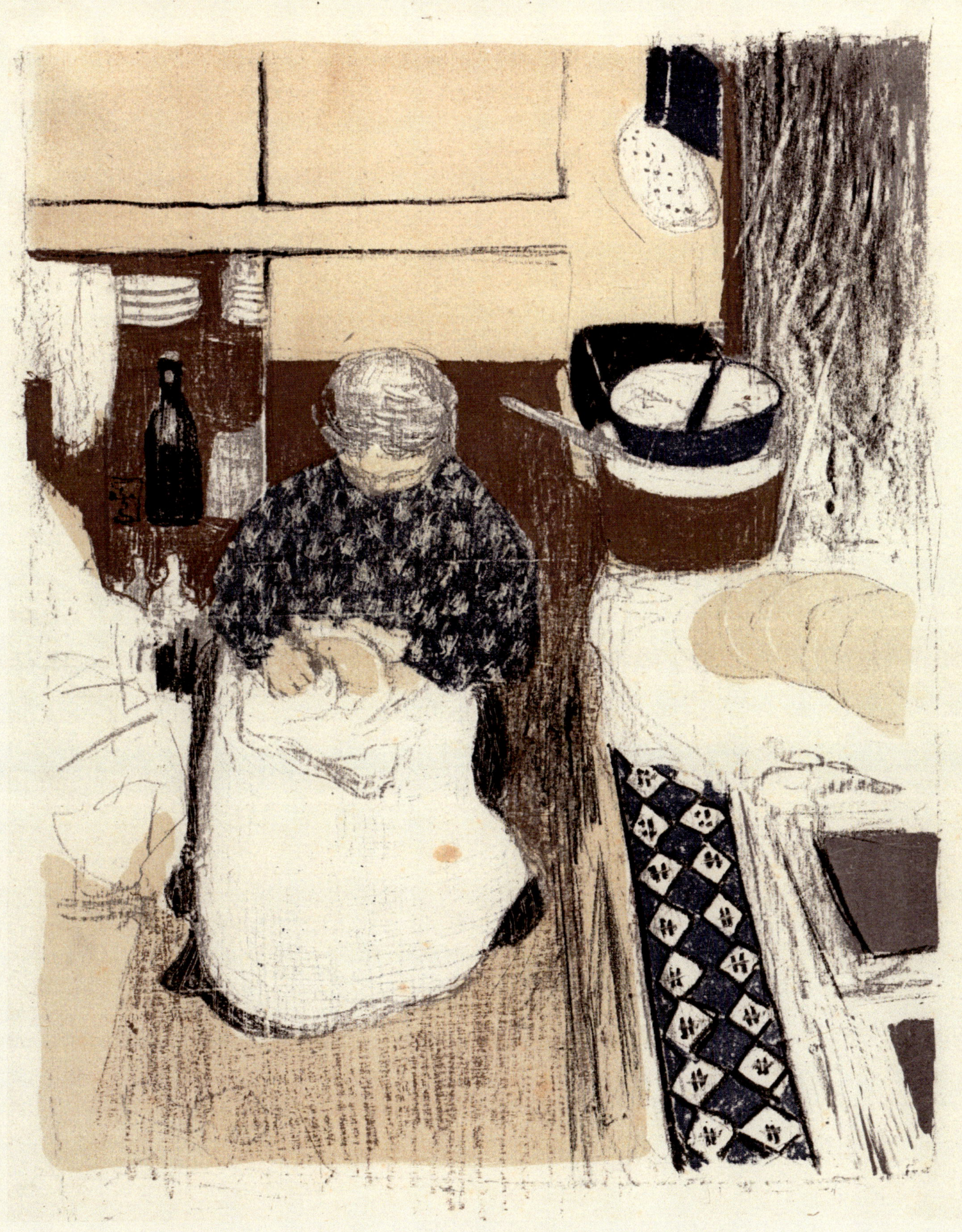

12.
Les deux belles-sœurs
*The Two Sisters-in-Law*

368 x 294 mm

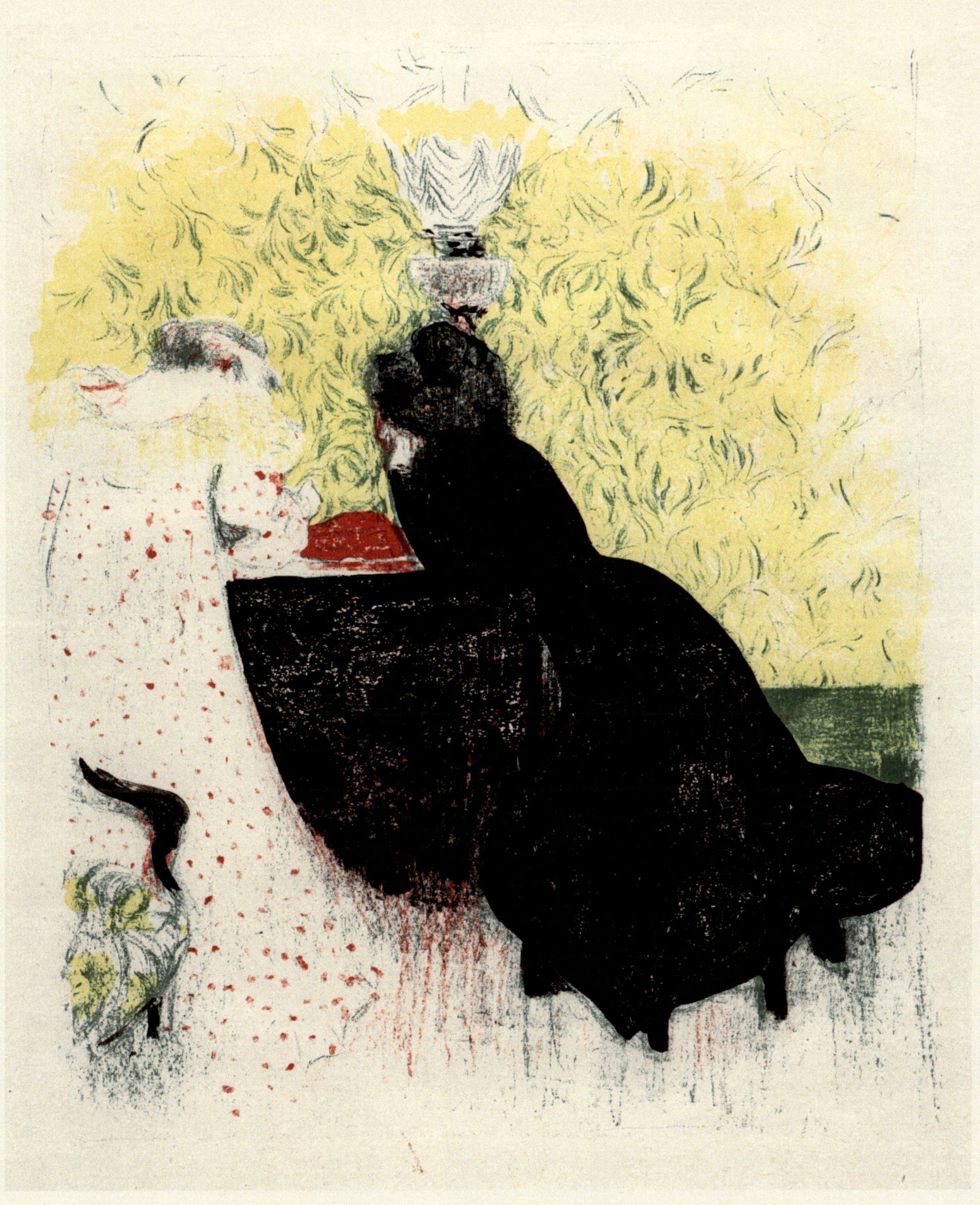

PAYSAGES ET INTÉRIEURS/
LANDSCAPES AND INTERIORS
Suite de 12 planches et une couverture,
imprimée par Auguste Clot. Éditée à
Paris par Ambroise Vollard en 1899,
et tirée à 100 exemplaires./
*Suite of 12 plates and a cover, printed
by Auguste Clot. Published in Paris by
Ambroise Vollard in 1899, in an edition
of 100 copies.*

Cette édition/*This edition*
© Pallas Athene (Publishers) Ltd,
London, 2026

Pallas Athene (Publishers) Ltd,
2 Birch Close, London N19 5XD

**www.pallasathene.co.uk**

ISBN 978 1 84368 299 8 (édition française)
ISBN 978 1 84368 298 1 (English edition)

Imprimé en Angleterre par Blissetts/
*Printed in England by Blissetts*

3

PAYSAGES
ET INTÉRIEURS

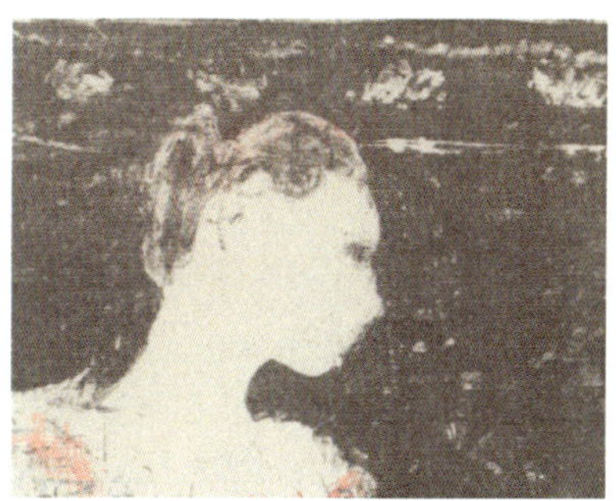

LANDSCAPES AND
INTERIORS

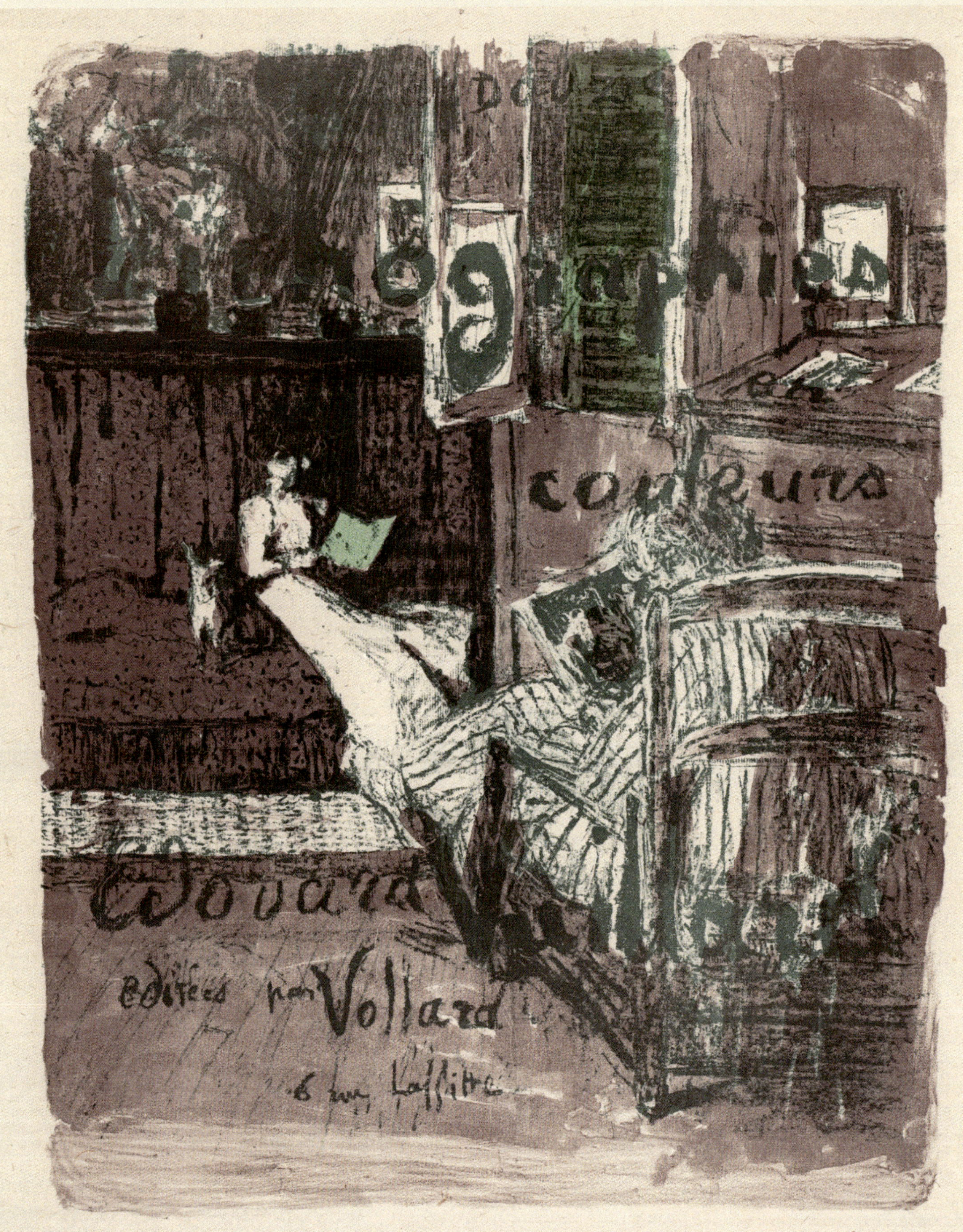
Lithographies en couleurs
Éditées par Vollard
6 rue Laffitte

# Paysages et intérieurs

# *Landscapes and Interiors*

## Édouard Vuillard

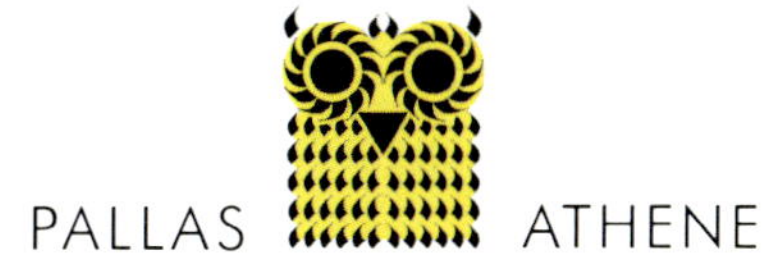

1.
La partie de dames
*The Game of Checkers*

330 x 257 mm

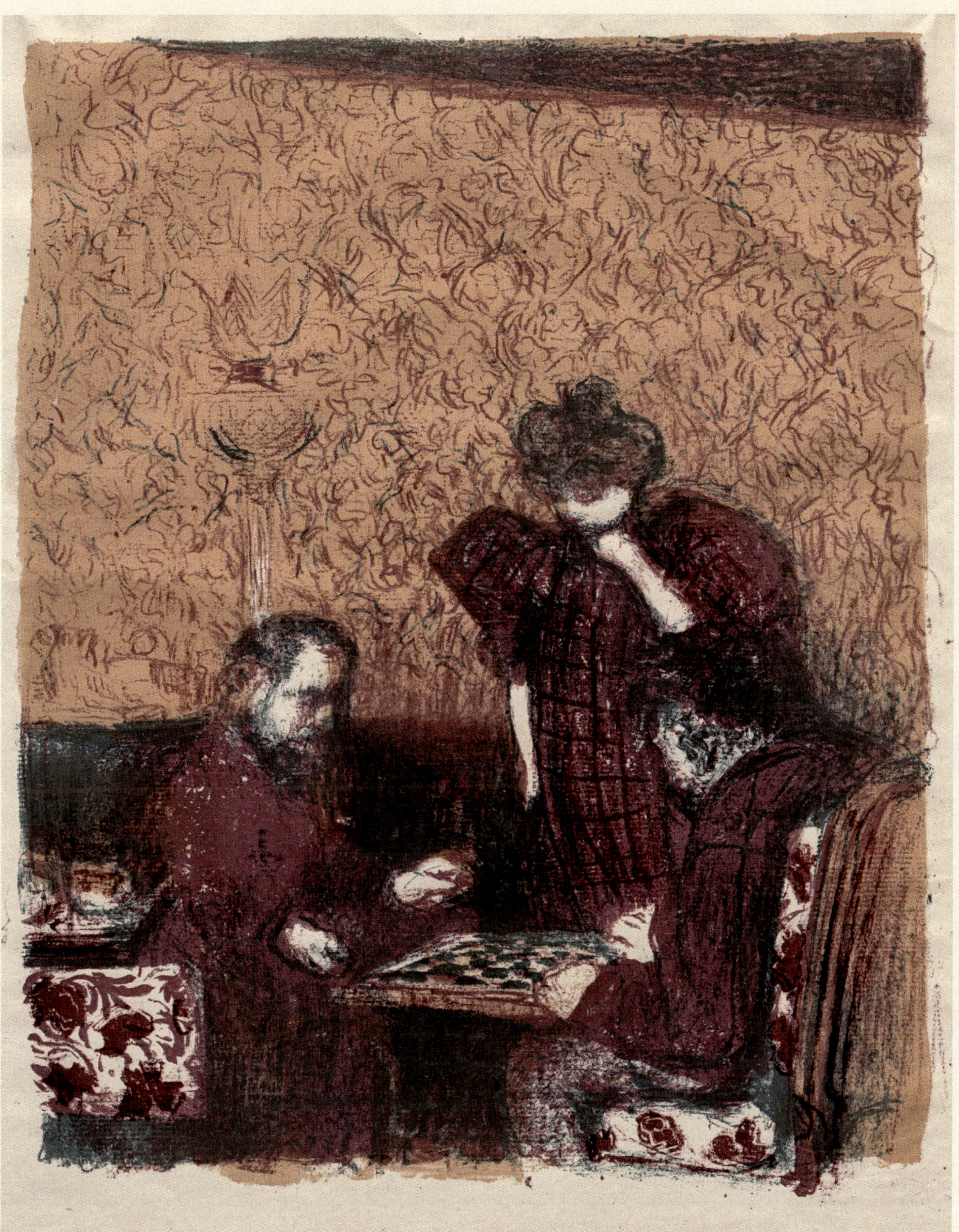

2.

L'Avenue

*The Avenue*

311 x 414 mm

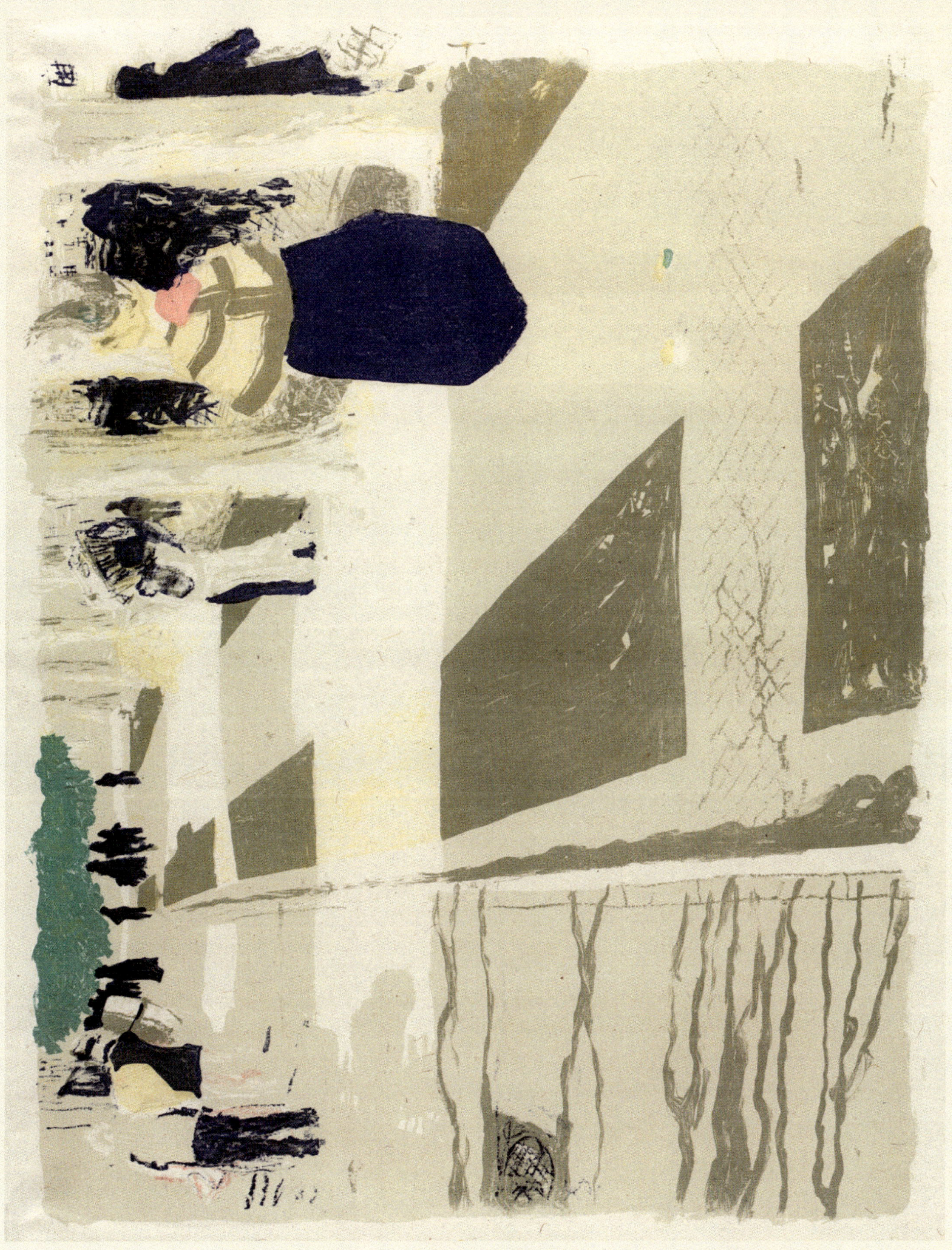

3.
À travers champs
*Across the Fields*

260 x 345 mm

4.
Intérieur à la suspension
*Interior with Ceiling Lamp*

356 x 282 mm

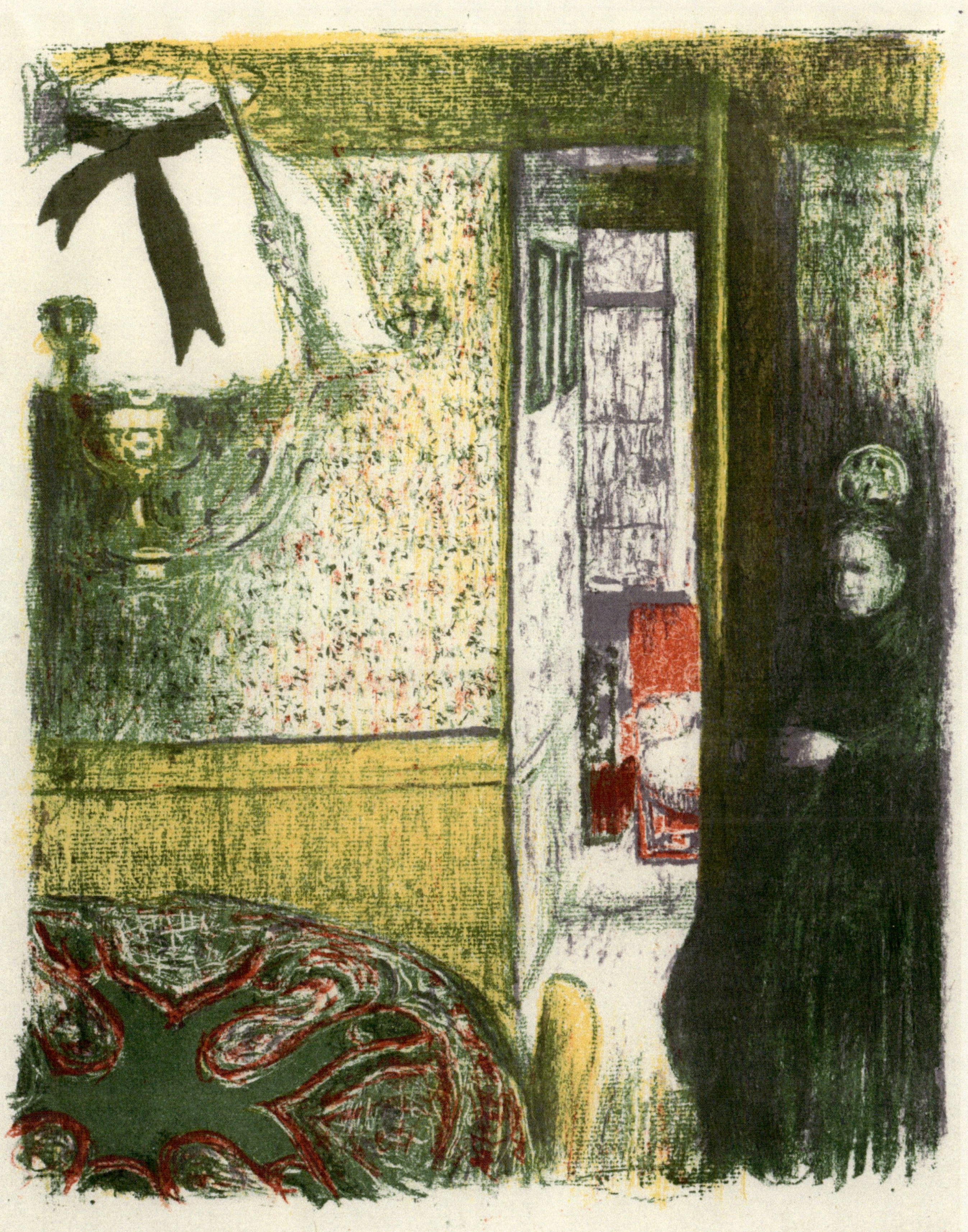

5.

Intérieur aux tentures roses I

*Interior with Pink Wallpaper I*

354 x 278 mm

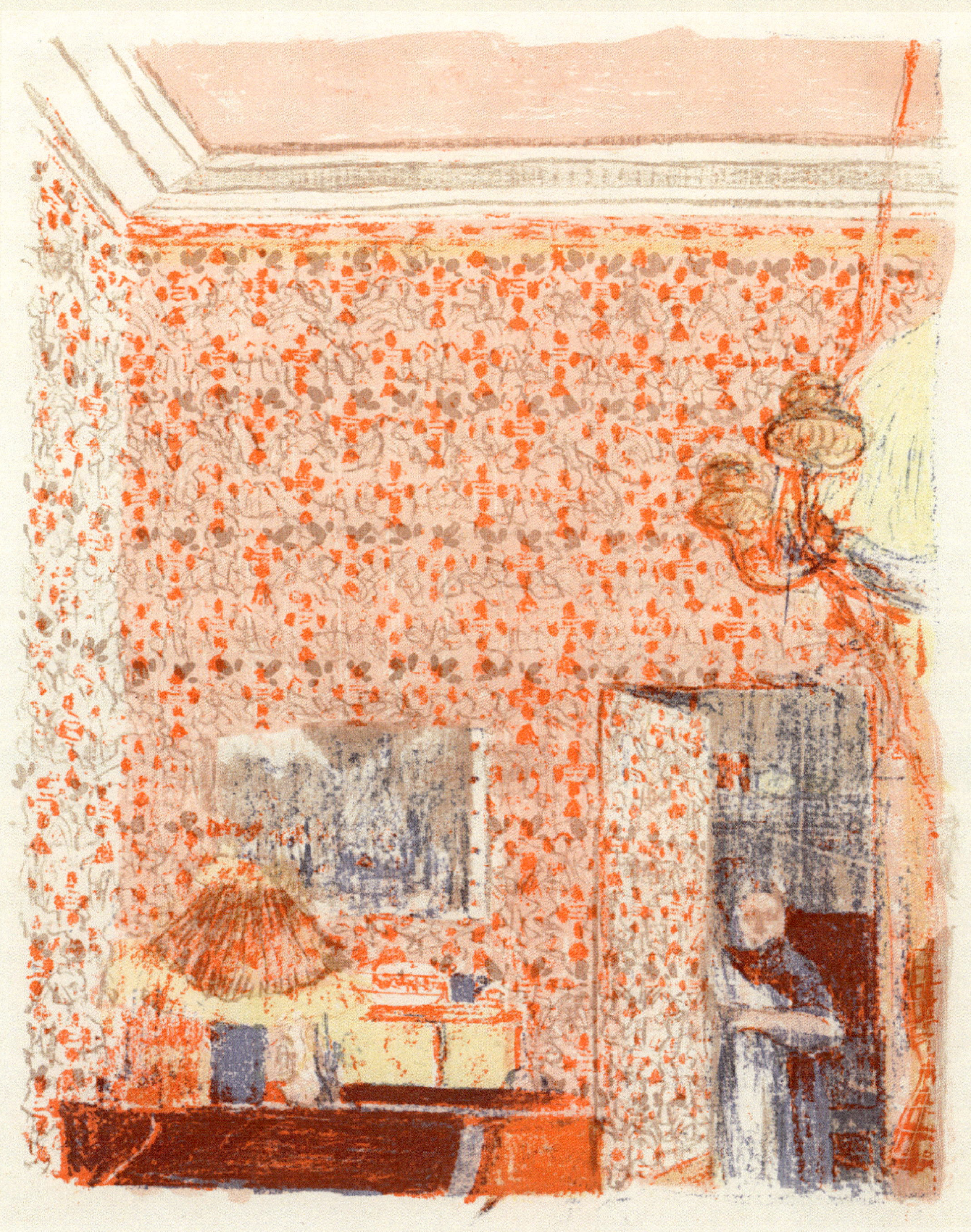

6.
Intérieur aux tentures roses II
*Interior with Pink Wallpaper II*

346 x 282 mm

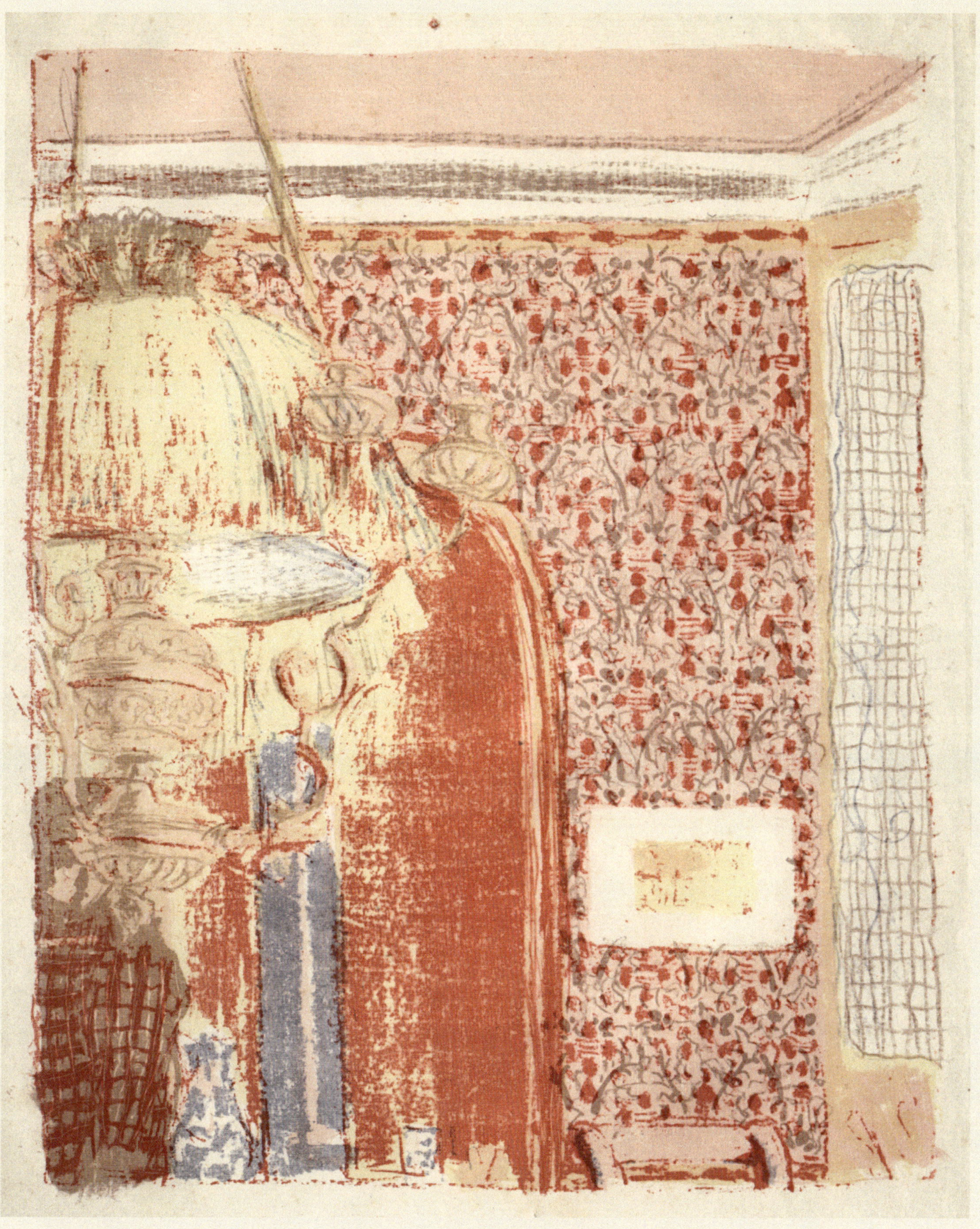

7.
Intérieur aux tentures roses III
*Interior with Pink Wallpaper III*

342 x 273 mm

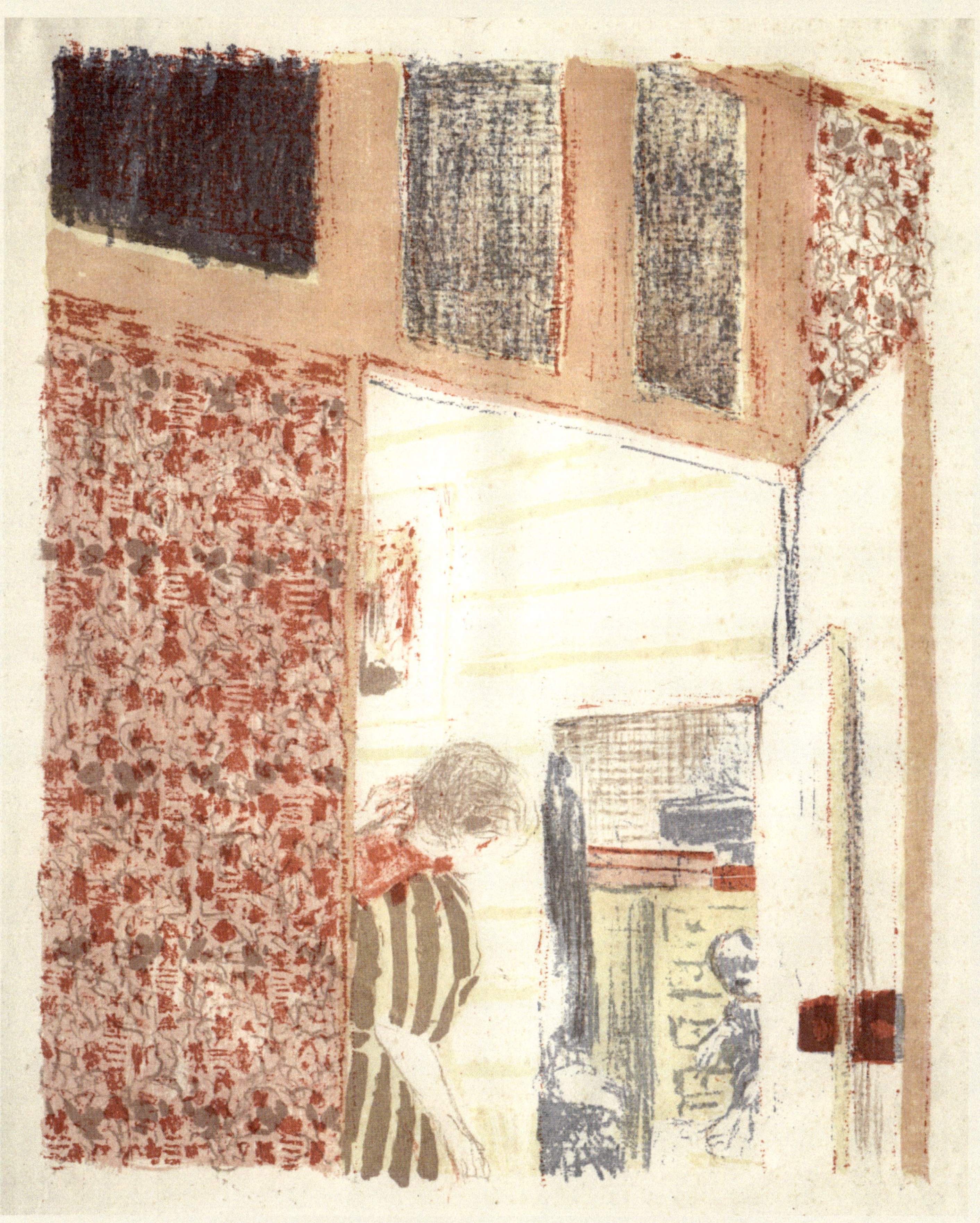

8.
L'Âtre
*The Hearth*

343 x 277 mm

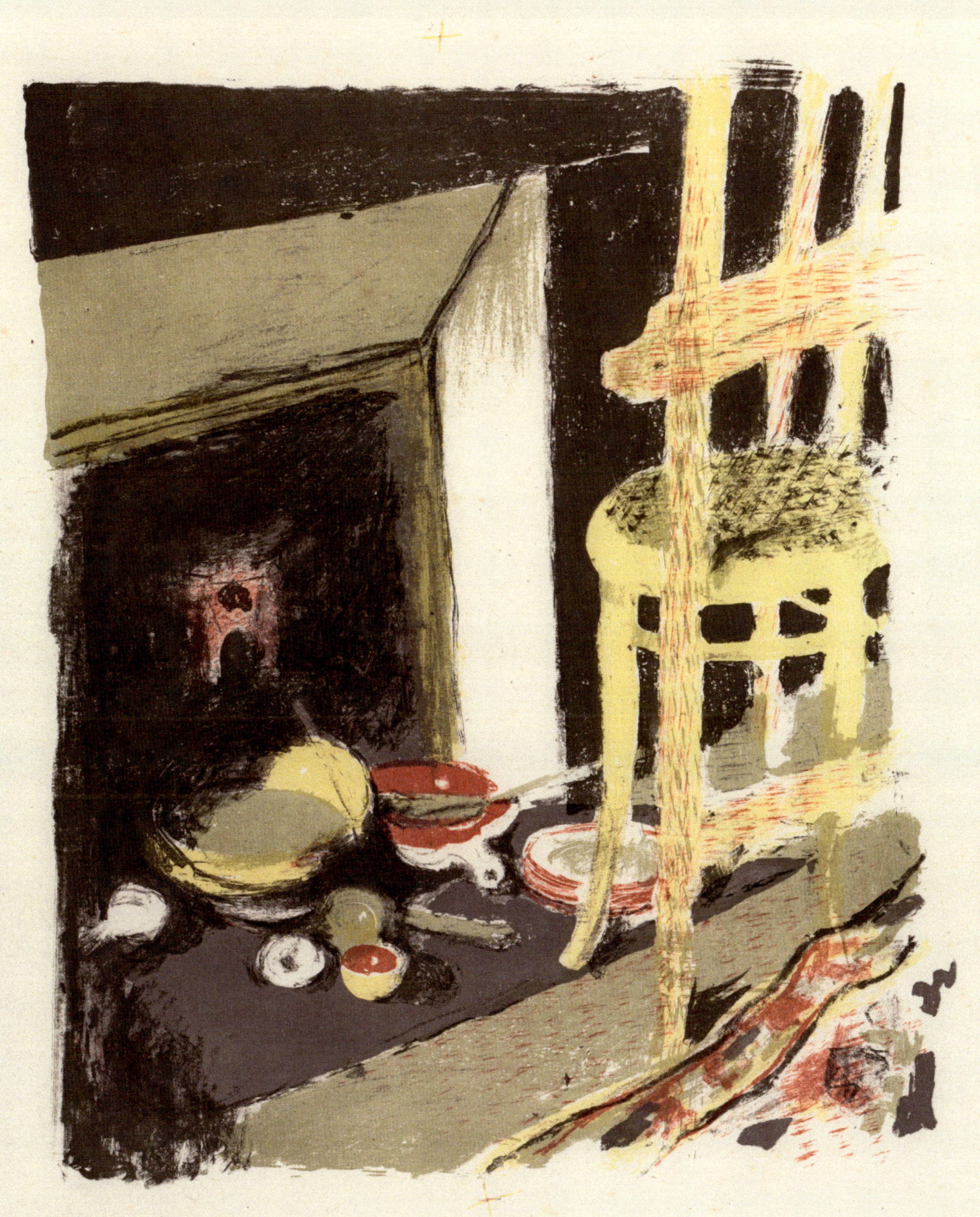

9.
Sur le pont de l'Europe
*On the Pont de l'Europe*

343 x 277 mm

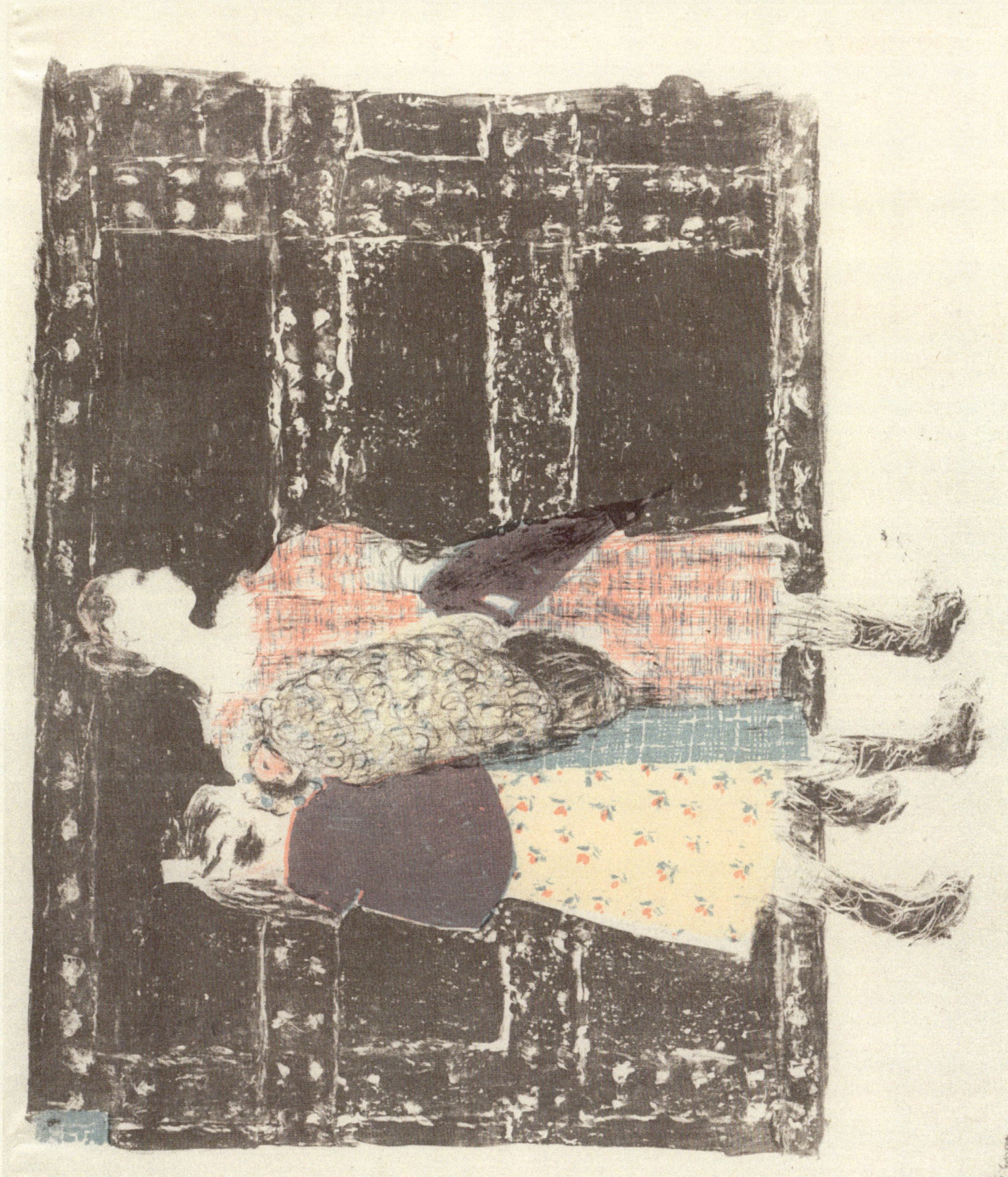

10.
La Pâtisserie
*The Pastry Shop*

351 x 275 mm

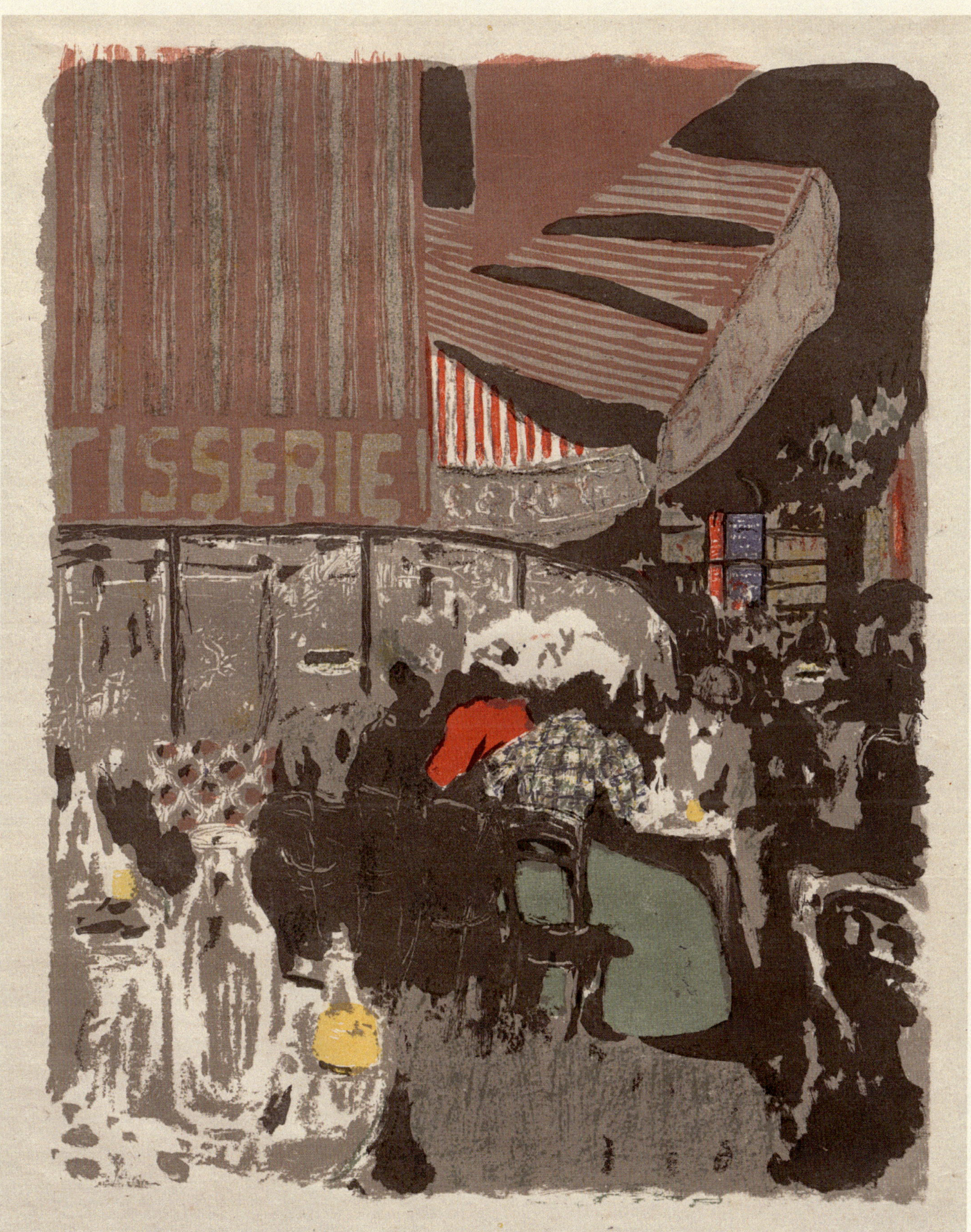
TISSERIE

II.

La Cuisinière (la mère de l'artiste)
*The Cook (the artist's mother)*

350 x 277 mm

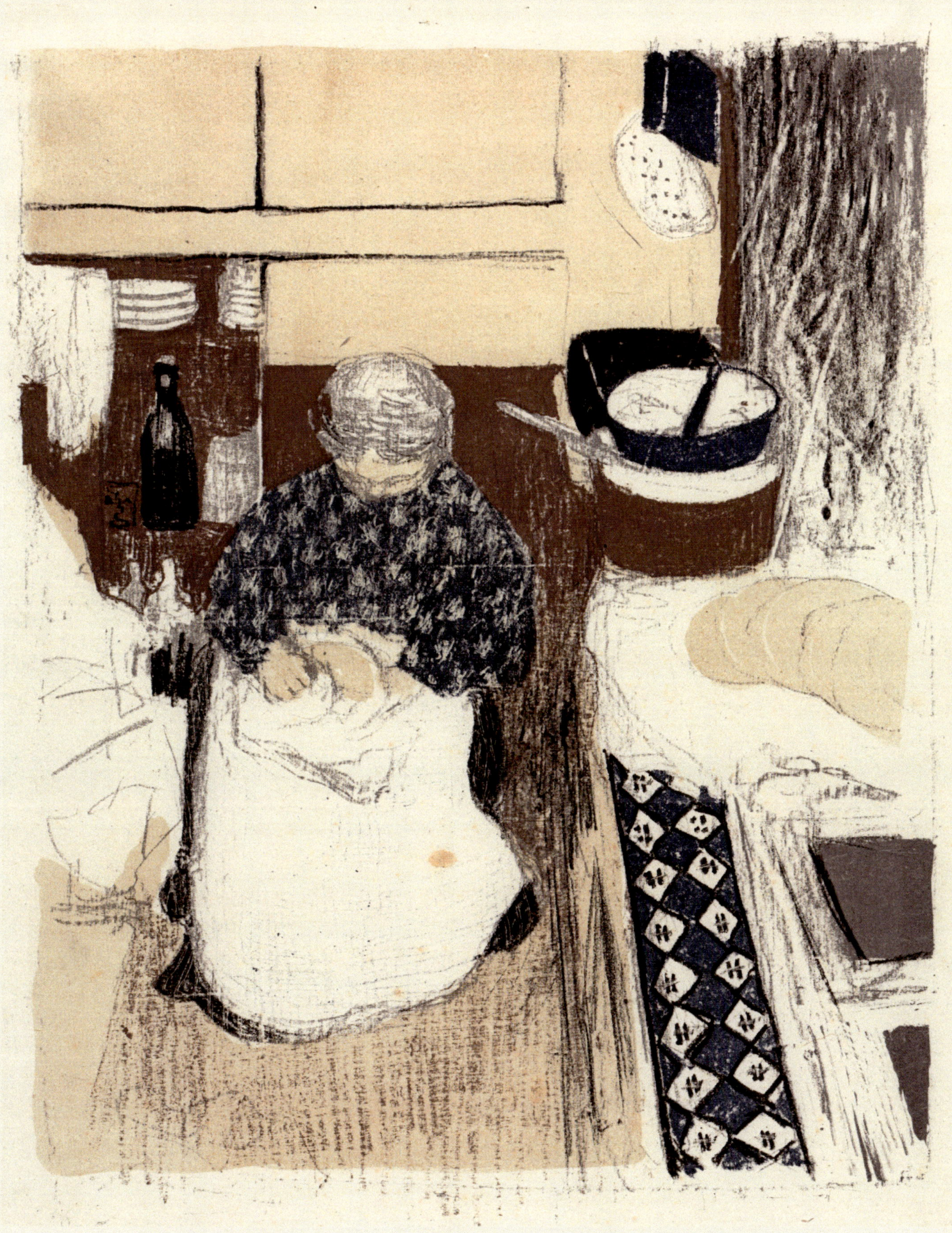

12.
Les deux belles-sœurs
*The Two Sisters-in-Law*

368 x 294 mm

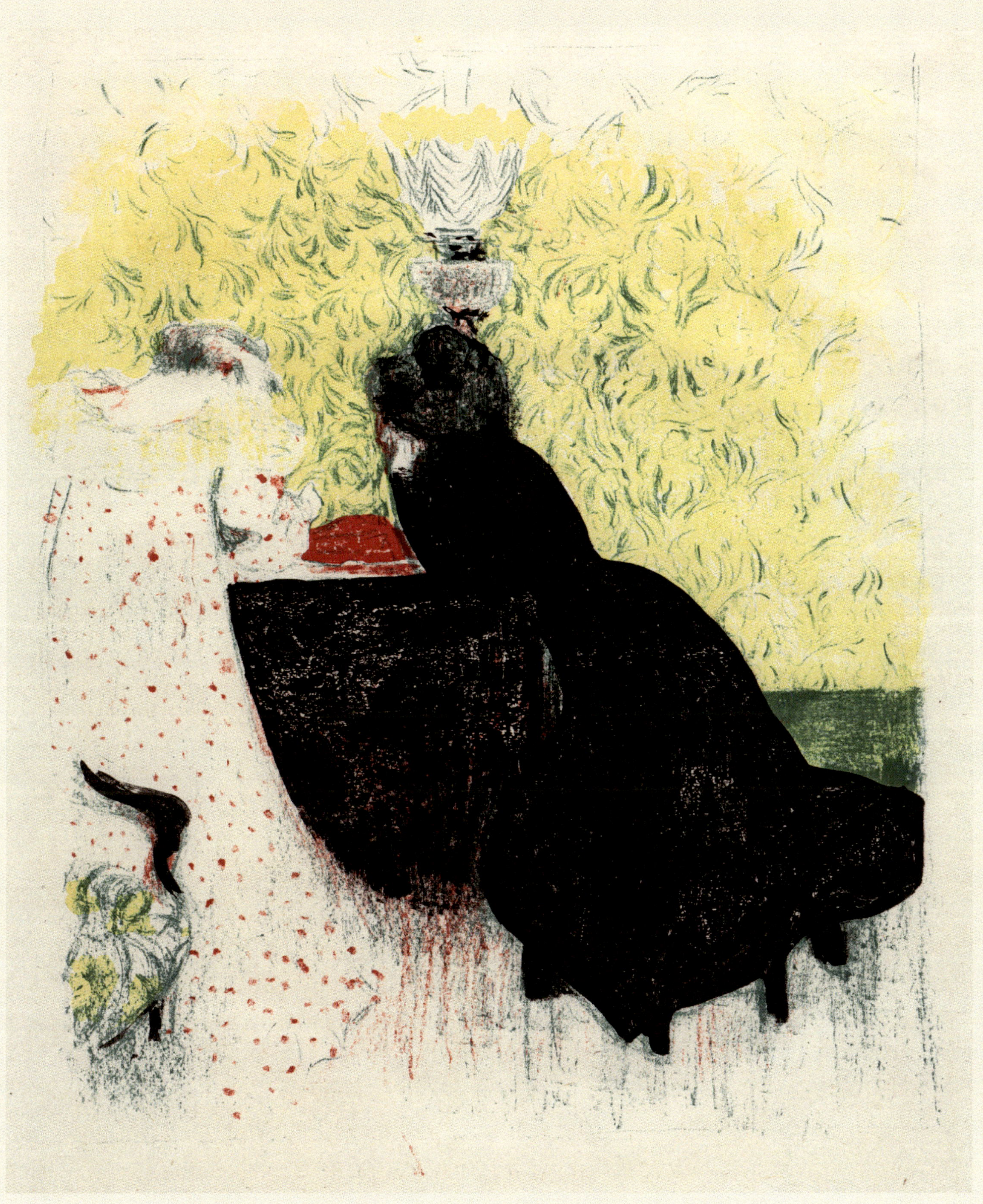

PAYSAGES ET INTÉRIEURS/
LANDSCAPES AND INTERIORS
Suite de 12 planches et une couverture,
imprimée par Auguste Clot. Éditée à
Paris par Ambroise Vollard en 1899,
et tirée à 100 exemplaires./
*Suite of 12 plates and a cover, printed
by Auguste Clot. Published in Paris by
Ambroise Vollard in 1899, in an edition
of 100 copies.*

Cette édition/*This edition*
© Pallas Athene (Publishers) Ltd,
London, 2026

Pallas Athene (Publishers) Ltd,
2 Birch Close, London N19 5XD

**www.pallasathene.co.uk**

ISBN 978 1 84368 299 8 (édition française)
ISBN 978 1 84368 298 1 (English edition)

Imprimé en Angleterre par Blissetts/
*Printed in England by Blissetts*

PAYSAGES
ET INTÉRIEURS

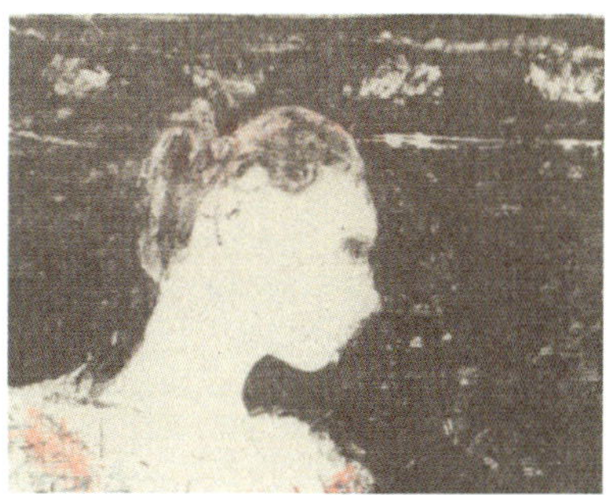

LANDSCAPES AND
INTERIORS

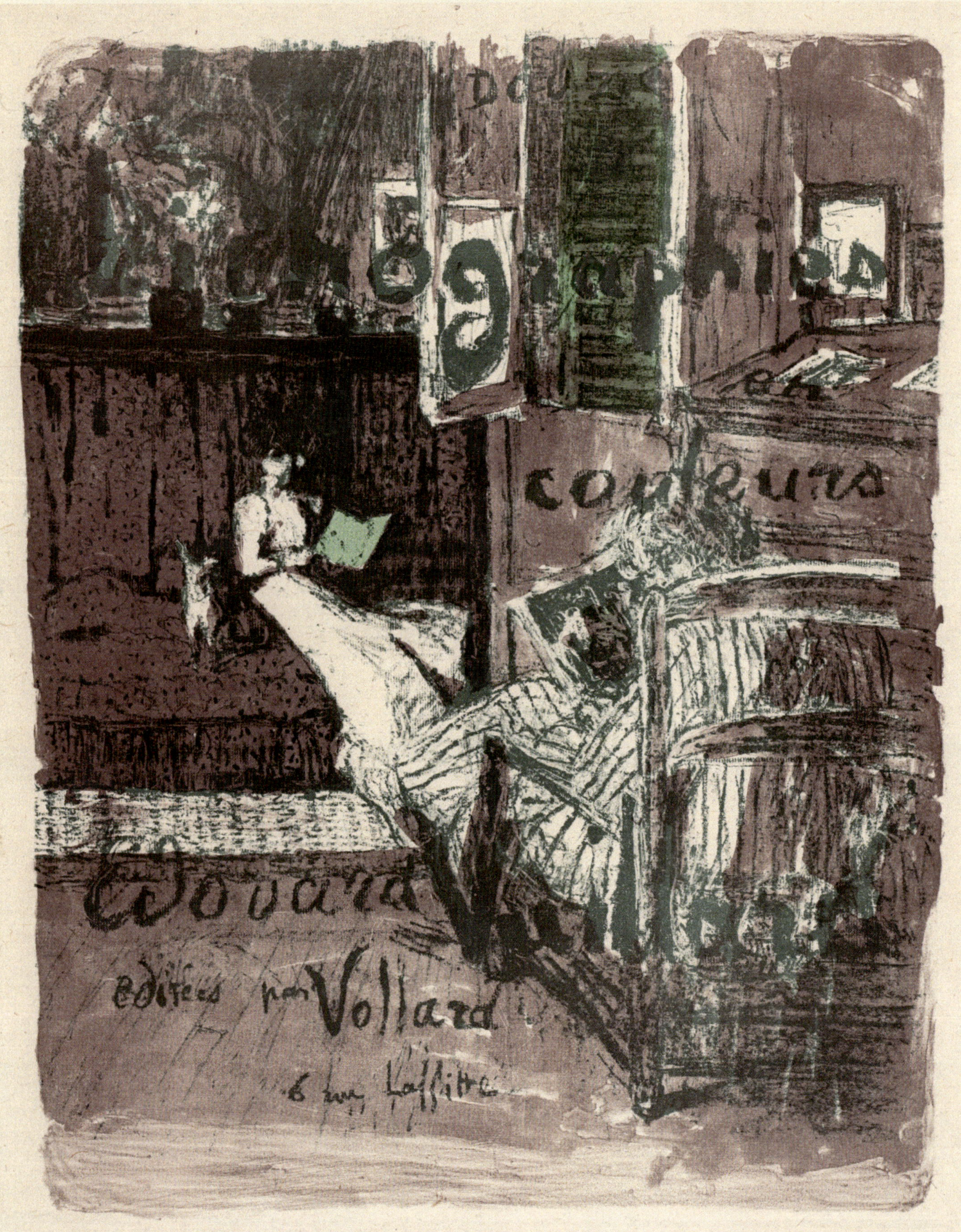

Deux
Lithographies
en
couleurs
Edouard Vuillard
Editées par Vollard
6 rue Laffitte

# Paysages et intérieurs

## *Landscapes and Interiors*

### Édouard Vuillard

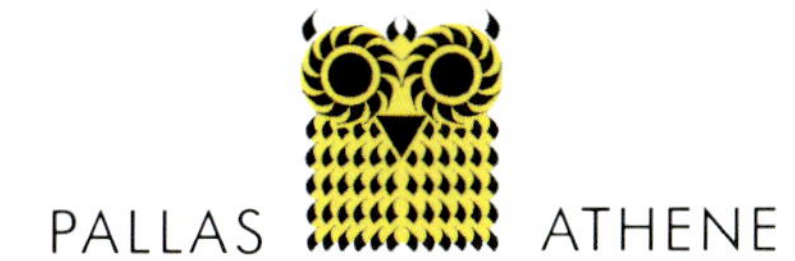

Pallas Athene

1.

La partie de dames
*The Game of Checkers*

330 x 257 mm

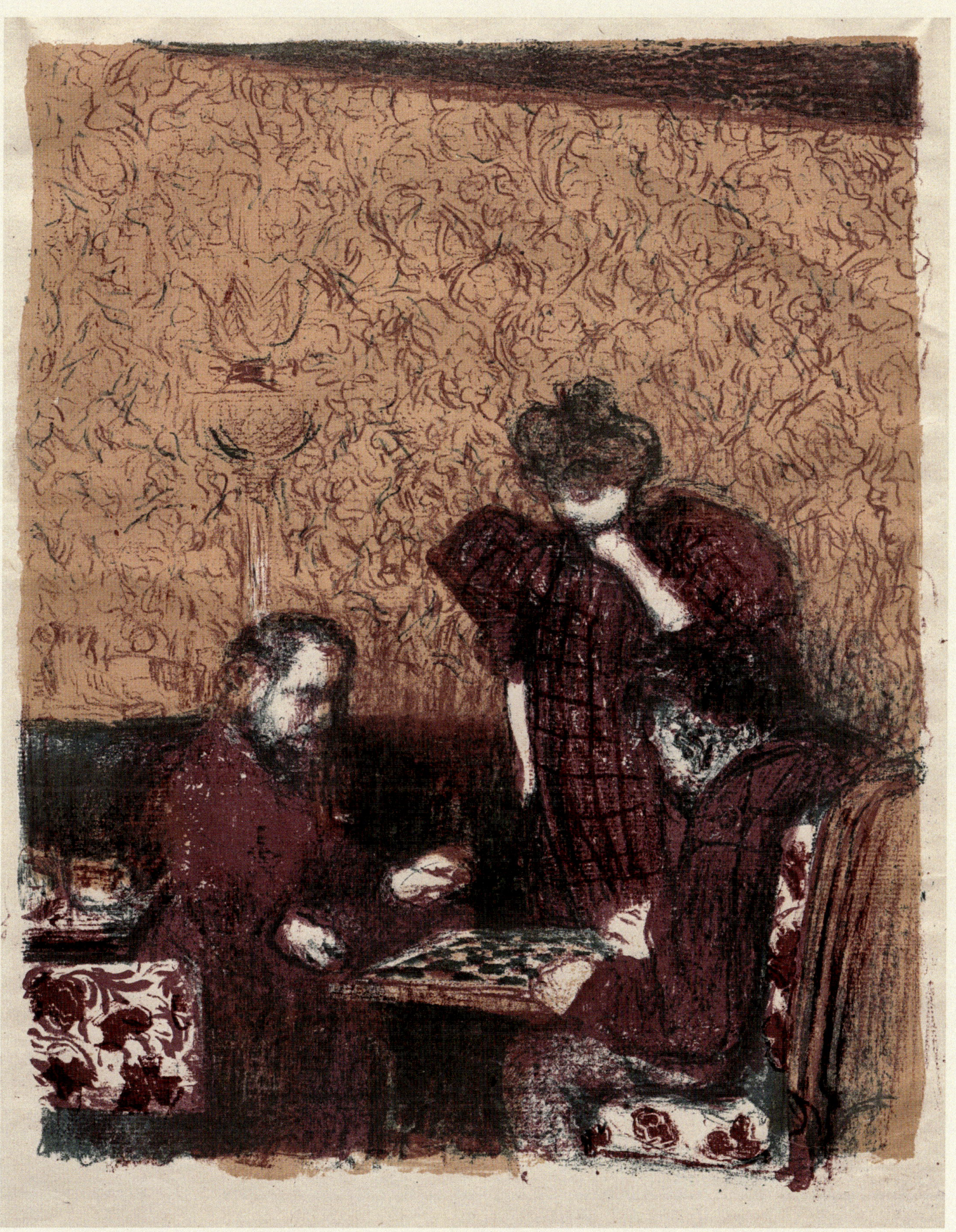

2.
L'Avenue
*The Avenue*

311 x 414 mm

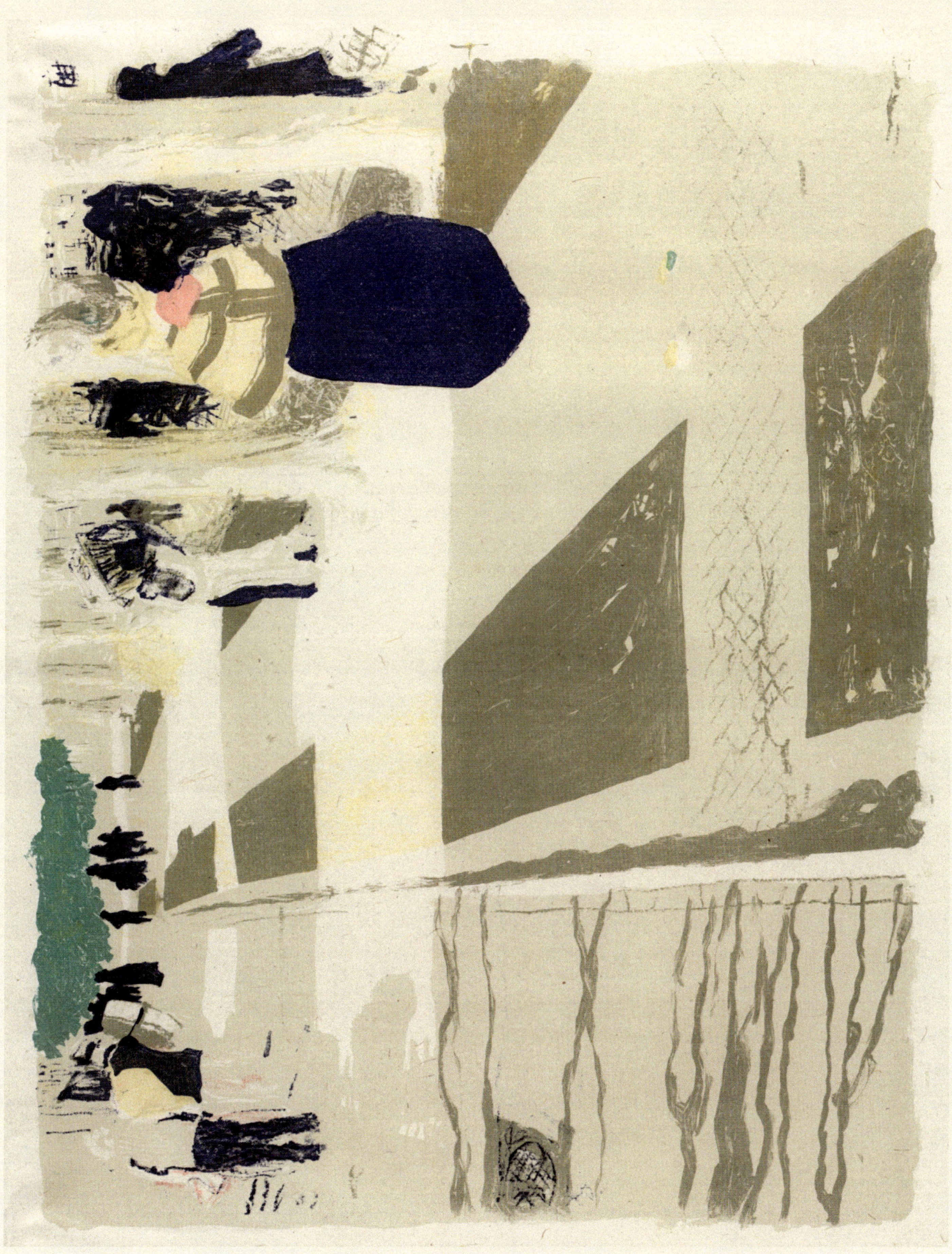

3.
À travers champs
*Across the Fields*

260 x 345 mm

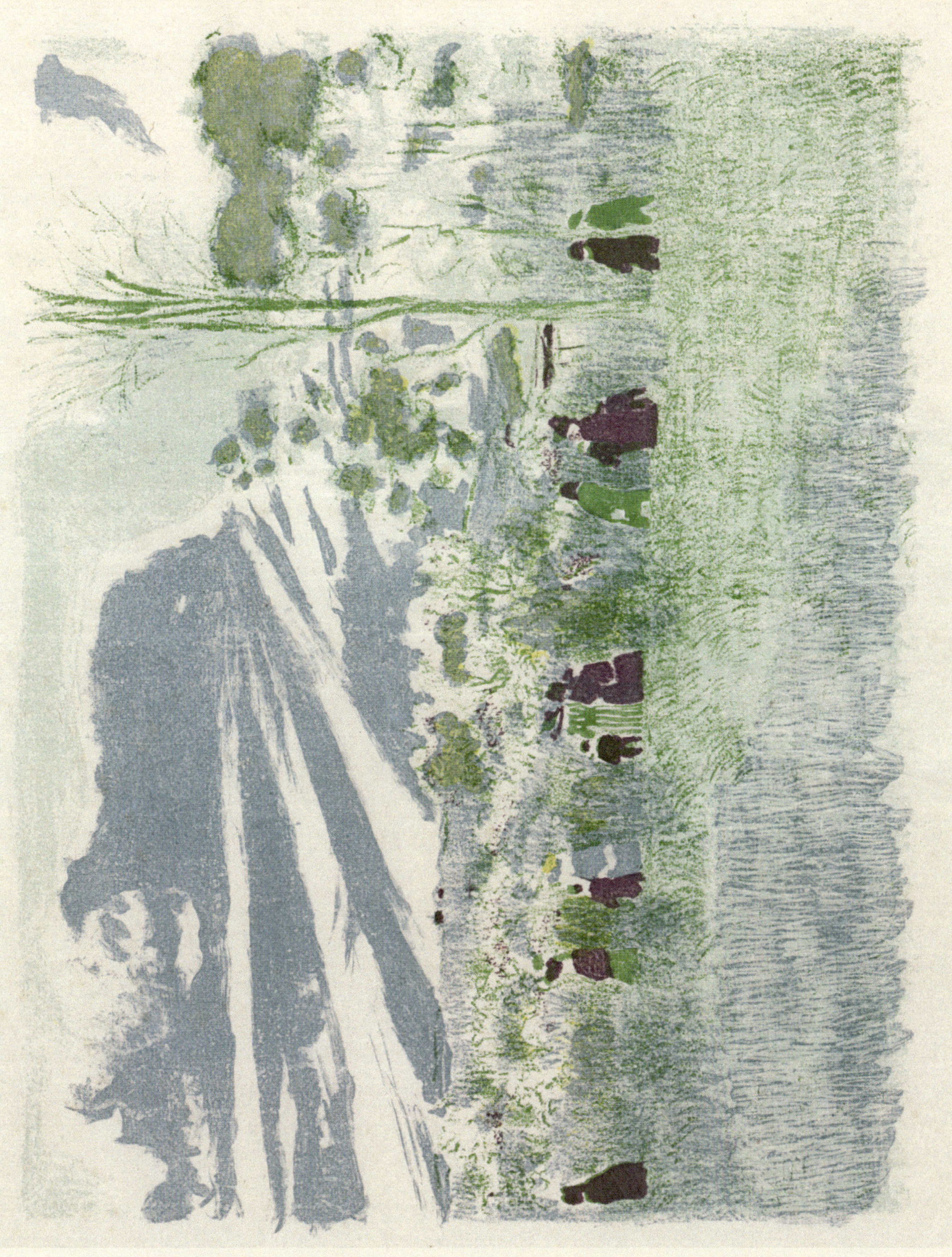

4.
Intérieur à la suspension
*Interior with Ceiling Lamp*

356 x 282 mm

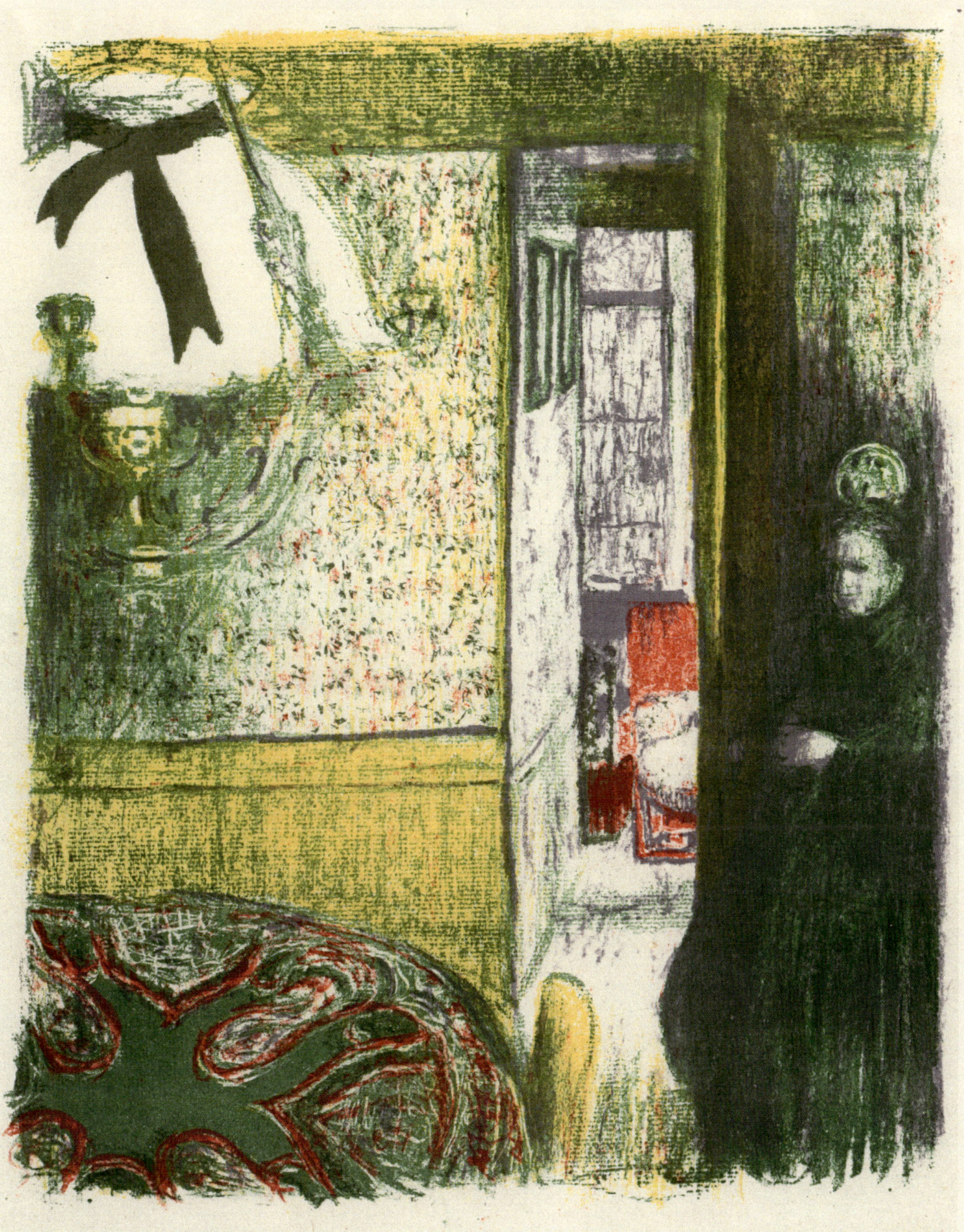

5.
Intérieur aux tentures roses I
*Interior with Pink Wallpaper I*

354 x 278 mm

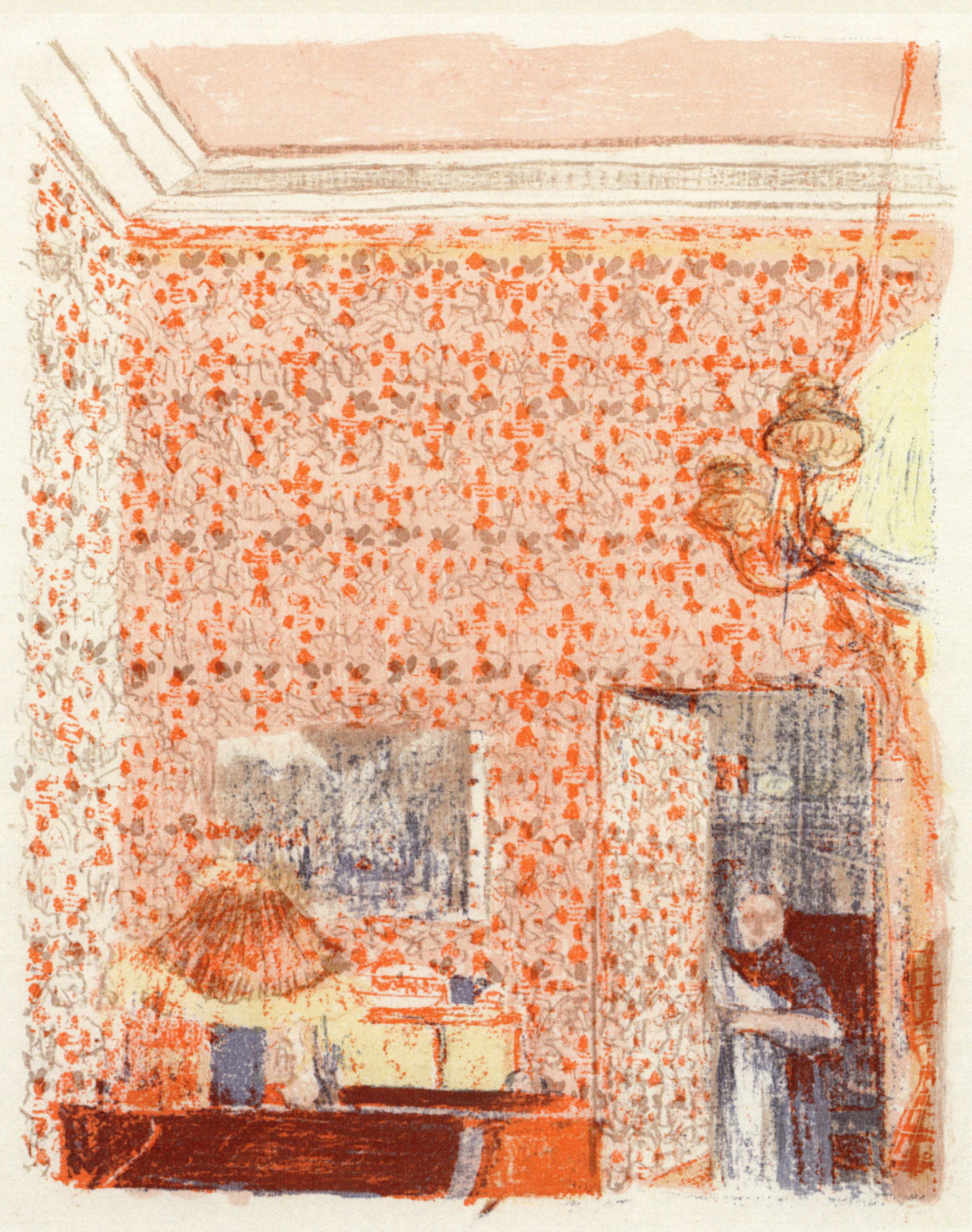

6.

Intérieur aux tentures roses II
*Interior with Pink Wallpaper II*

346 x 282 mm

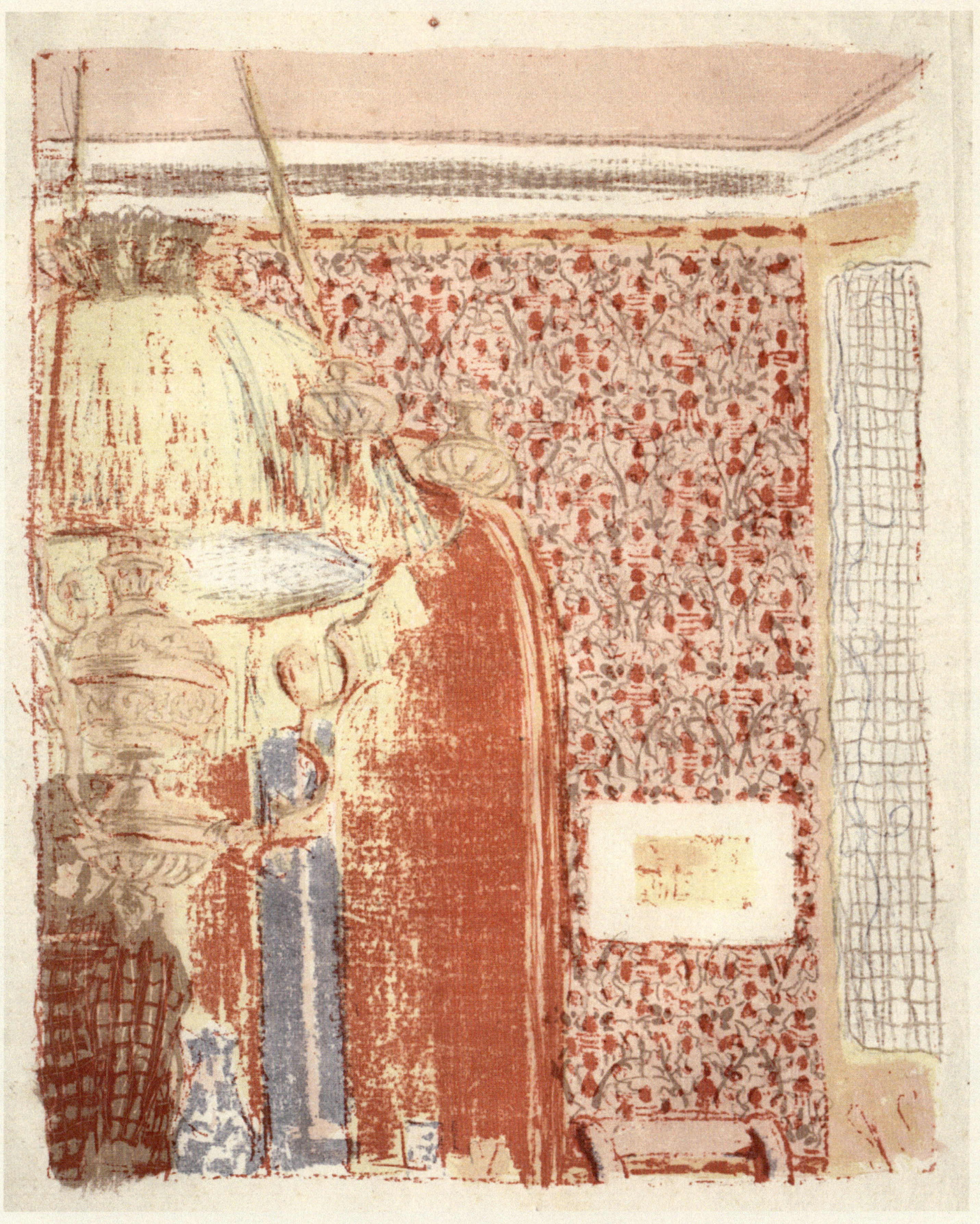

7.
Intérieur aux tentures roses III
*Interior with Pink Wallpaper III*

342 x 273 mm

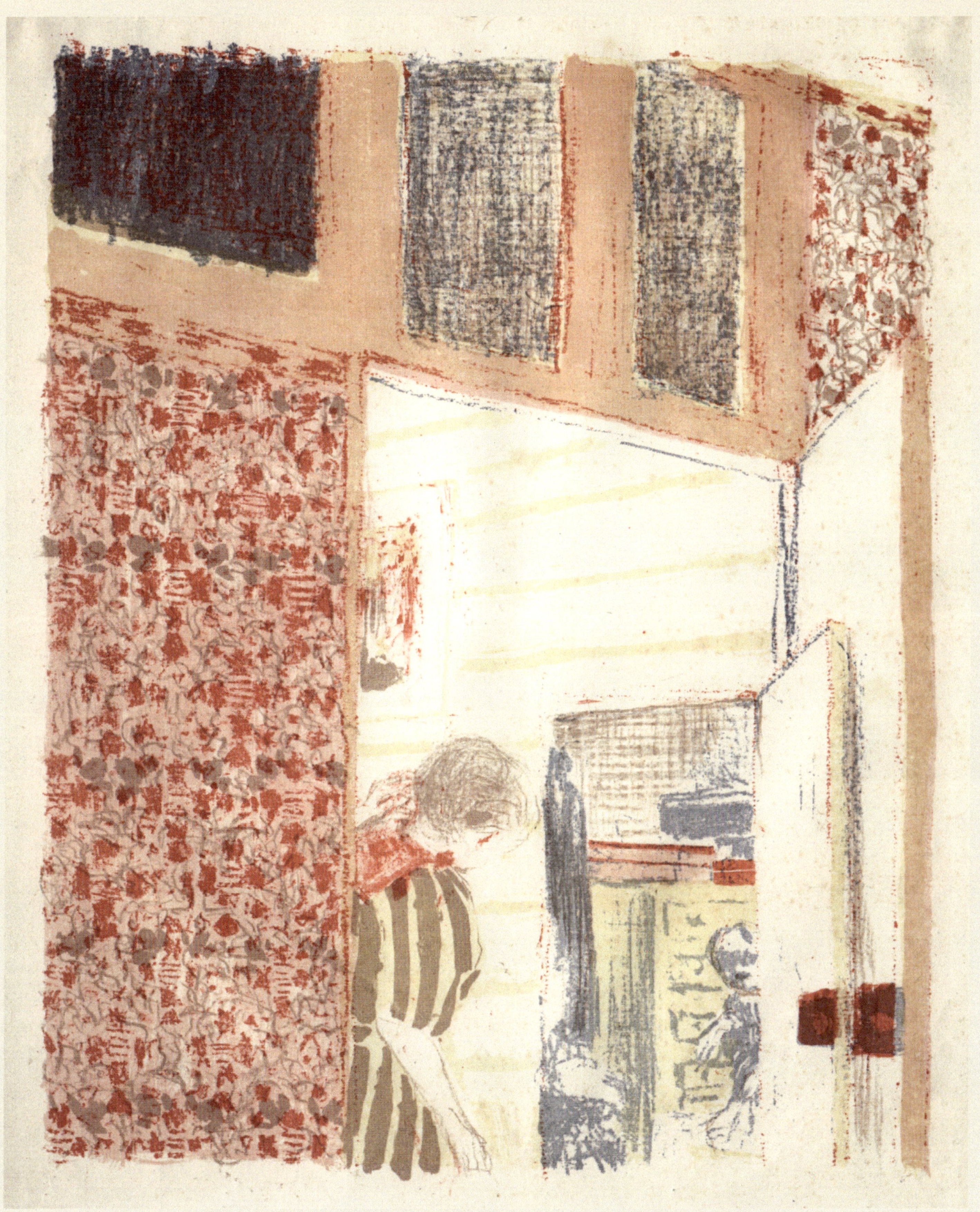

8.
L'Âtre
*The Hearth*

343 x 277 mm

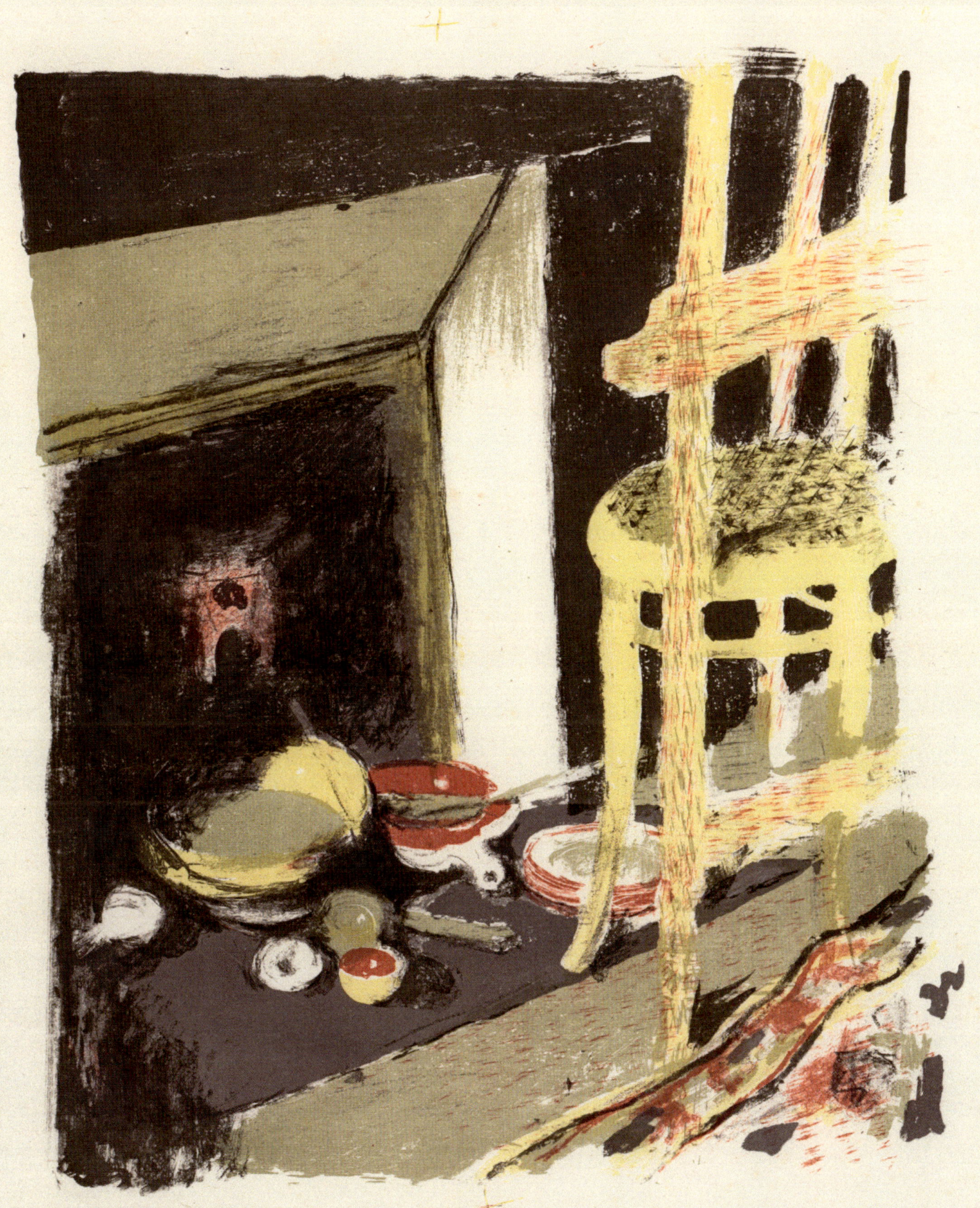

9.
Sur le pont de l'Europe
*On the Pont de l'Europe*

343 X 277 mm

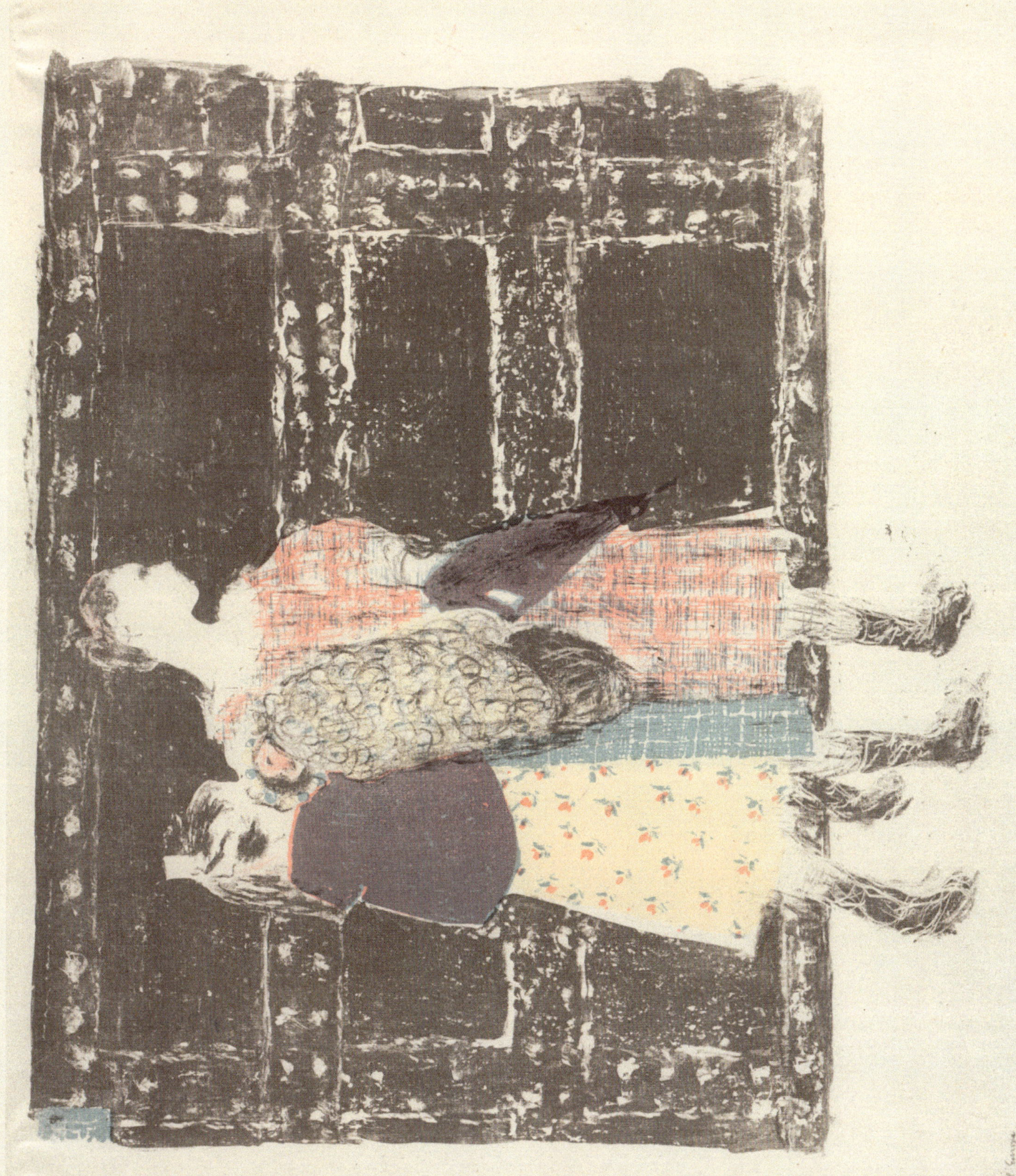

10.

La Pâtisserie
*The Pastry Shop*

351 x 275 mm

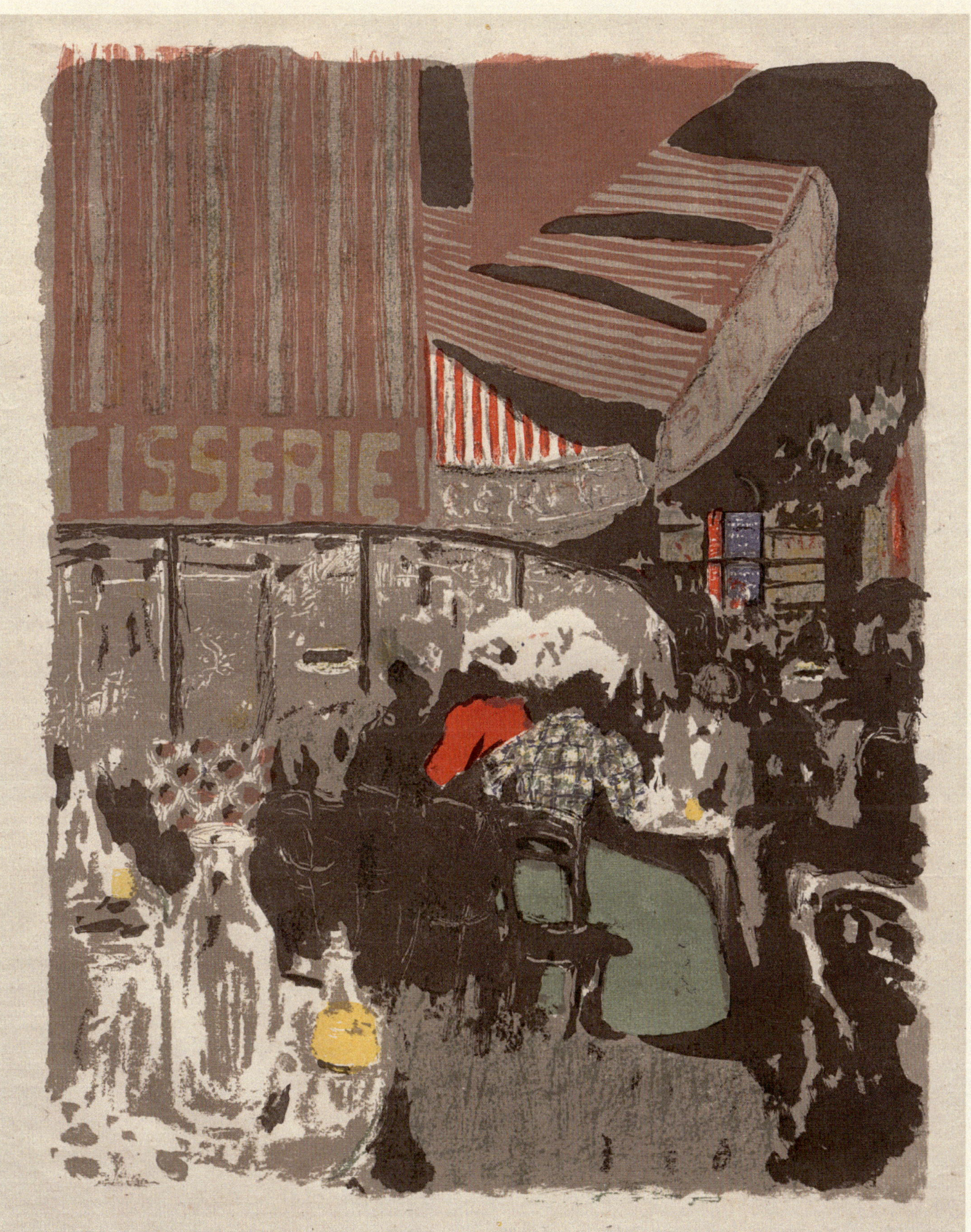
TISSERIE

11.

La Cuisinière (la mère de l'artiste)
*The Cook (the artist's mother)*

350 x 277 mm

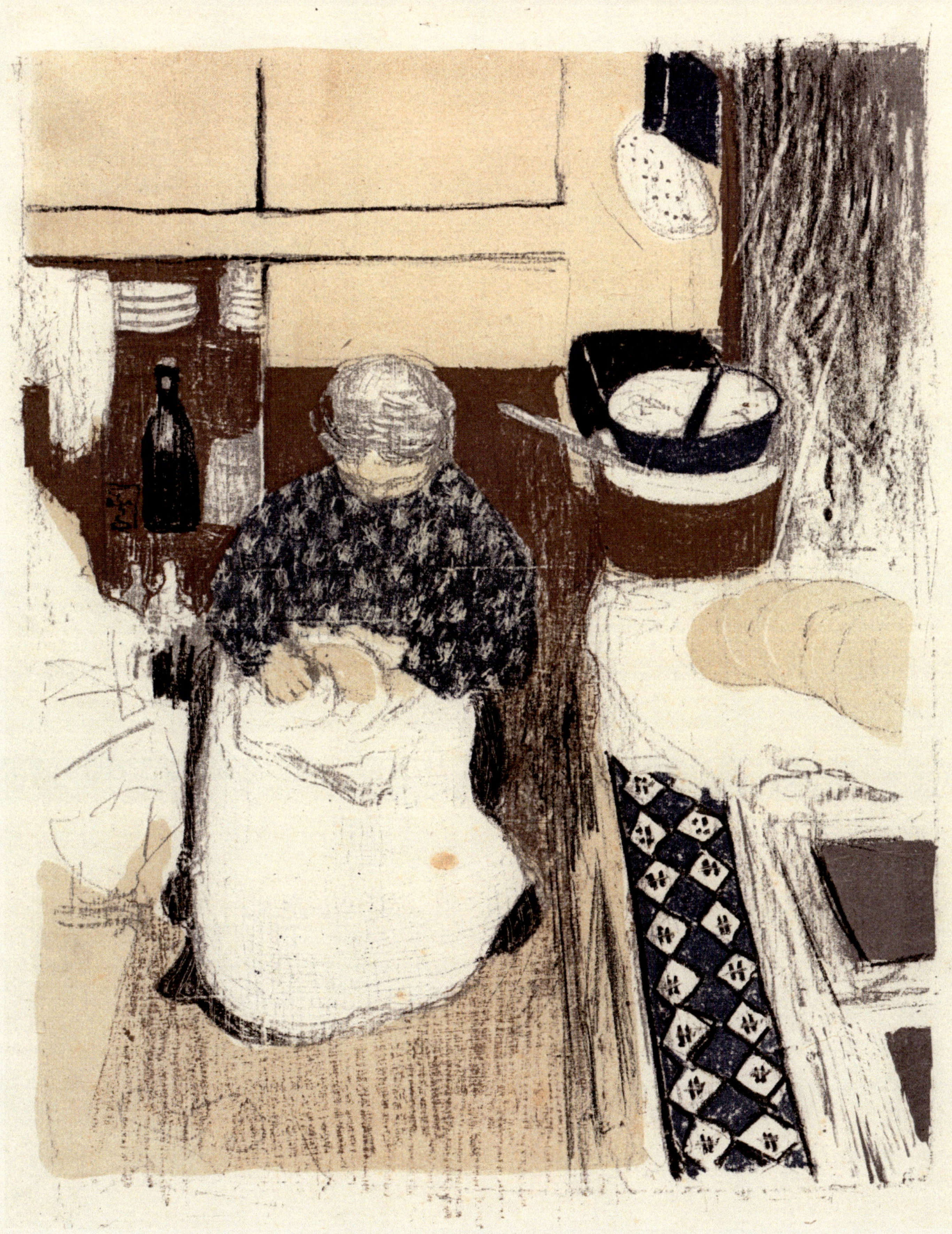

12.

Les deux belles-sœurs
*The Two Sisters-in-Law*

368 x 294 mm

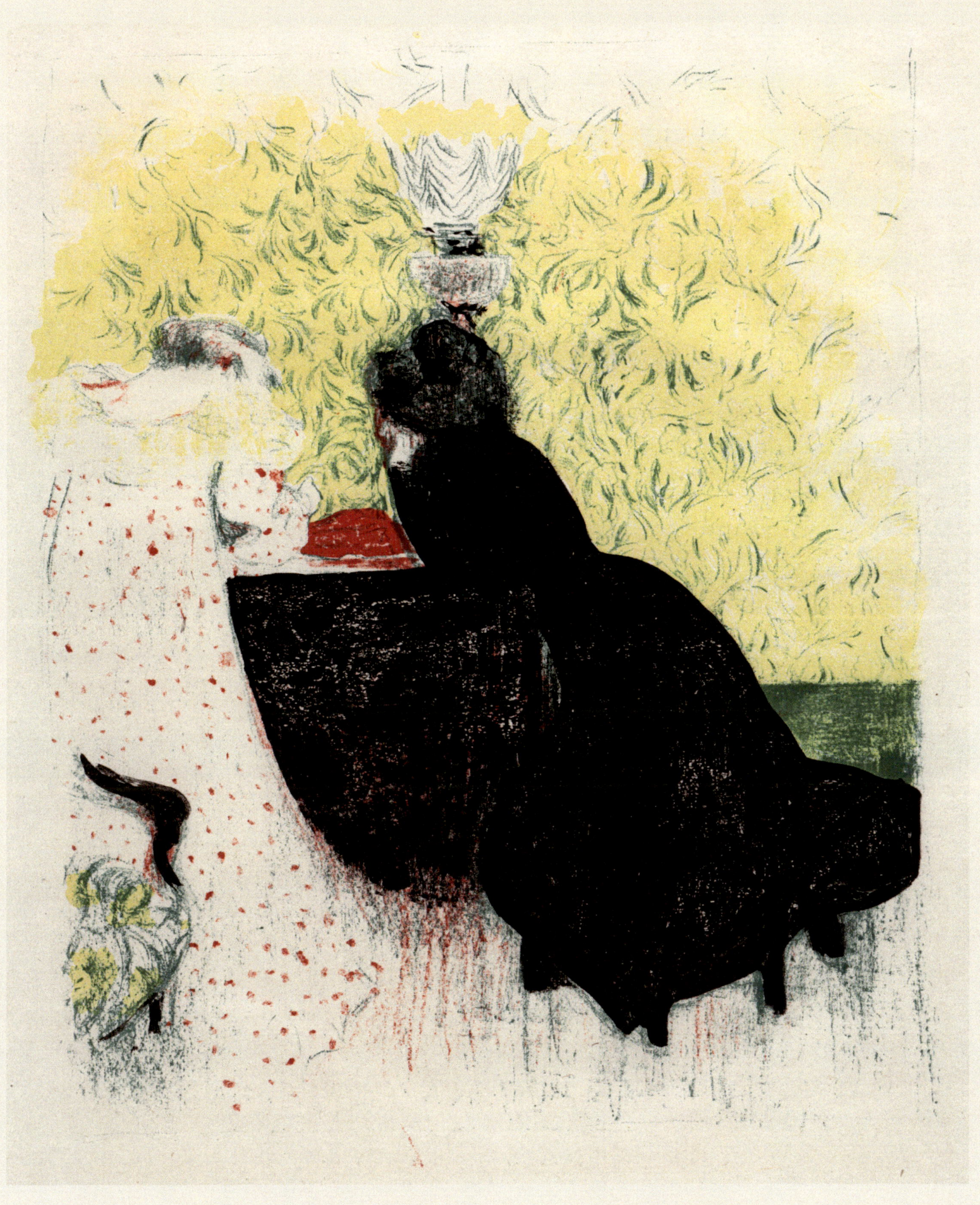

PAYSAGES ET INTÉRIEURS/
LANDSCAPES AND INTERIORS
Suite de 12 planches et une couverture,
imprimée par Auguste Clot. Éditée à
Paris par Ambroise Vollard en 1899,
et tirée à 100 exemplaires./
*Suite of 12 plates and a cover, printed
by Auguste Clot. Published in Paris by
Ambroise Vollard in 1899, in an edition
of 100 copies.*

Cette édition/*This edition*
© Pallas Athene (Publishers) Ltd,
London, 2026

Pallas Athene (Publishers) Ltd,
2 Birch Close, London N19 5XD

**www.pallasathene.co.uk**

ISBN 978 1 84368 299 8 (édition française)
ISBN 978 1 84368 298 1 (English edition)

Imprimé en Angleterre par Blissetts/
*Printed in England by Blissetts*

3

# PAYSAGES
# ET INTÉRIEURS

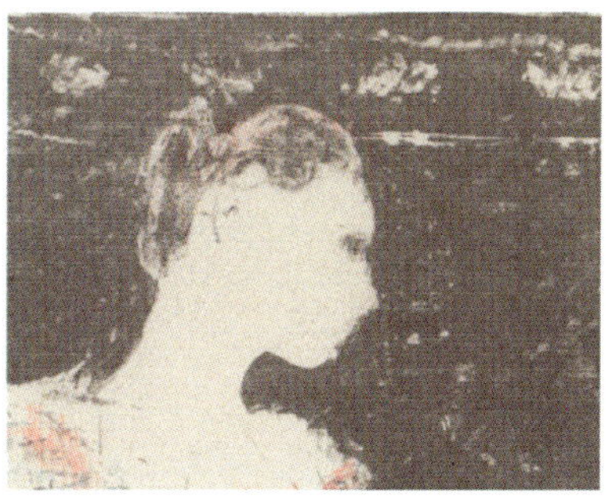

# LANDSCAPES AND
# INTERIORS

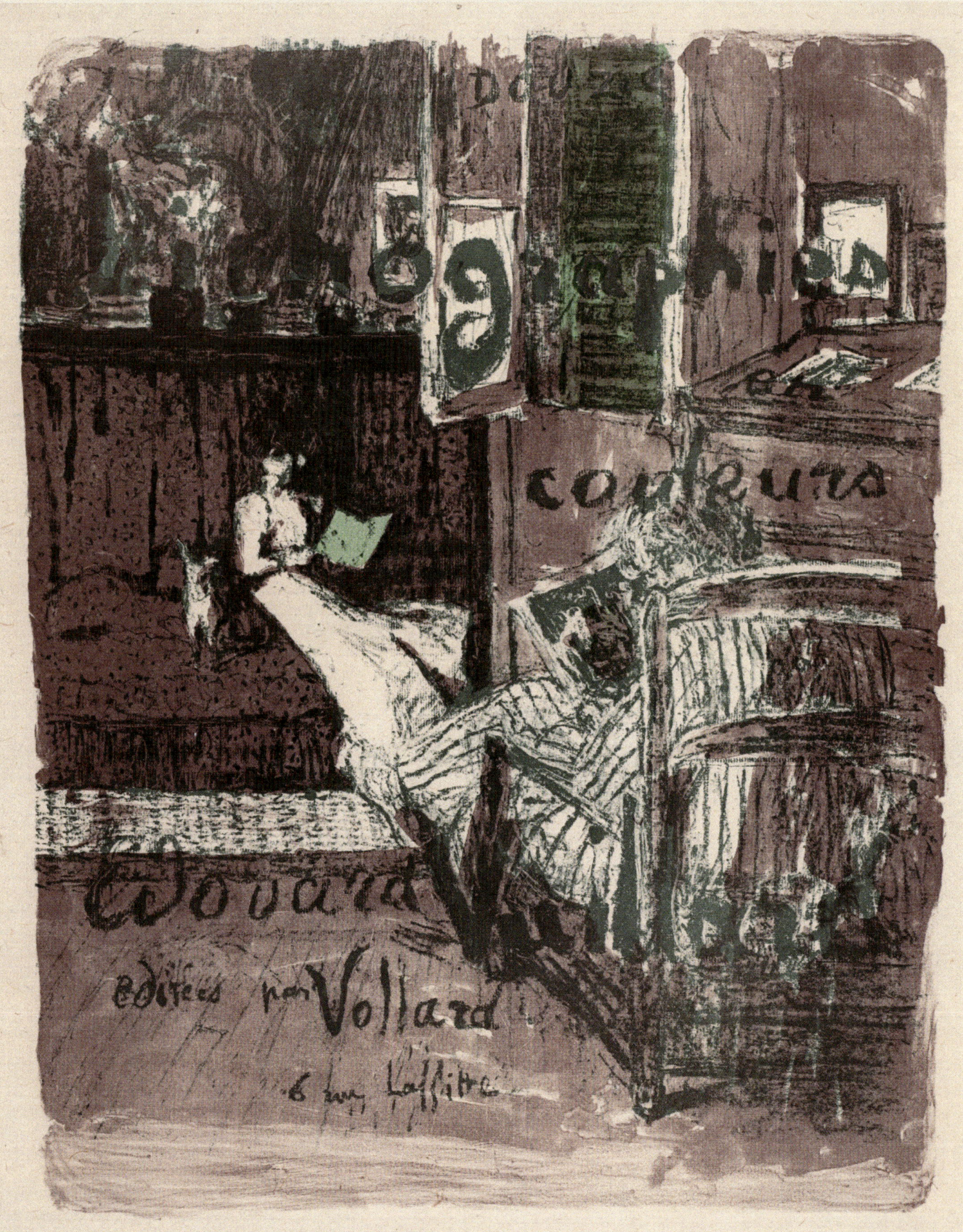
Douze
lithographies en
couleurs
Edouard Vuillard
Editées par Vollard
6 rue Laffitte

# Paysages et intérieurs

## Landscapes and Interiors

### Édouard Vuillard

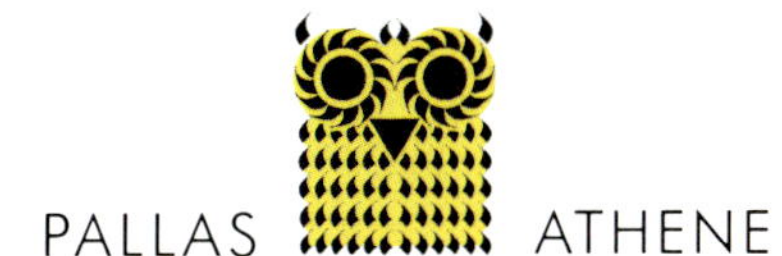

I.

La partie de dames
*The Game of Checkers*

330 X 257 mm

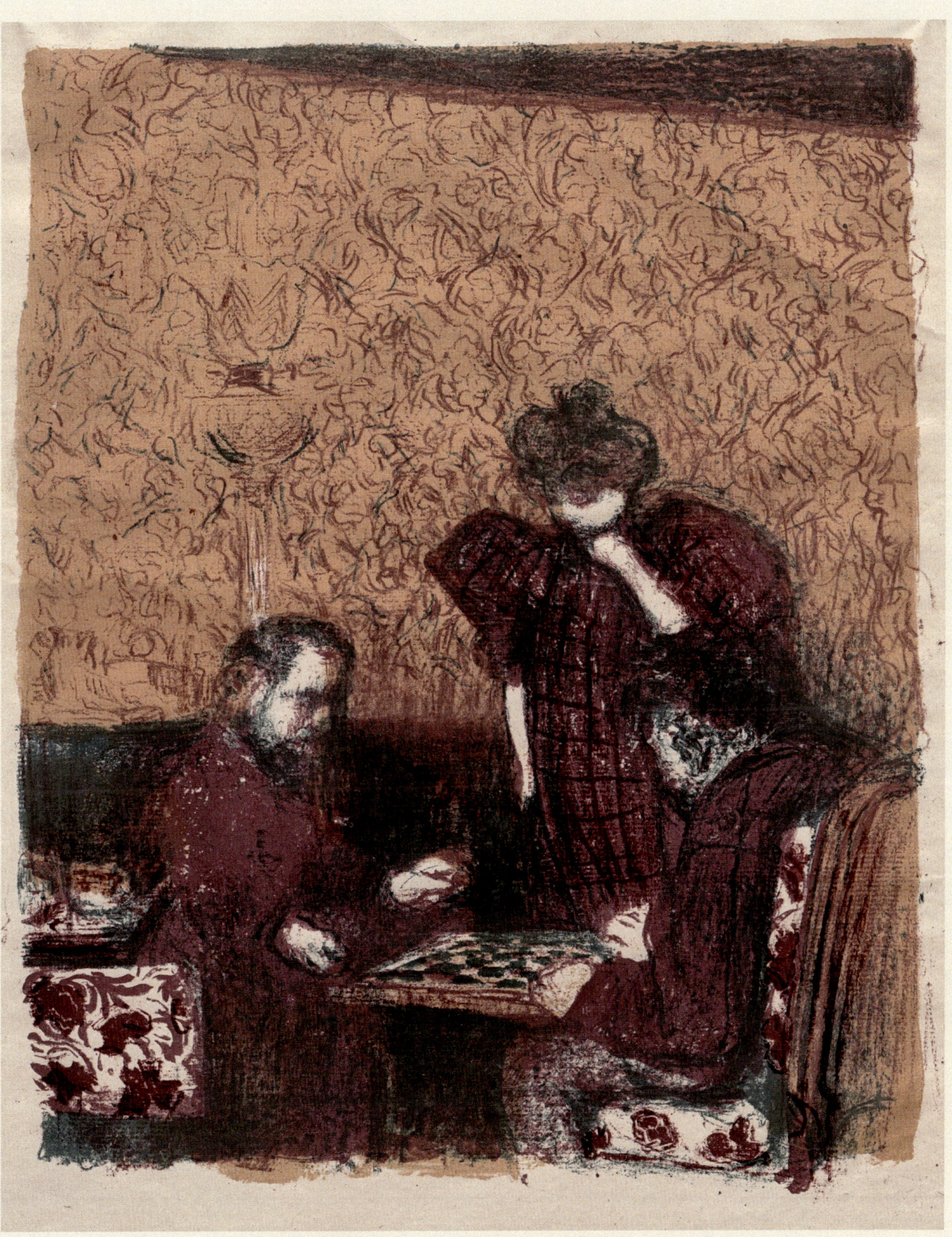

2.

L'Avenue

*The Avenue*

311 x 414 mm

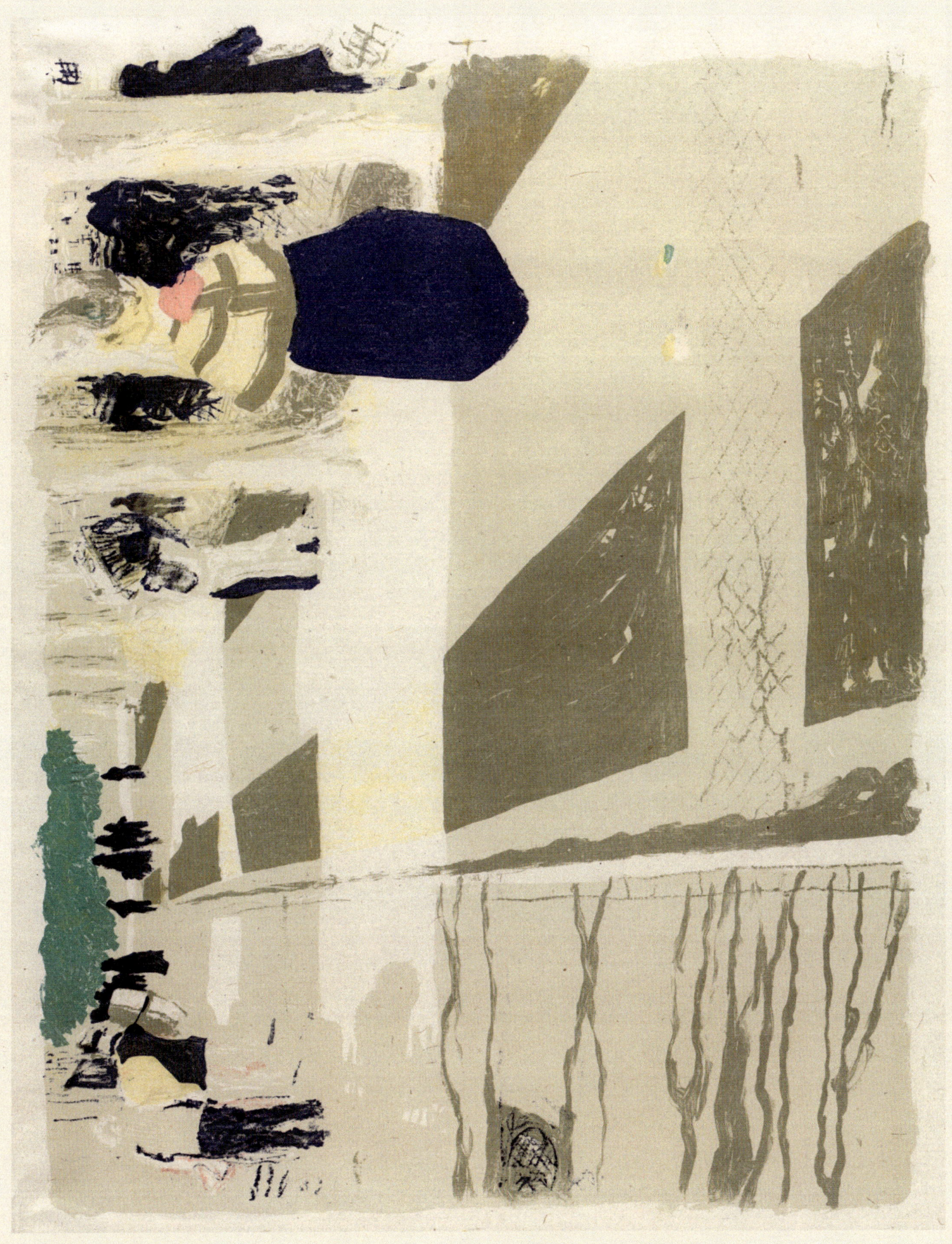

3.
À travers champs
*Across the Fields*

260 x 345 mm

4.
Intérieur à la suspension
*Interior with Ceiling Lamp*

356 x 282 mm

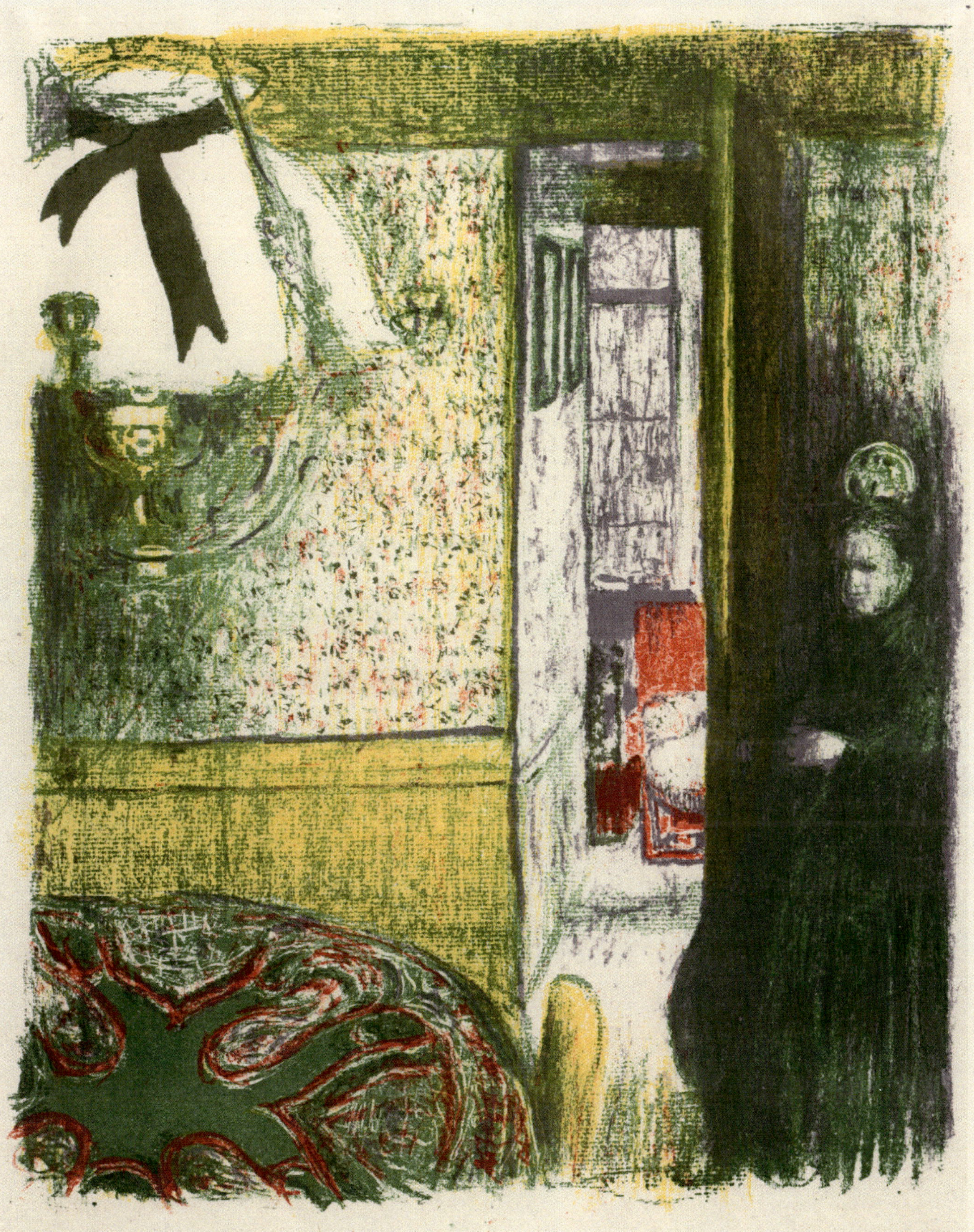

5.
Intérieur aux tentures roses I
*Interior with Pink Wallpaper I*

354 x 278 mm

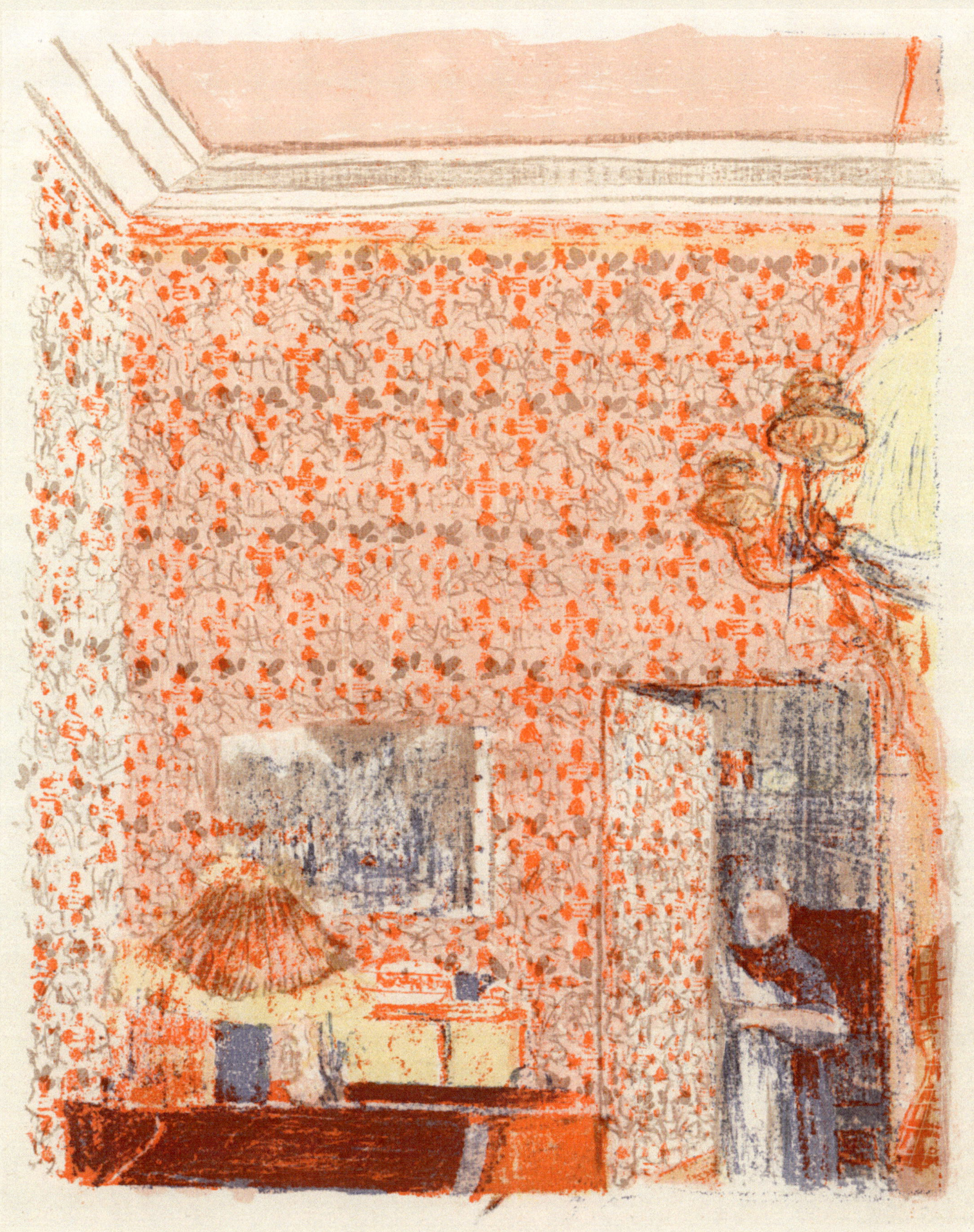

6.

Intérieur aux tentures roses II
*Interior with Pink Wallpaper II*

346 x 282 mm

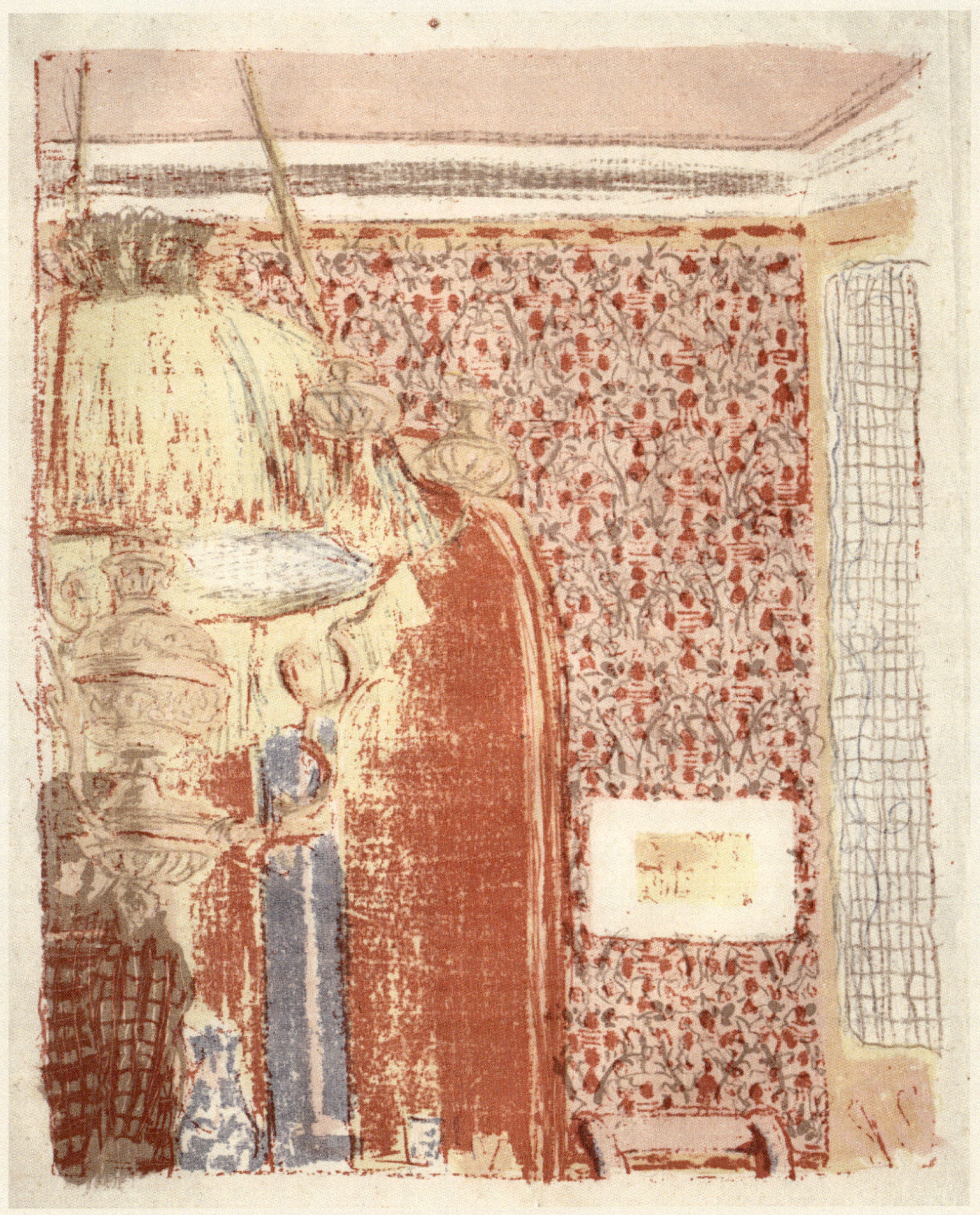

7.
Intérieur aux tentures roses III
*Interior with Pink Wallpaper III*

342 X 273 mm

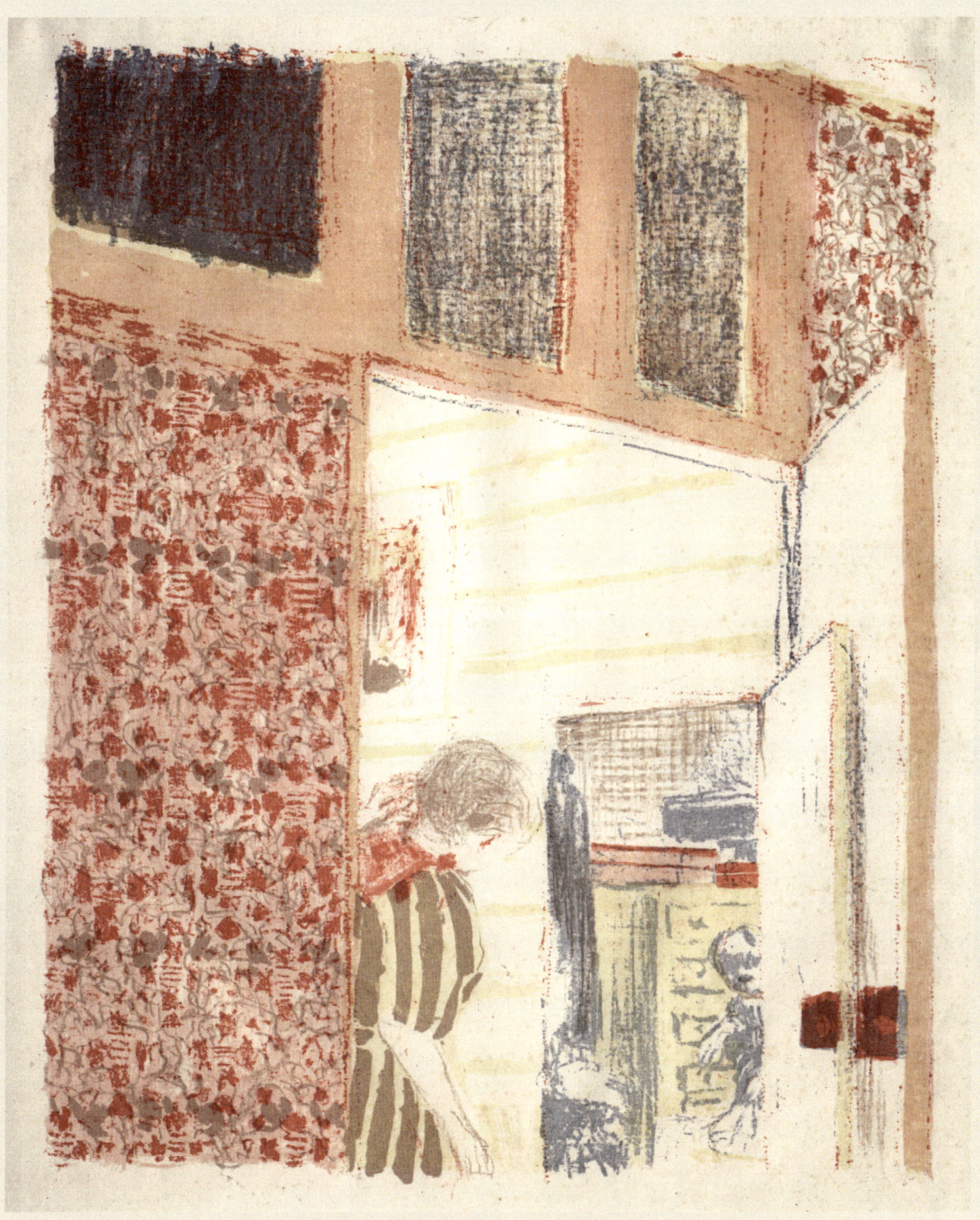

8.

L'Âtre

*The Hearth*

343 x 277 mm

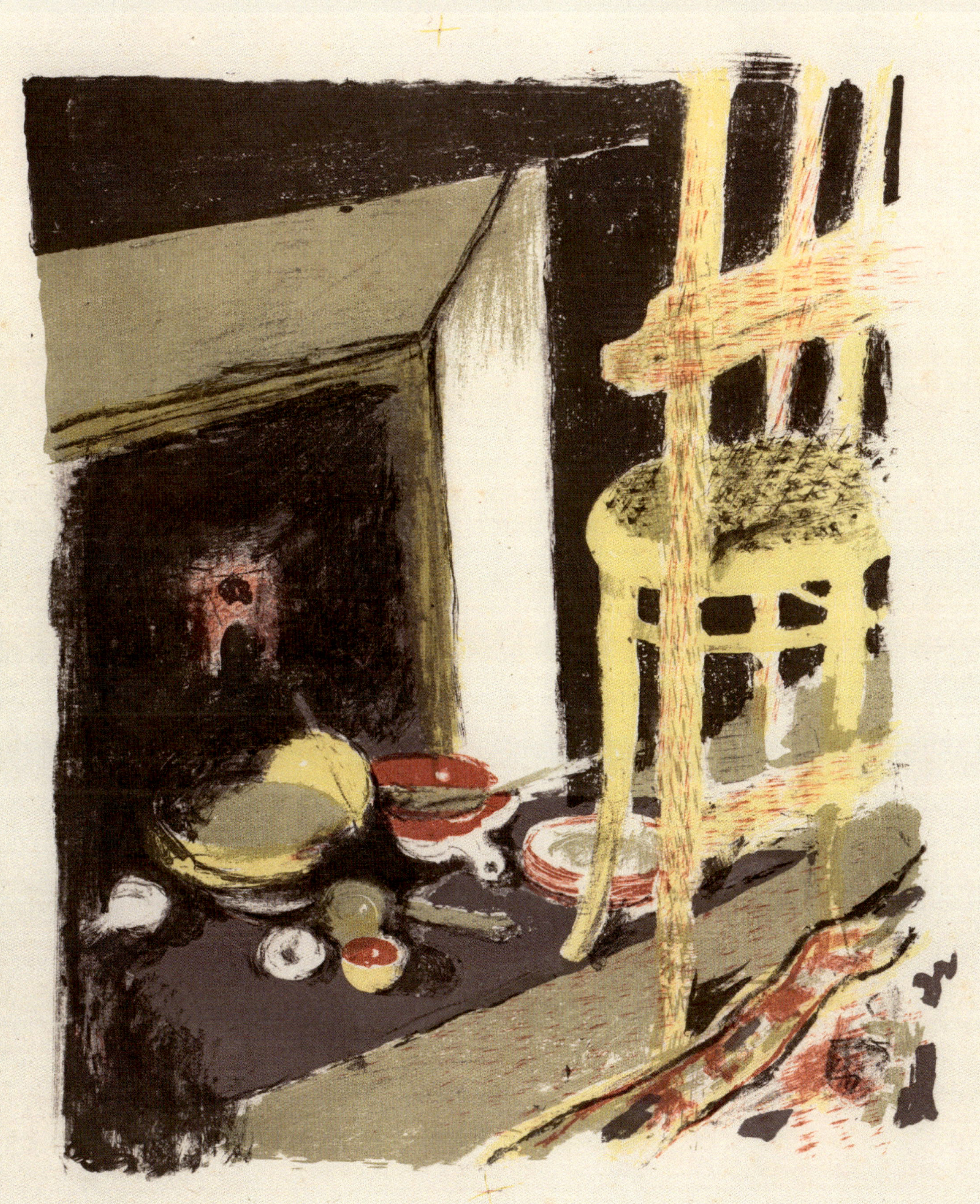

9.
Sur le pont de l'Europe
*On the Pont de l'Europe*

343 x 277 mm

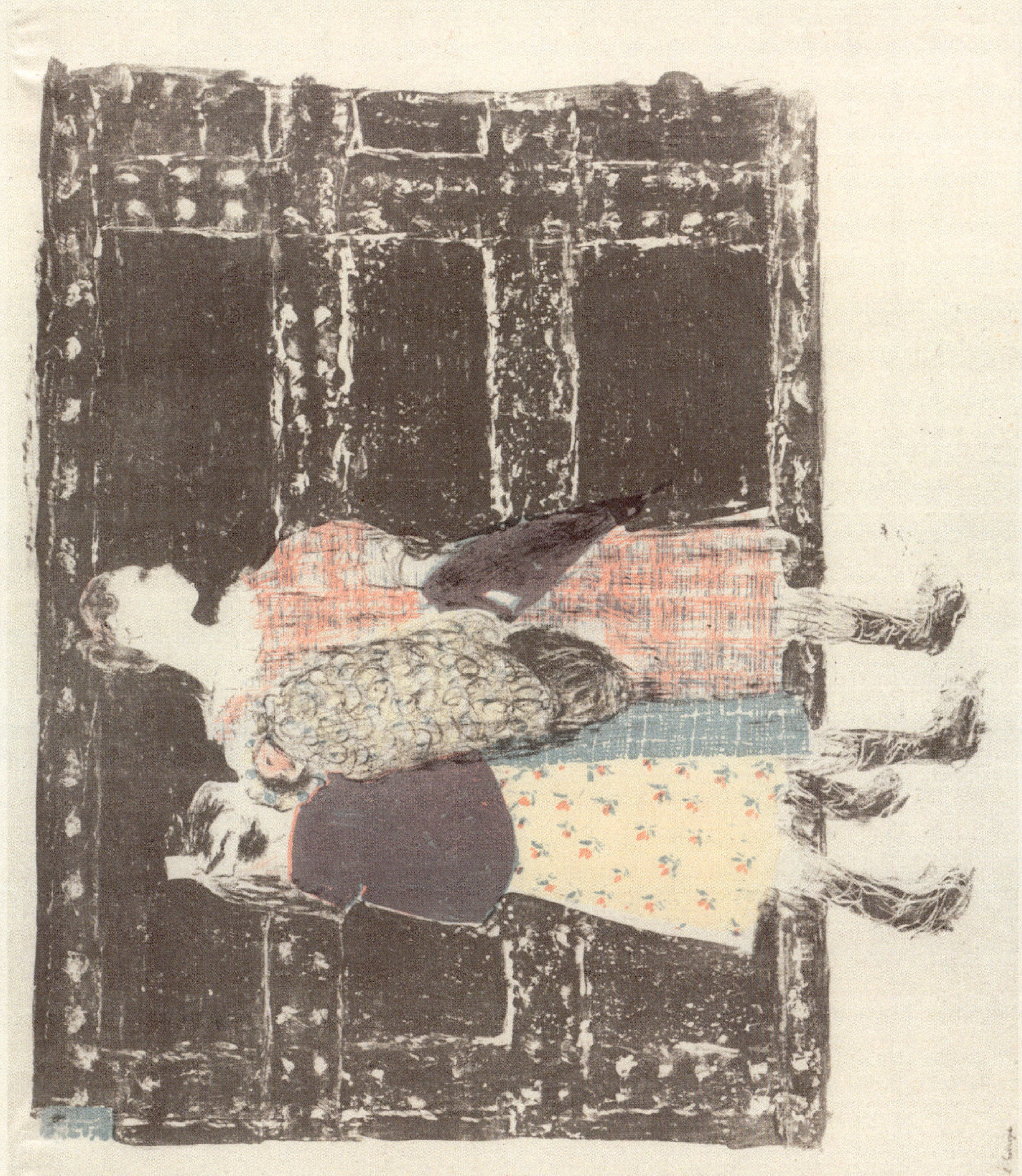

10.

La Pâtisserie
*The Pastry Shop*

351 x 275 mm

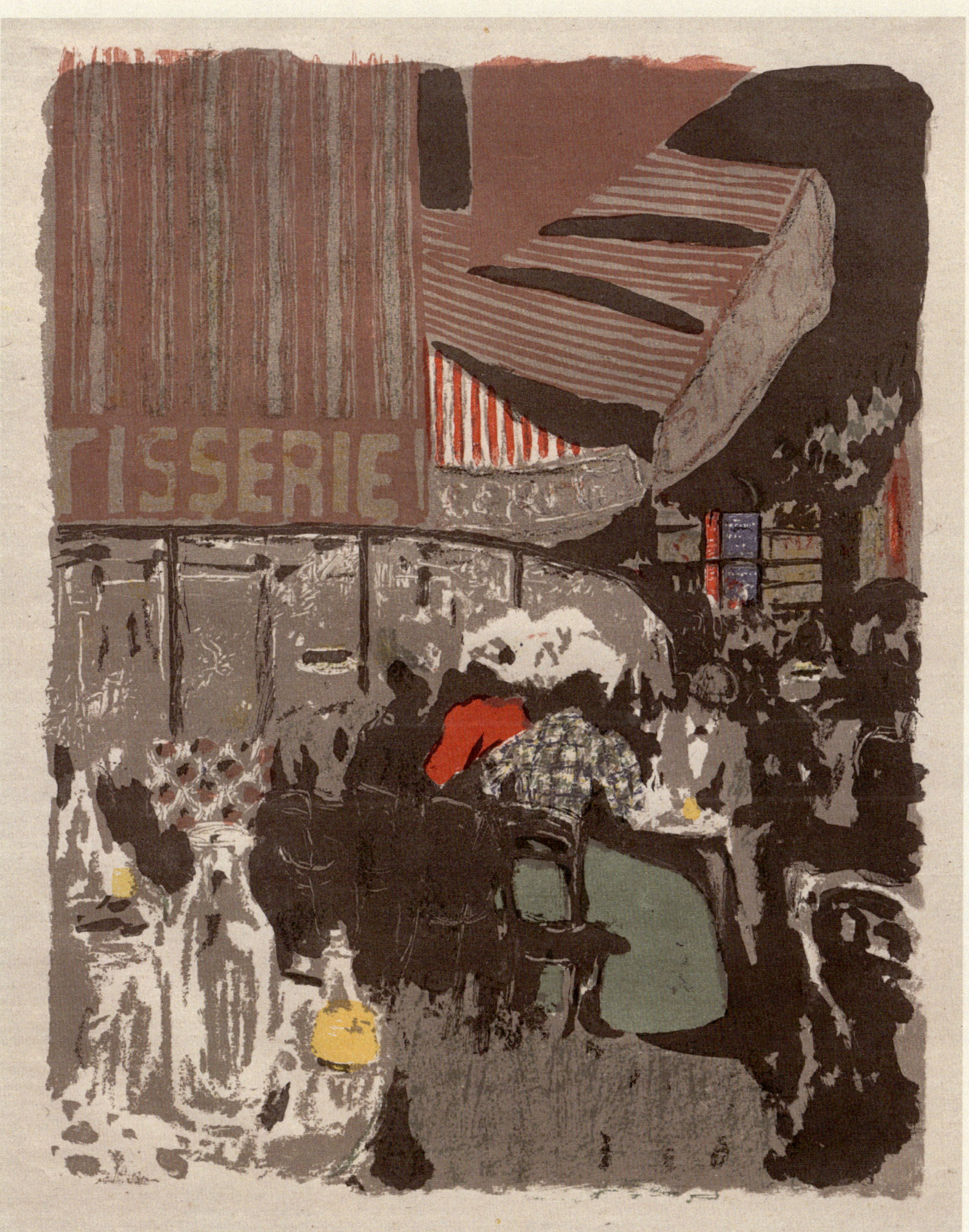
TISSERIE

II.

La Cuisinière (la mère de l'artiste)
*The Cook (the artist's mother)*

350 x 277 mm

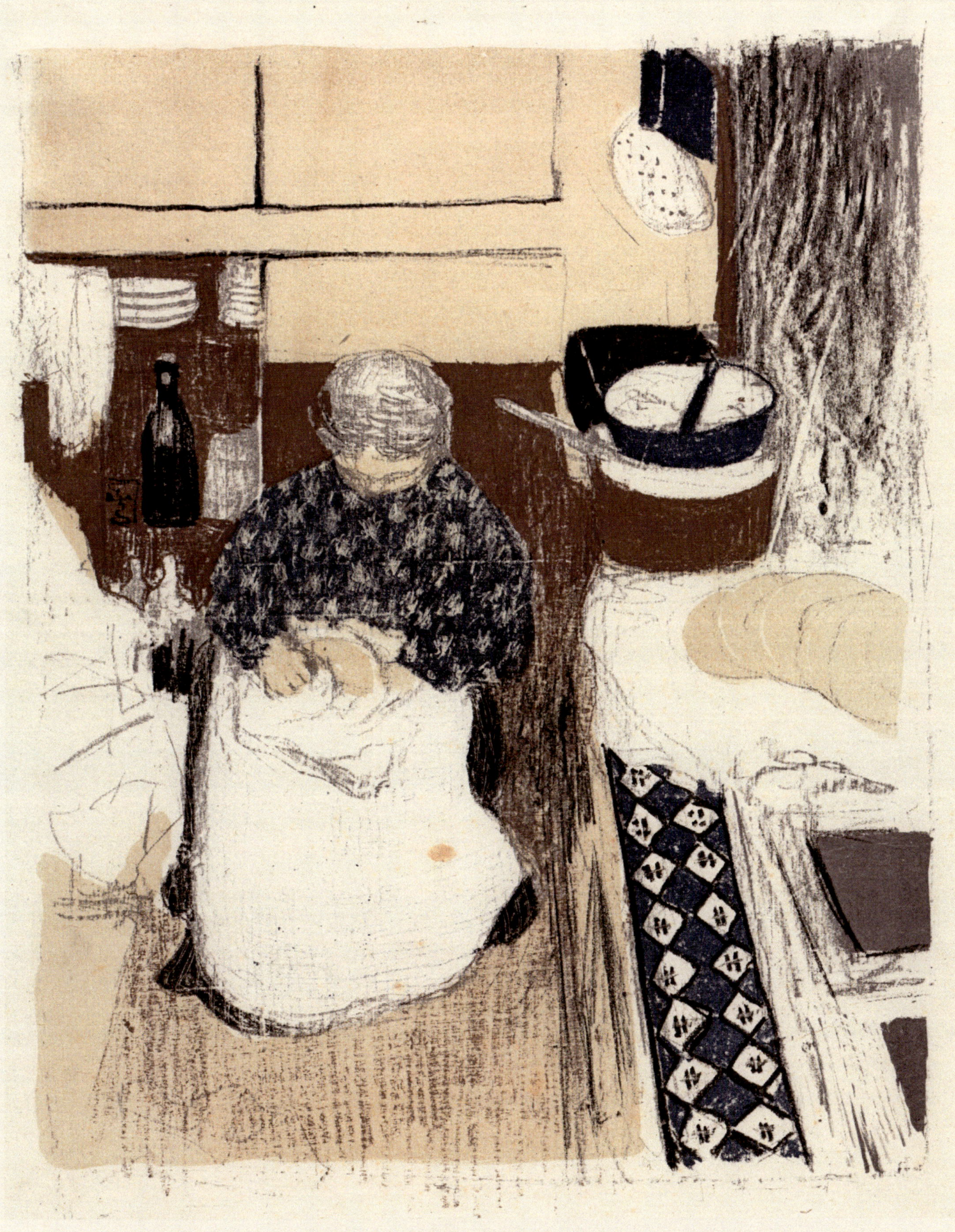

12.
Les deux belles-sœurs
*The Two Sisters-in-Law*

368 x 294 mm

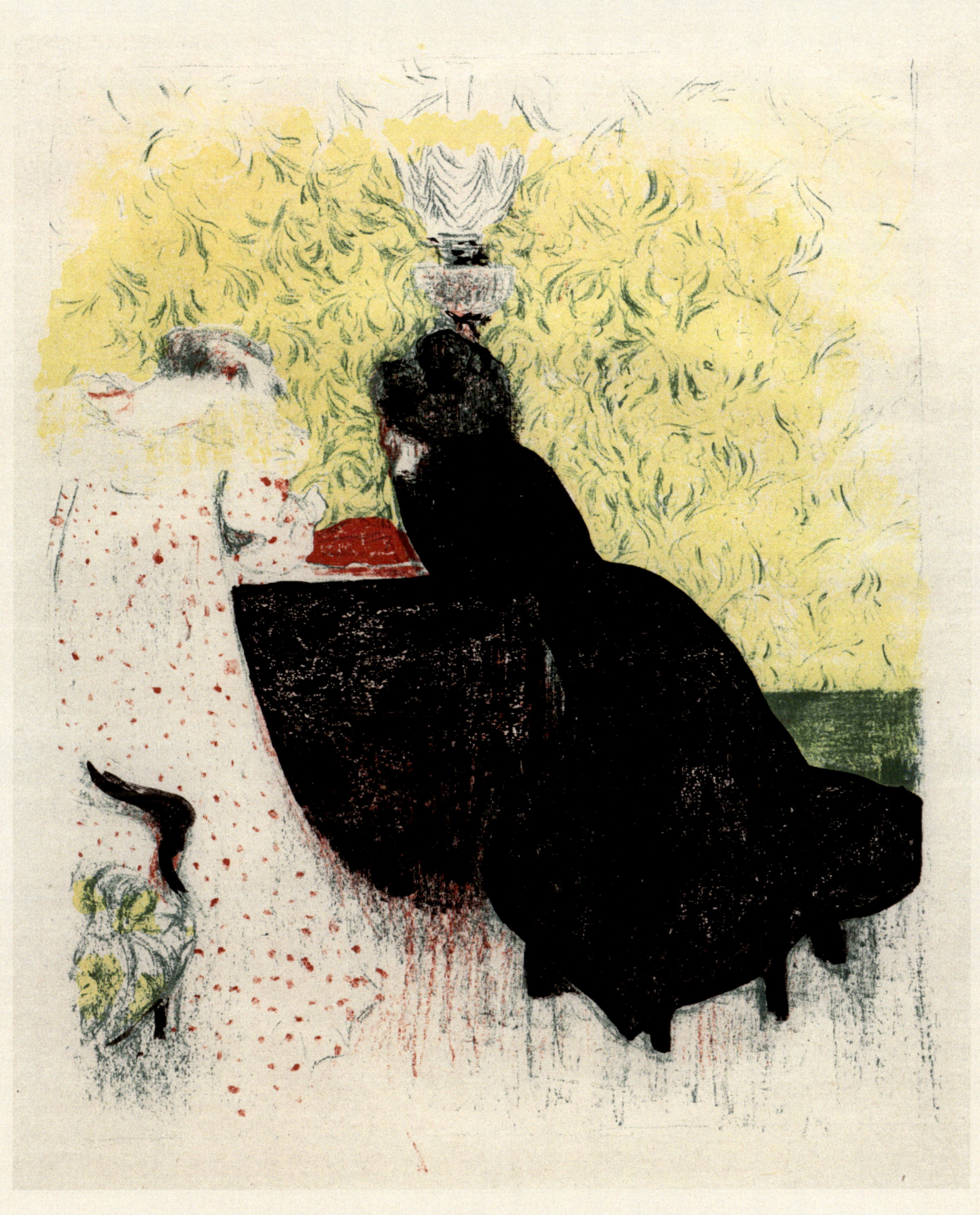

PAYSAGES ET INTÉRIEURS/
LANDSCAPES AND INTERIORS
Suite de 12 planches et une couverture,
imprimée par Auguste Clot. Éditée à
Paris par Ambroise Vollard en 1899,
et tirée à 100 exemplaires./
*Suite of 12 plates and a cover, printed
by Auguste Clot. Published in Paris by
Ambroise Vollard in 1899, in an edition
of 100 copies.*

Cette édition/*This edition*
© Pallas Athene (Publishers) Ltd,
London, 2026

Pallas Athene (Publishers) Ltd,
2 Birch Close, London N19 5XD

**www.pallasathene.co.uk**

ISBN 978 1 84368 299 8 (édition française)
ISBN 978 1 84368 298 1 (English edition)

Imprimé en Angleterre par Blissetts/
*Printed in England by Blissetts*

# PAYSAGES
# ET INTÉRIEURS

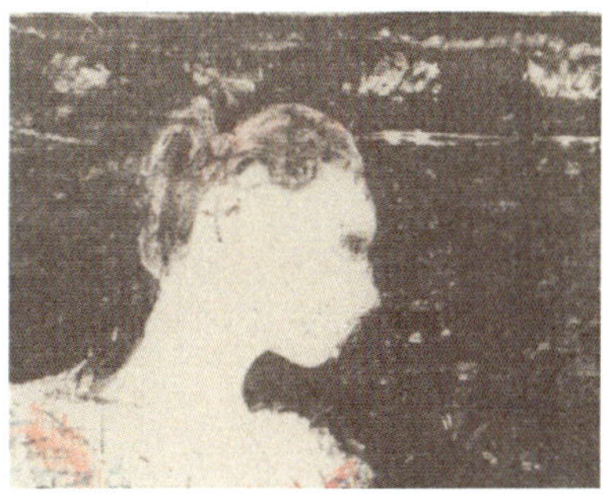

# LANDSCAPES AND
# INTERIORS

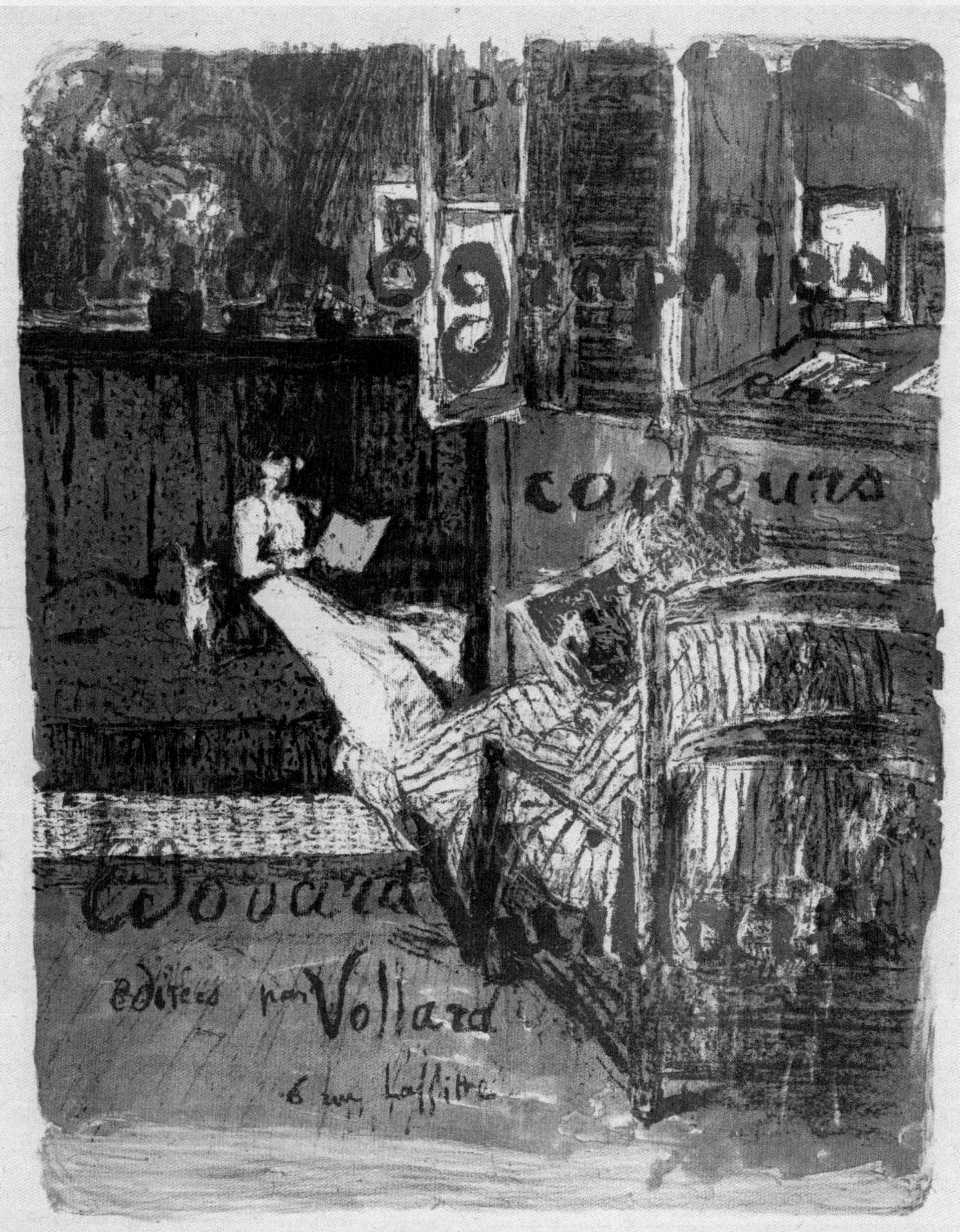
Lithographies en couleurs
Édités par Vollard
8 rue Laffitte

# Paysages et intérieurs

# *Landscapes and Interiors*

## Édouard Vuillard

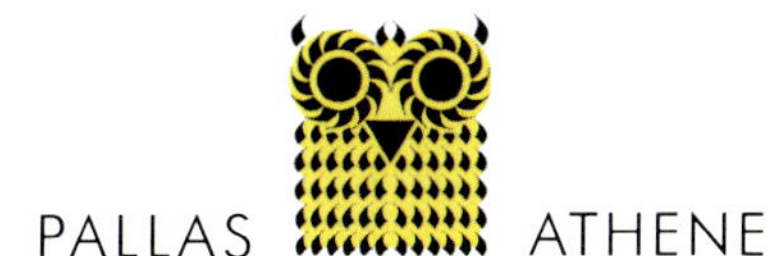

Pallas Athene

I.

La partie de dames
*The Game of Checkers*

330 X 257 mm

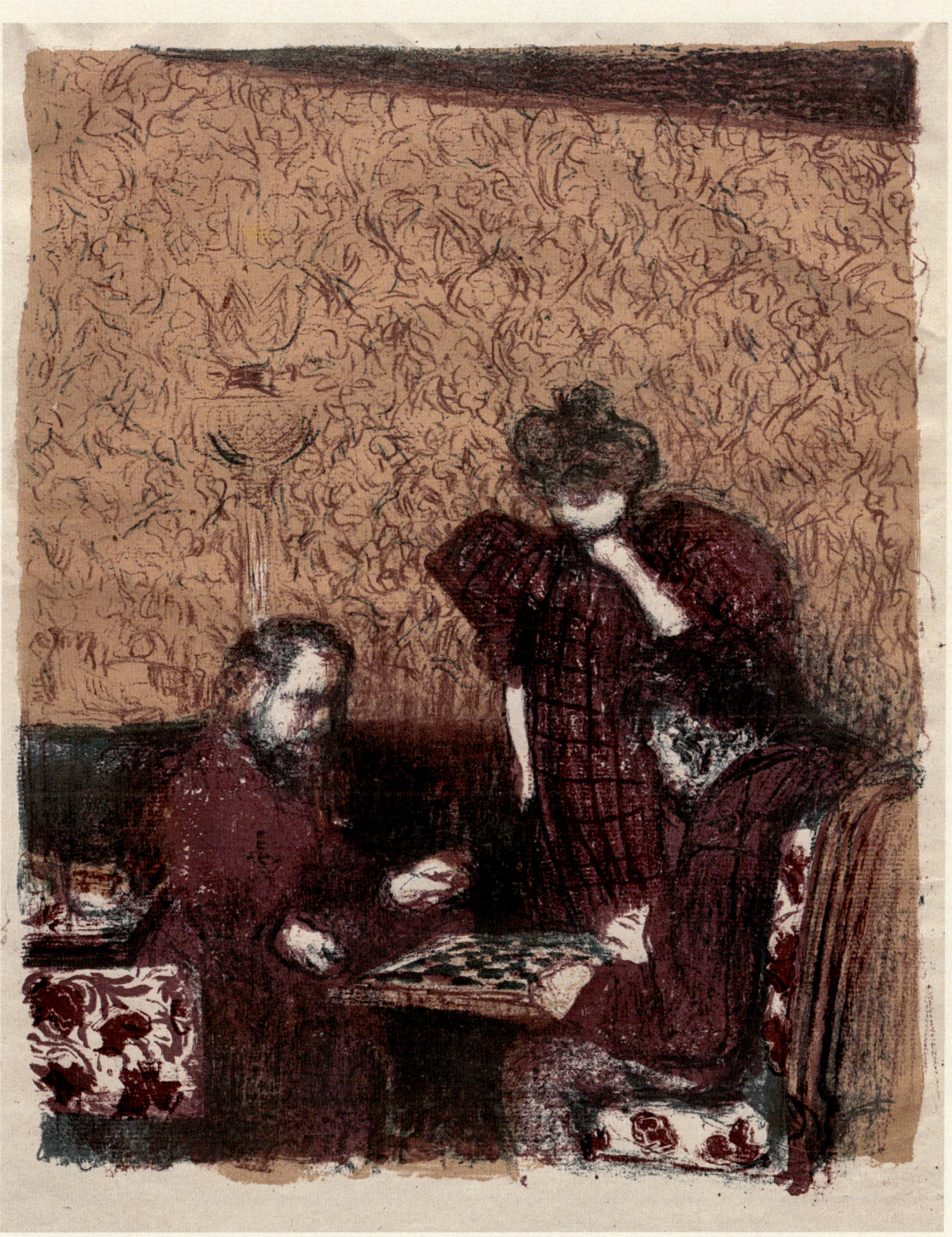

2.

L'Avenue

*The Avenue*

311 x 414 mm

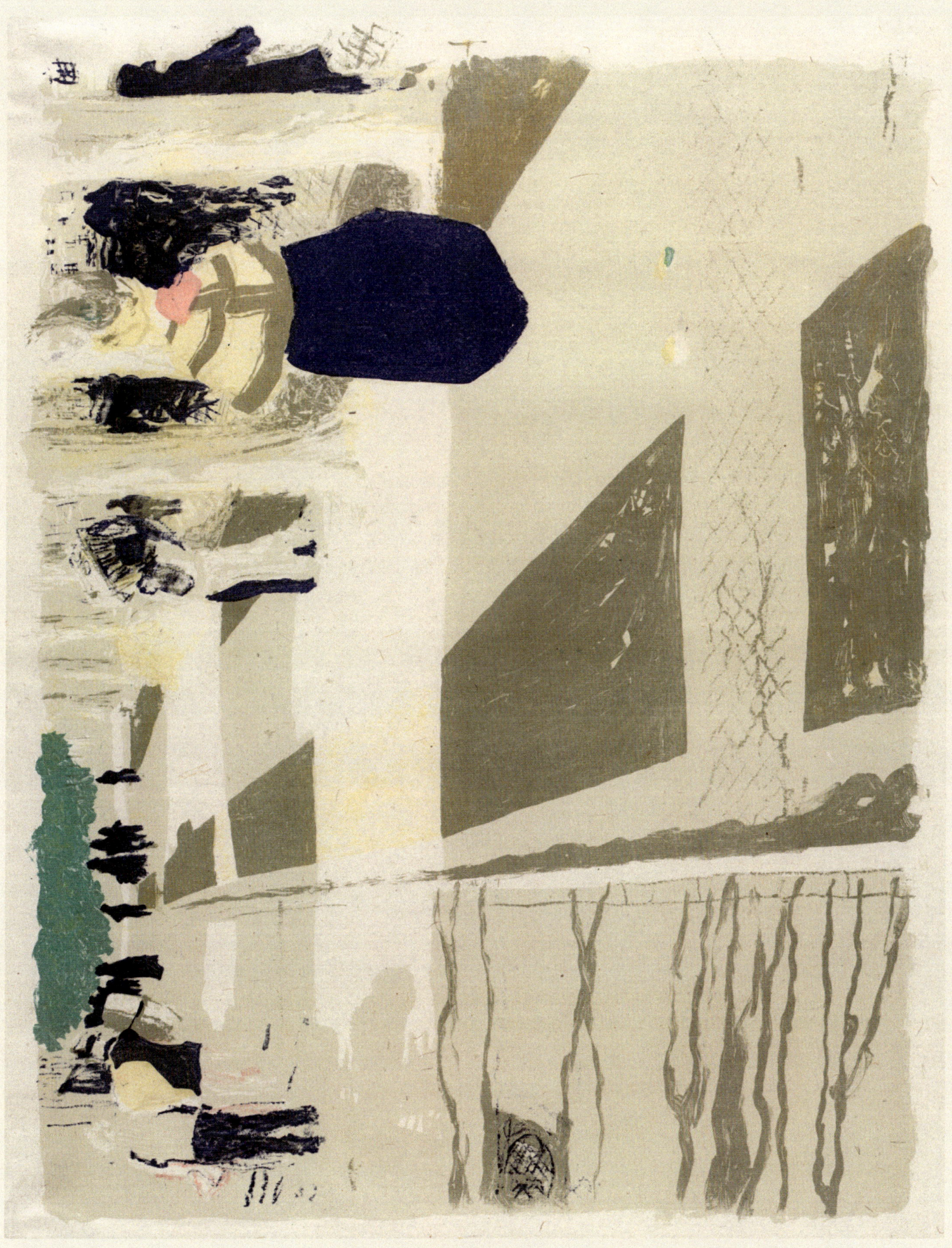

3.
À travers champs
*Across the Fields*

260 x 345 mm

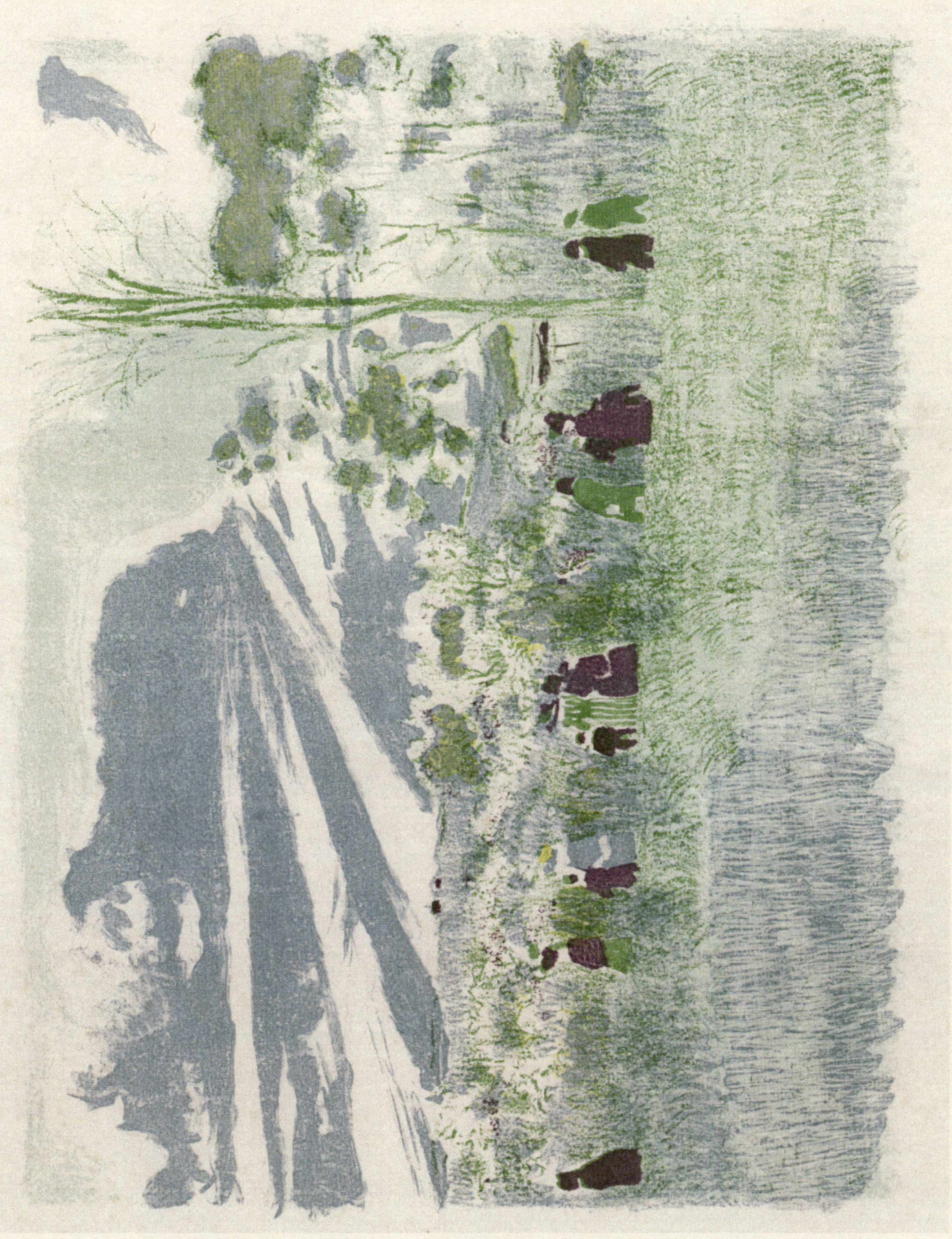

4.
Intérieur à la suspension
*Interior with Ceiling Lamp*

356 x 282 mm

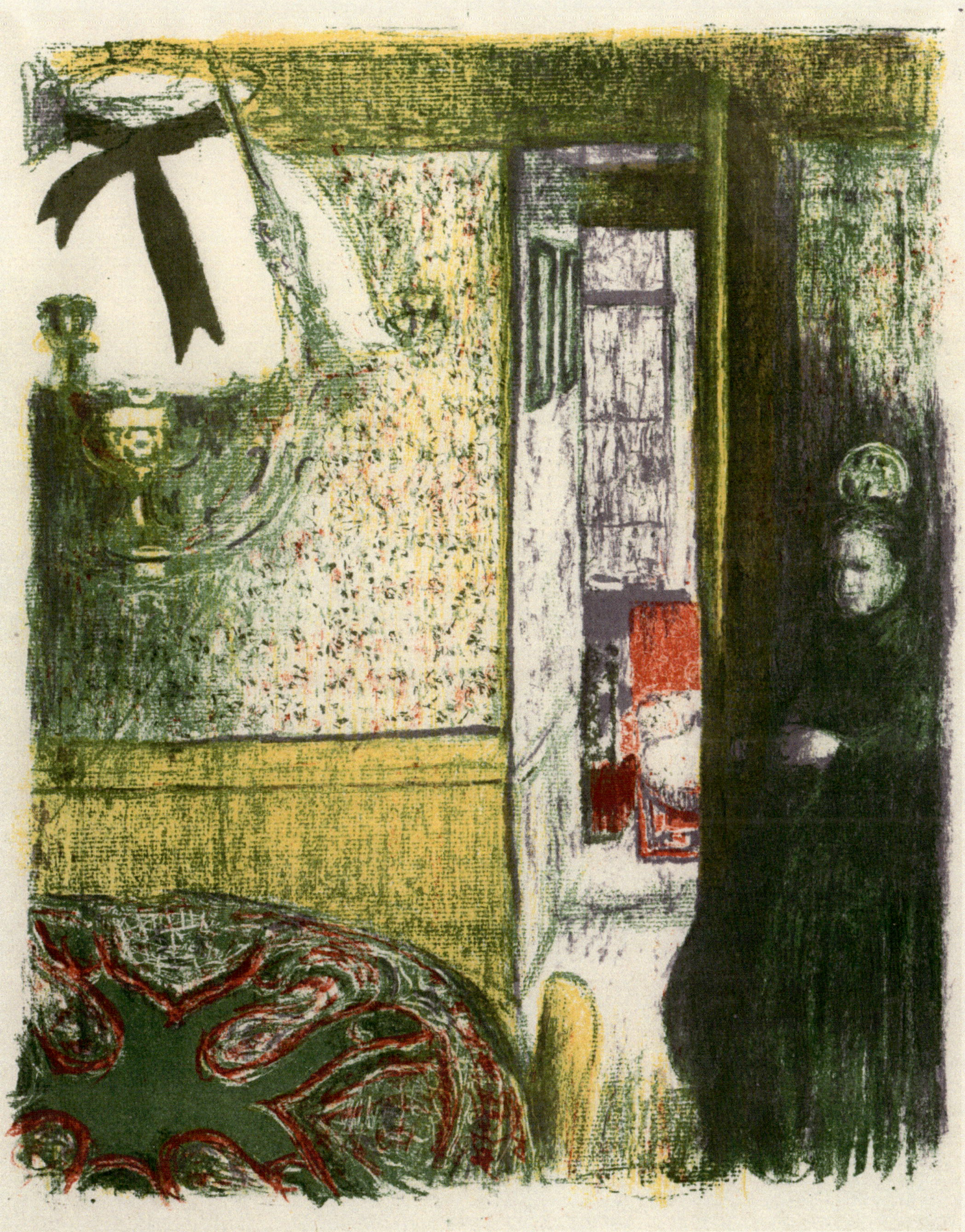

5.
Intérieur aux tentures roses I
*Interior with Pink Wallpaper I*

354 x 278 mm

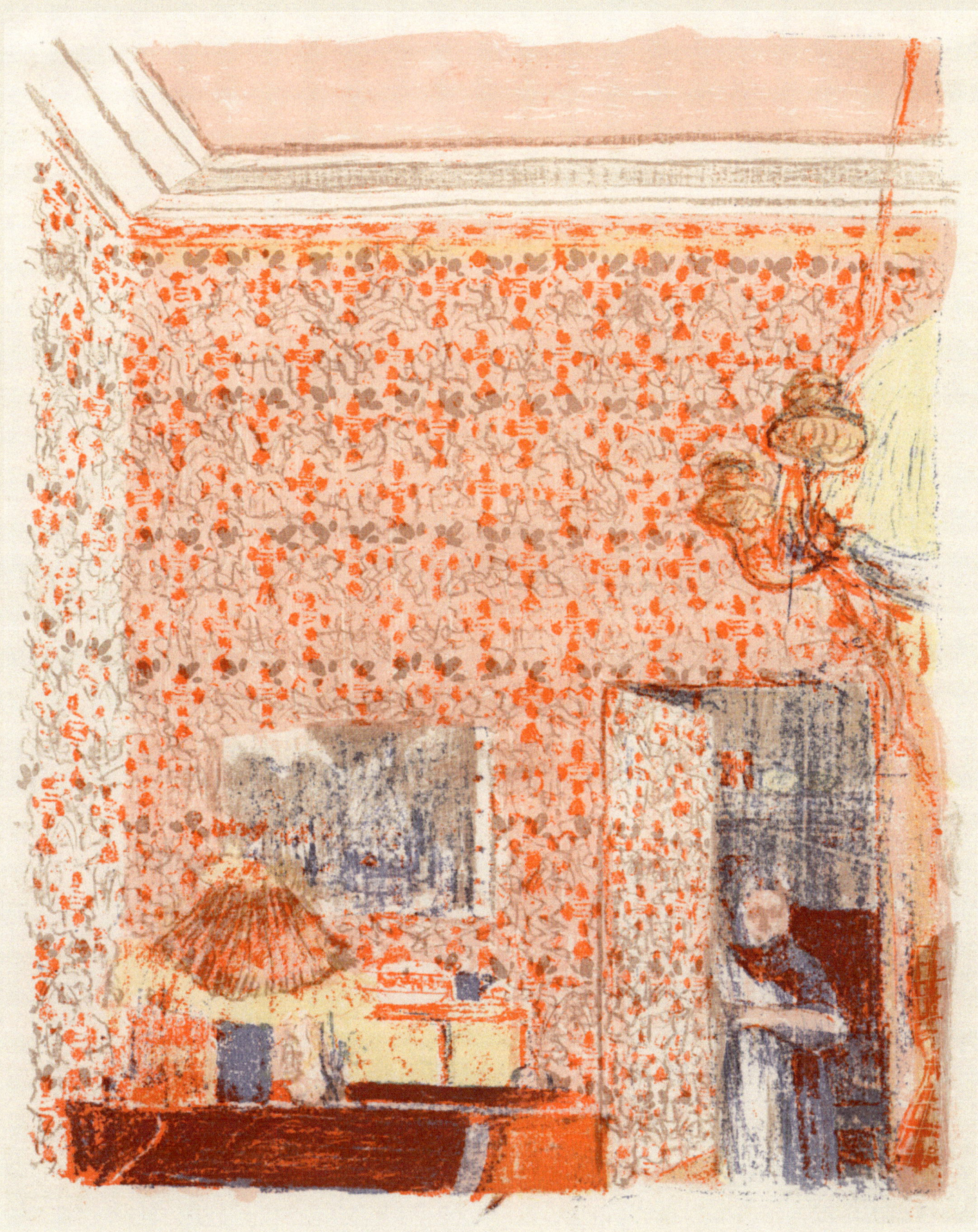

6.
Intérieur aux tentures roses II
*Interior with Pink Wallpaper II*

346 x 282 mm

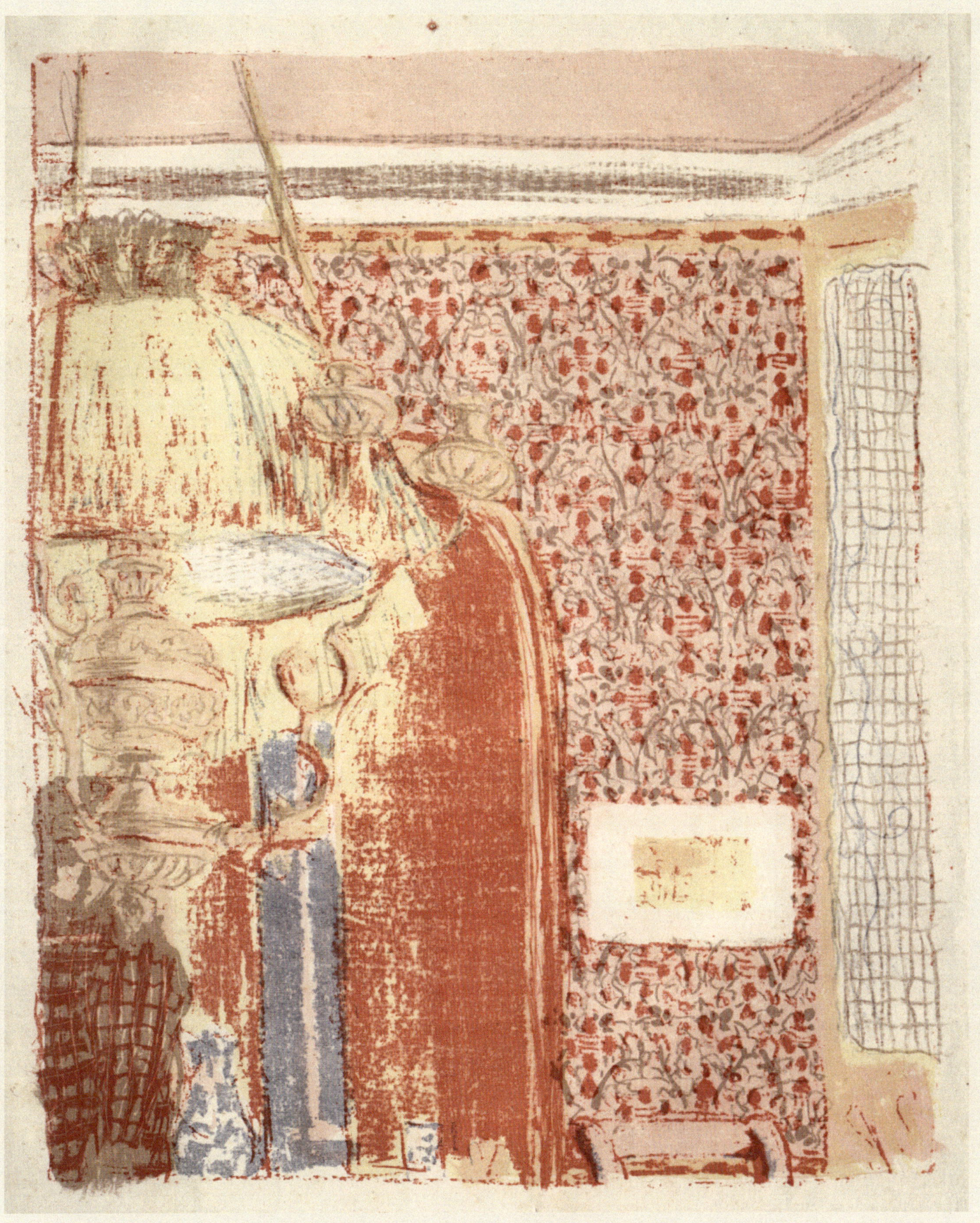

7.
Intérieur aux tentures roses III
*Interior with Pink Wallpaper III*

342 x 273 mm

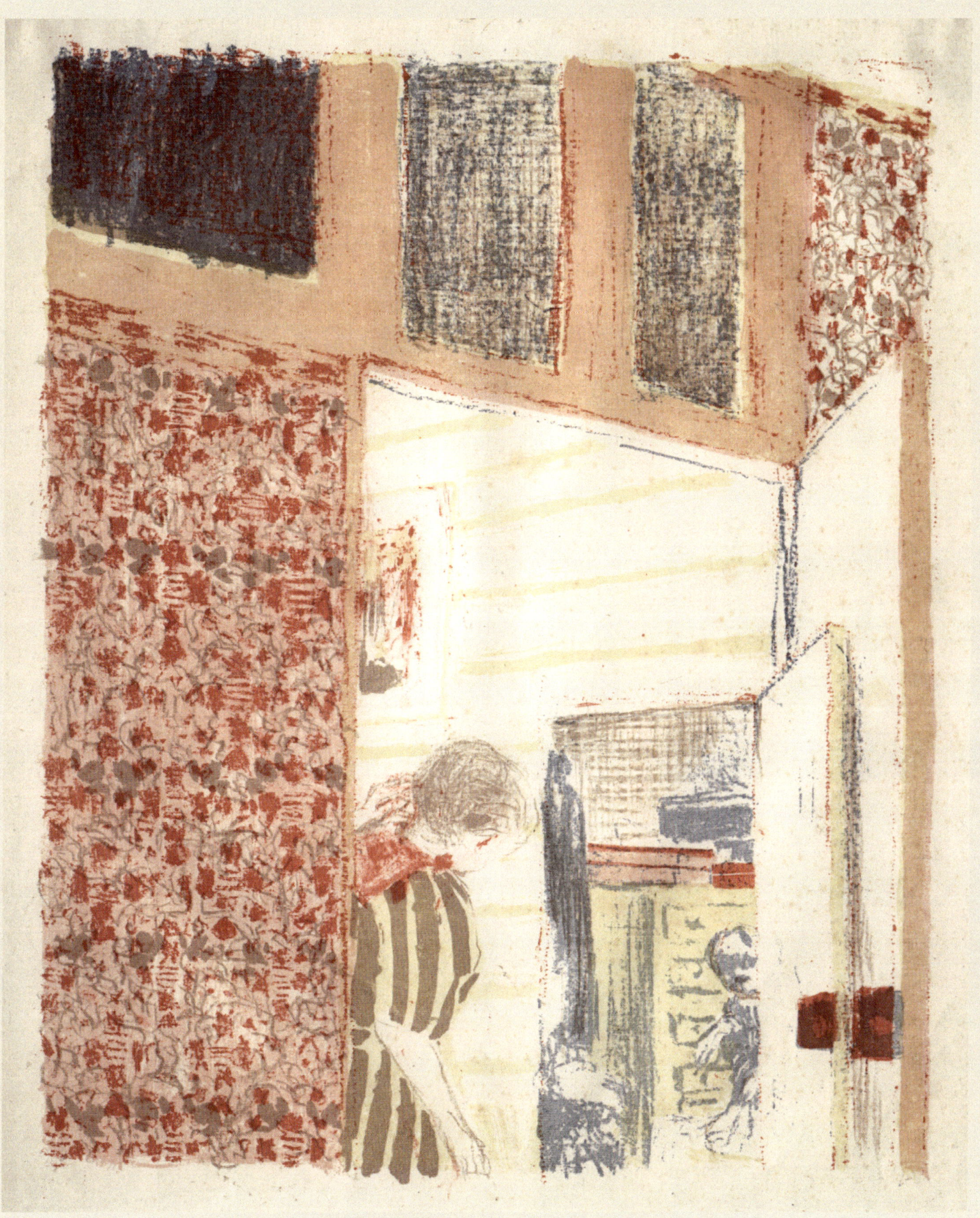

8.
L'Âtre
*The Hearth*

343 x 277 mm

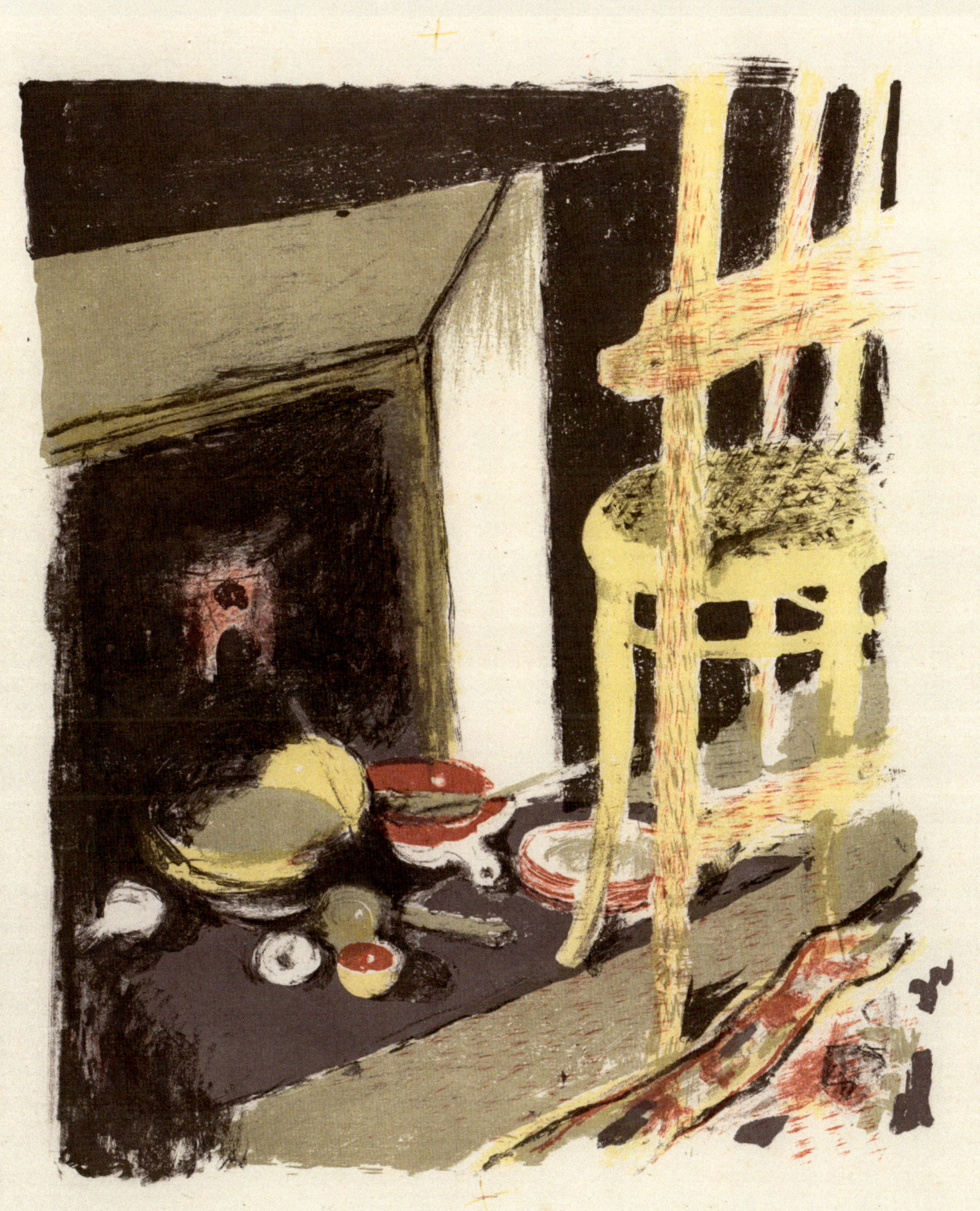

9.

Sur le pont de l'Europe
*On the Pont de l'Europe*

343 x 277 mm

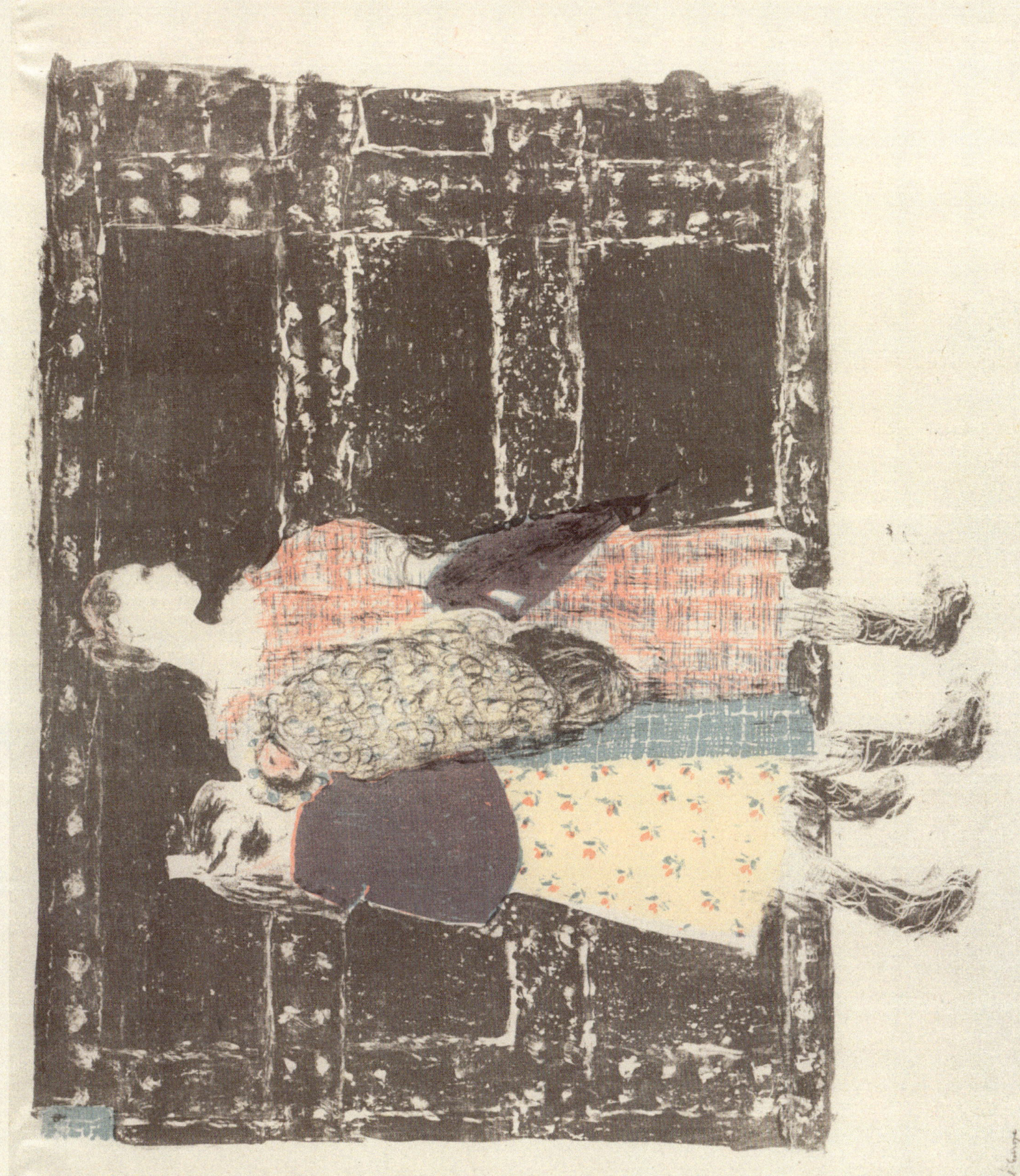

10.
La Pâtisserie
*The Pastry Shop*

351 X 275 mm

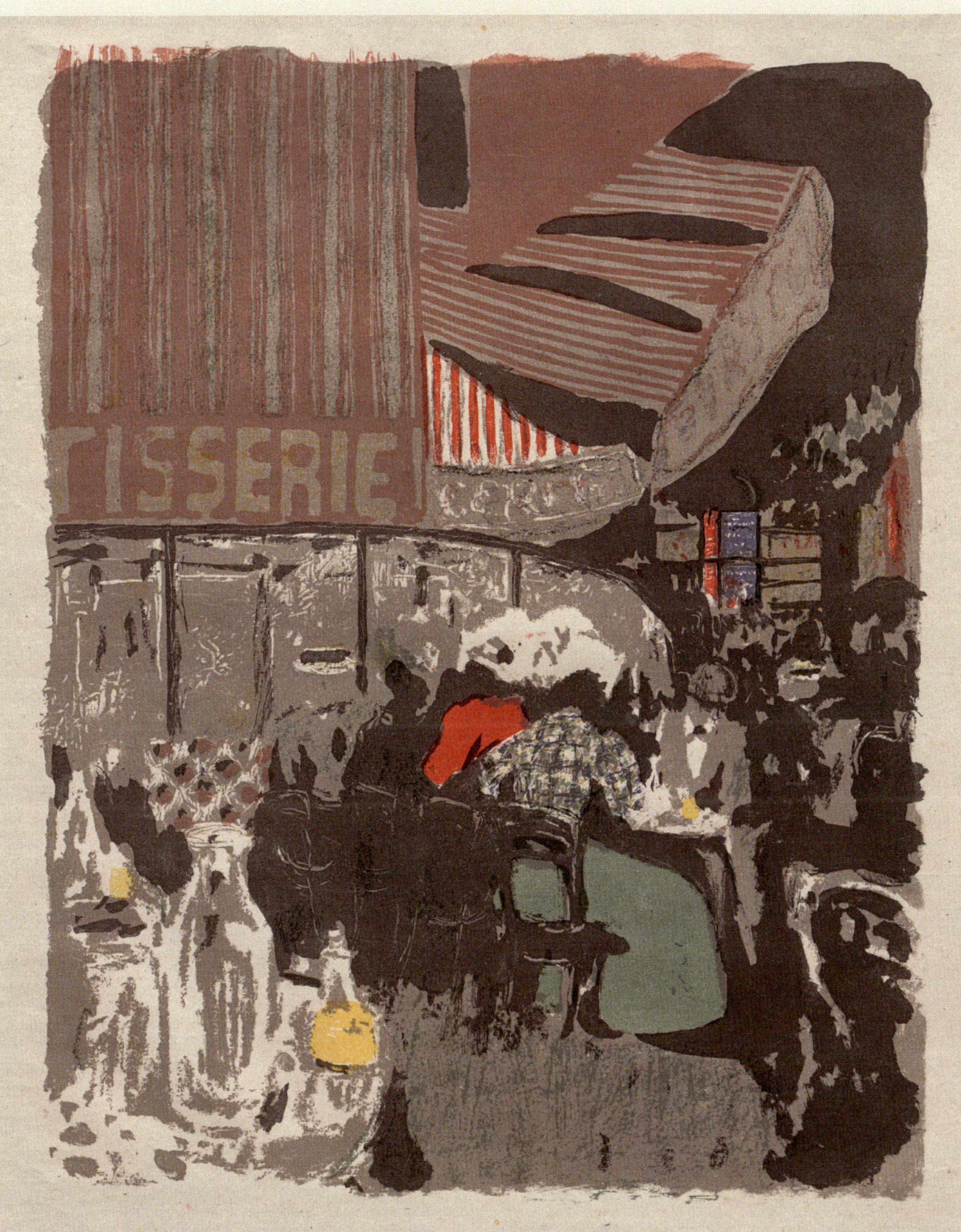
TISSERIE

II.

La Cuisinière (la mère de l'artiste)
*The Cook (the artist's mother)*

350 x 277 mm

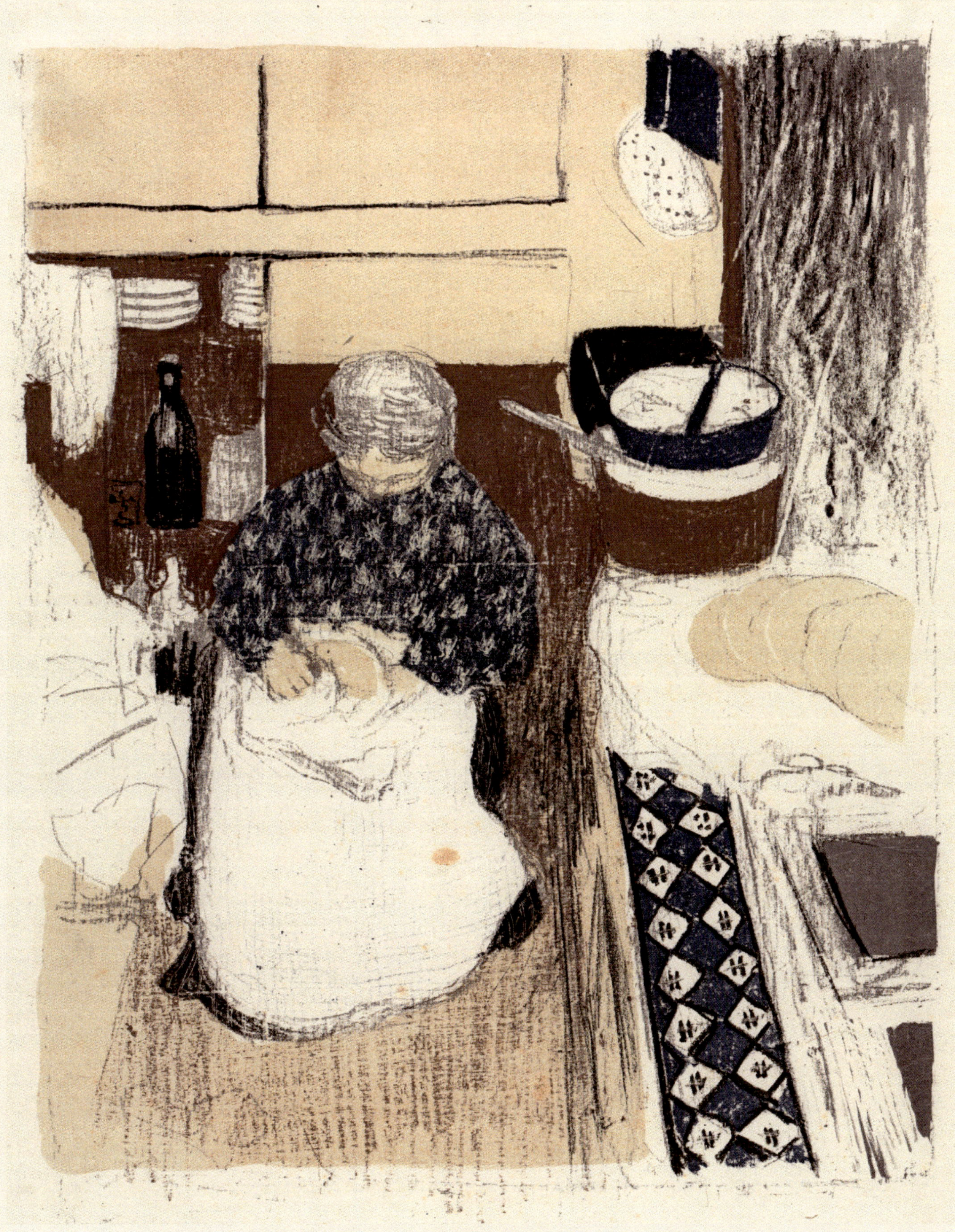

12.
Les deux belles-sœurs
*The Two Sisters-in-Law*

368 x 294 mm

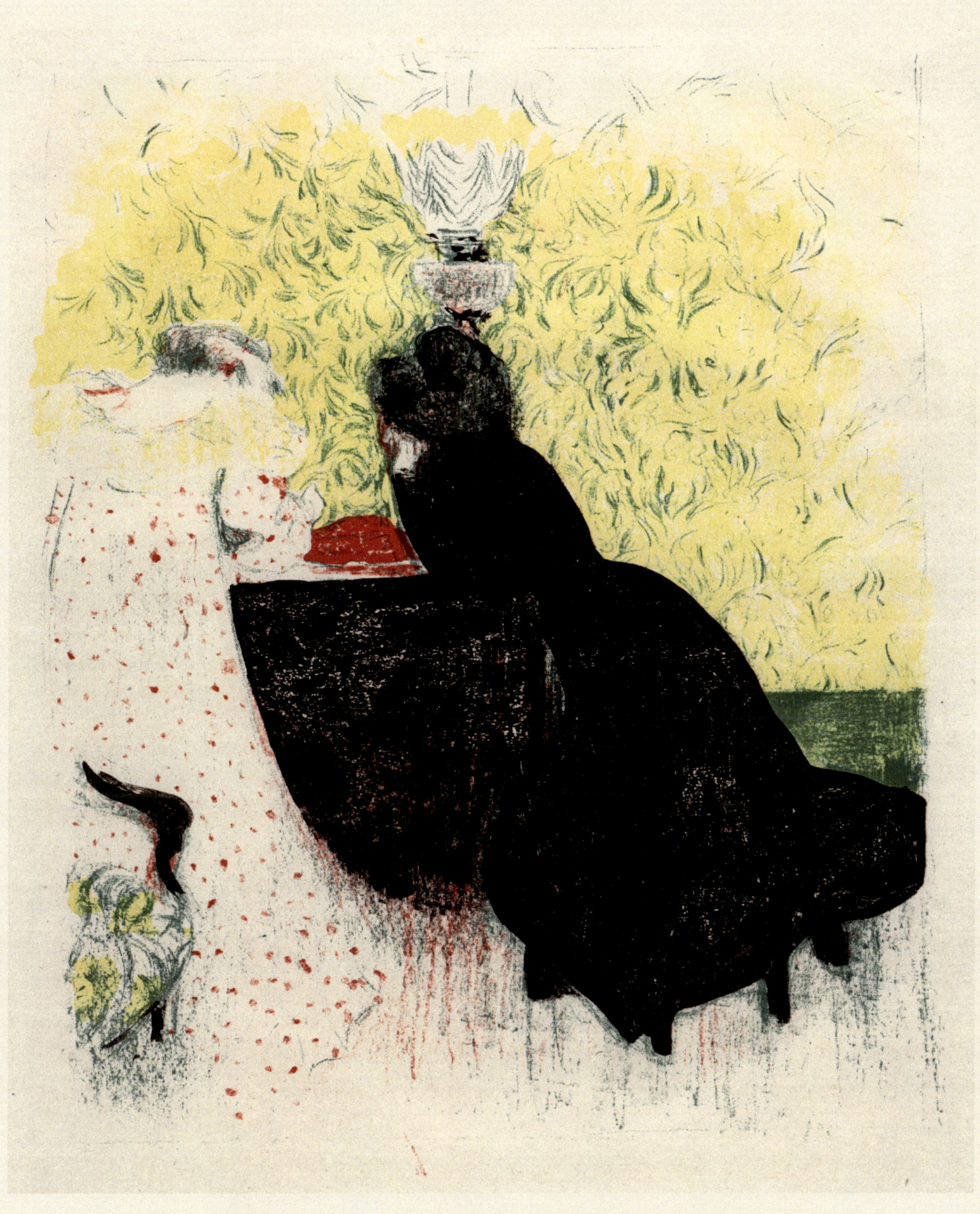

PAYSAGES ET INTÉRIEURS/
LANDSCAPES AND INTERIORS
Suite de 12 planches et une couverture,
imprimée par Auguste Clot. Éditée à
Paris par Ambroise Vollard en 1899,
et tirée à 100 exemplaires./
*Suite of 12 plates and a cover, printed
by Auguste Clot. Published in Paris by
Ambroise Vollard in 1899, in an edition
of 100 copies.*

Cette édition/*This edition*
© Pallas Athene (Publishers) Ltd,
London, 2026

Pallas Athene (Publishers) Ltd,
2 Birch Close, London N19 5XD

**www.pallasathene.co.uk**

ISBN 978 1 84368 299 8 (édition française)
ISBN 978 1 84368 298 1 (English edition)

Imprimé en Angleterre par Blissetts/
*Printed in England by Blissetts*

3

# PAYSAGES
## ET INTÉRIEURS

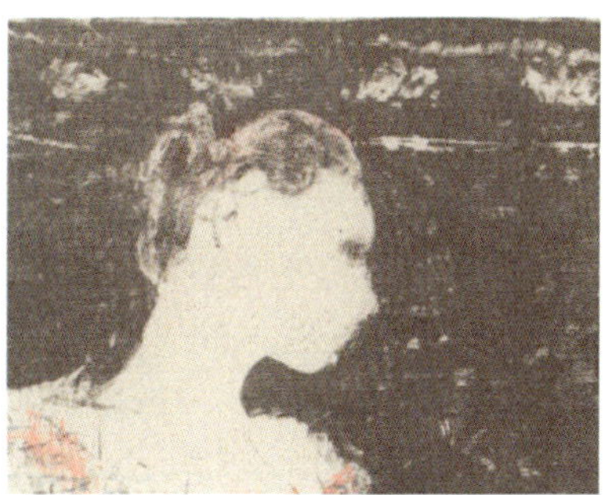

# LANDSCAPES AND
## INTERIORS

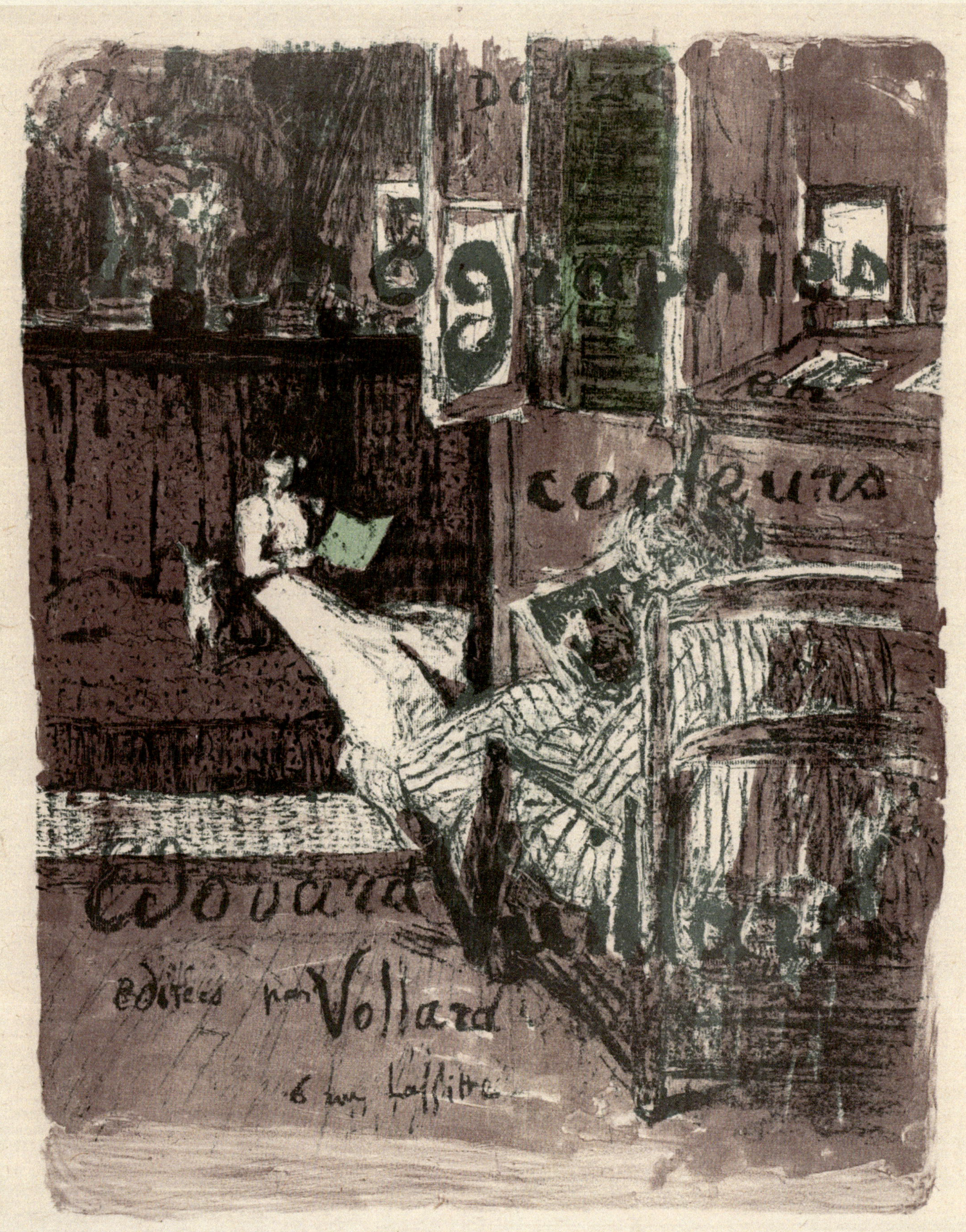
Douze
Lithographies en
couleurs
Édouard Vuillard
Éditées par Vollard
8 rue Laffitte

# Paysages et intérieurs

# *Landscapes and Interiors*

## Édouard Vuillard

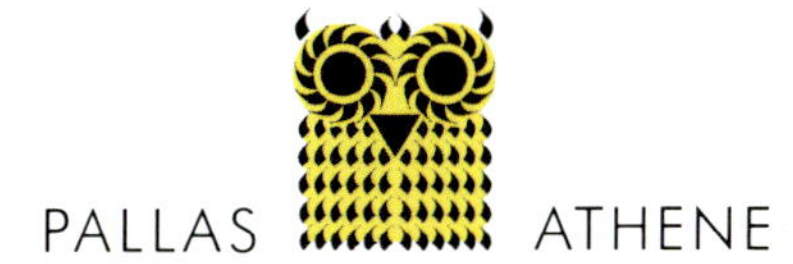

1.

La partie de dames

*The Game of Checkers*

330 x 257 mm

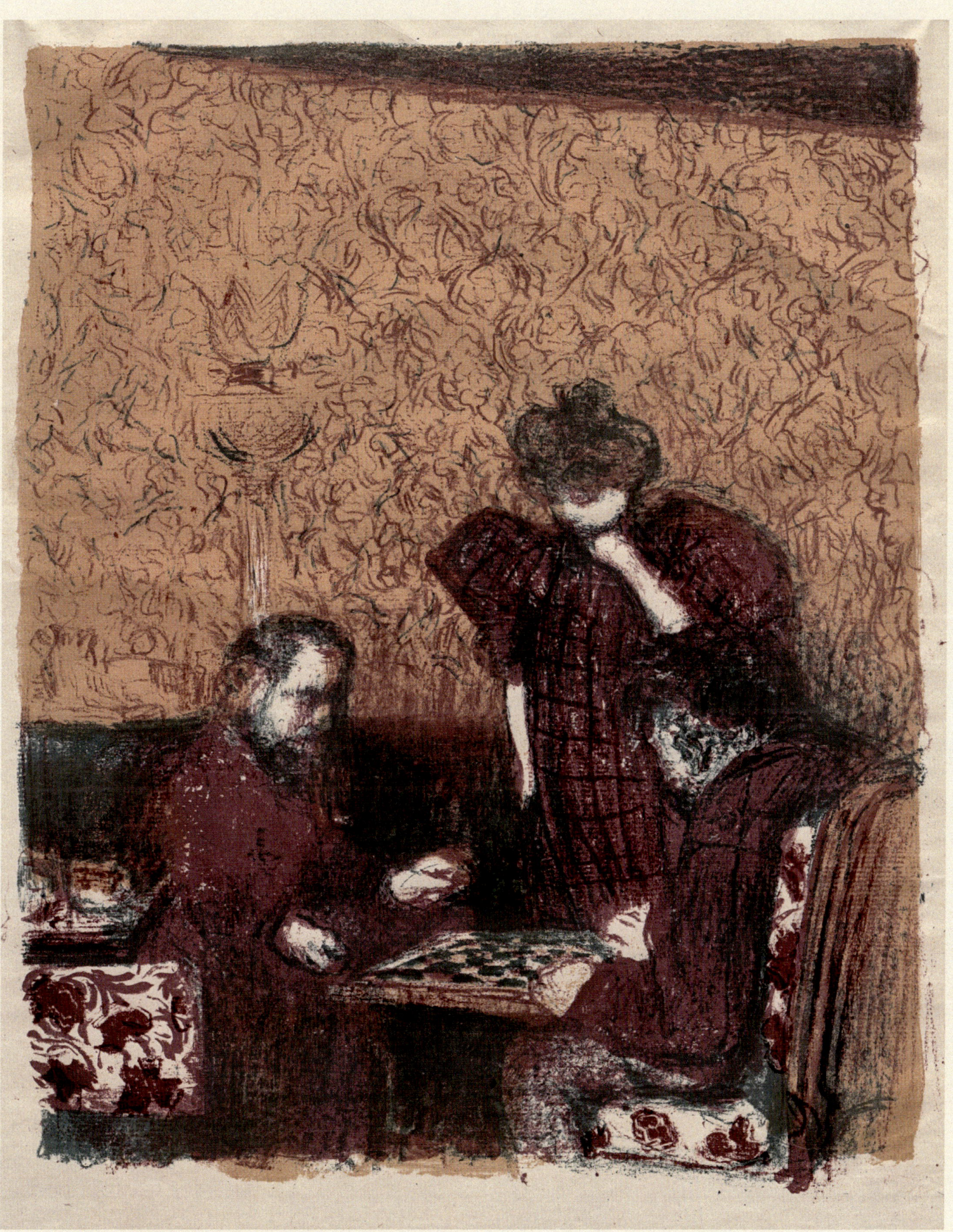

2.

L'Avenue

*The Avenue*

311 x 414 mm

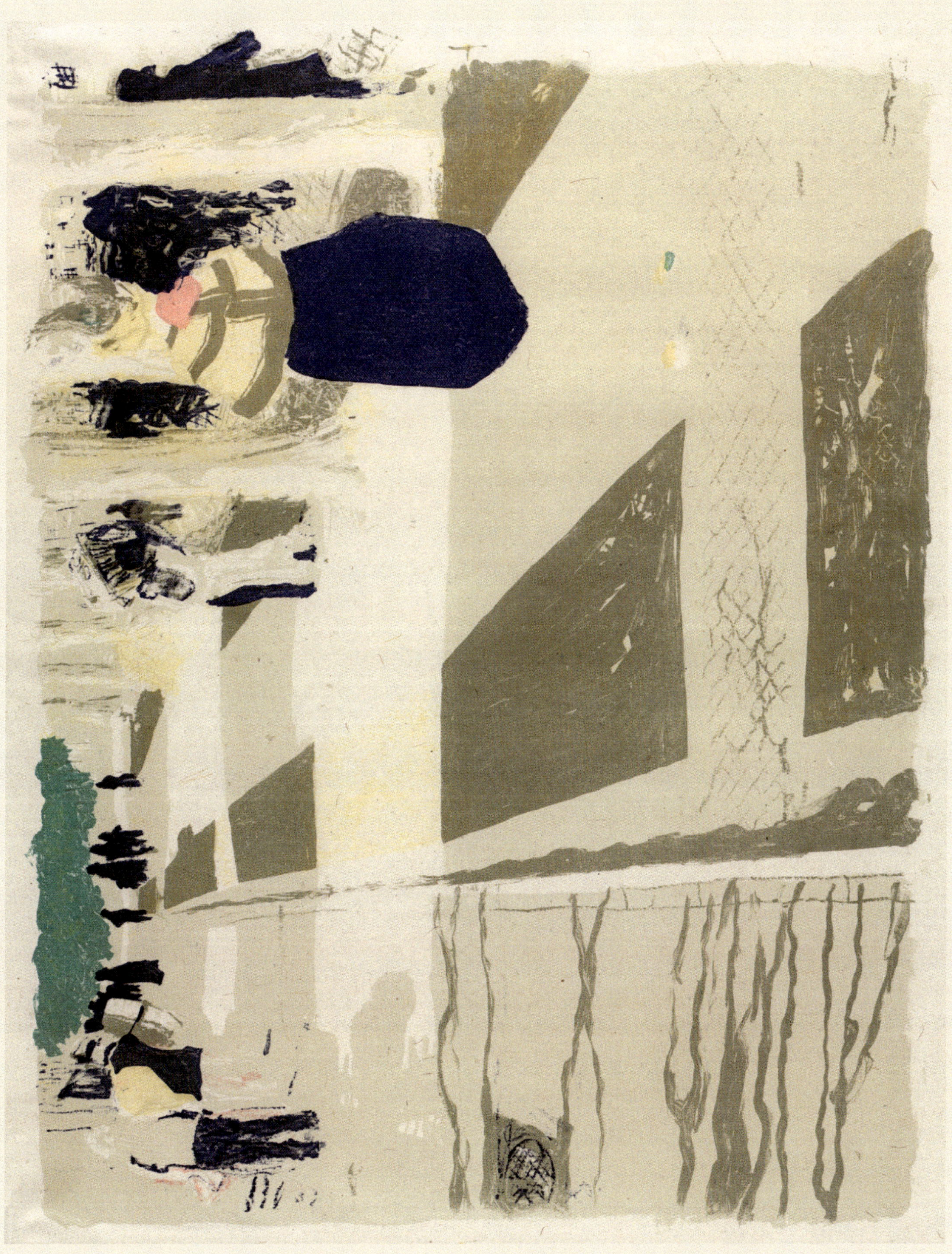

3.
À travers champs
*Across the Fields*

260 x 345 mm

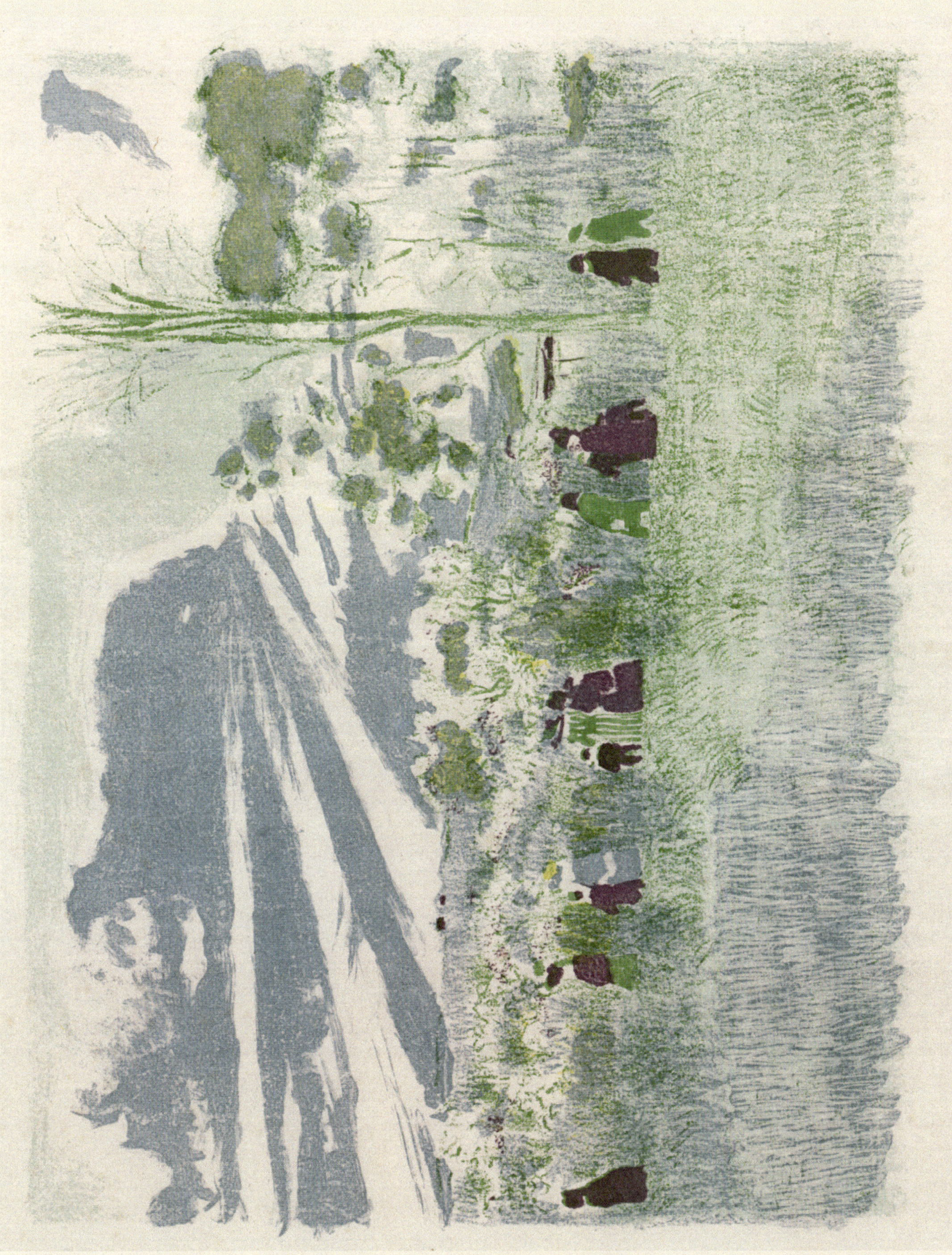

4.
Intérieur à la suspension
*Interior with Ceiling Lamp*

356 x 282 mm

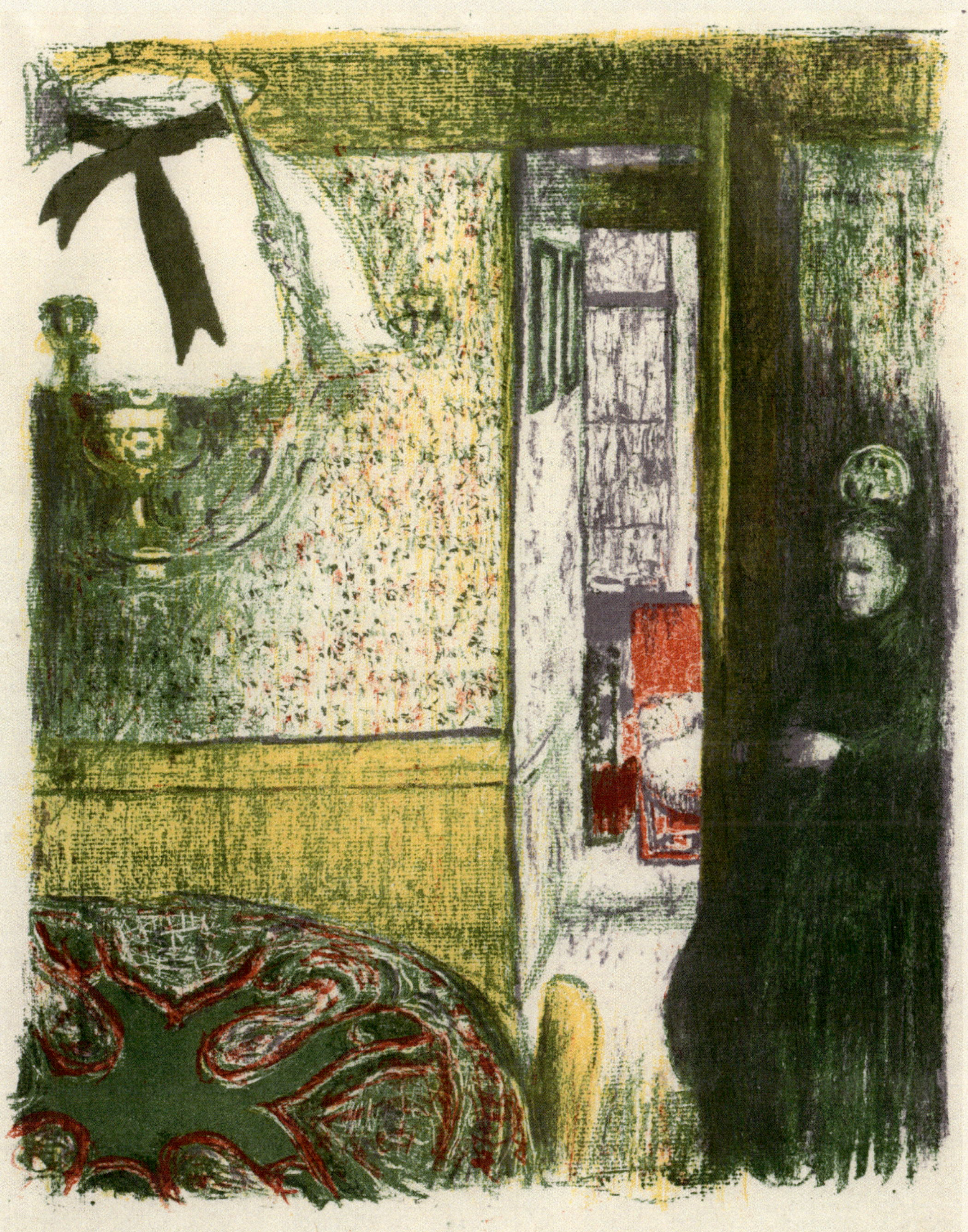

5.
Intérieur aux tentures roses I
*Interior with Pink Wallpaper I*

354 x 278 mm

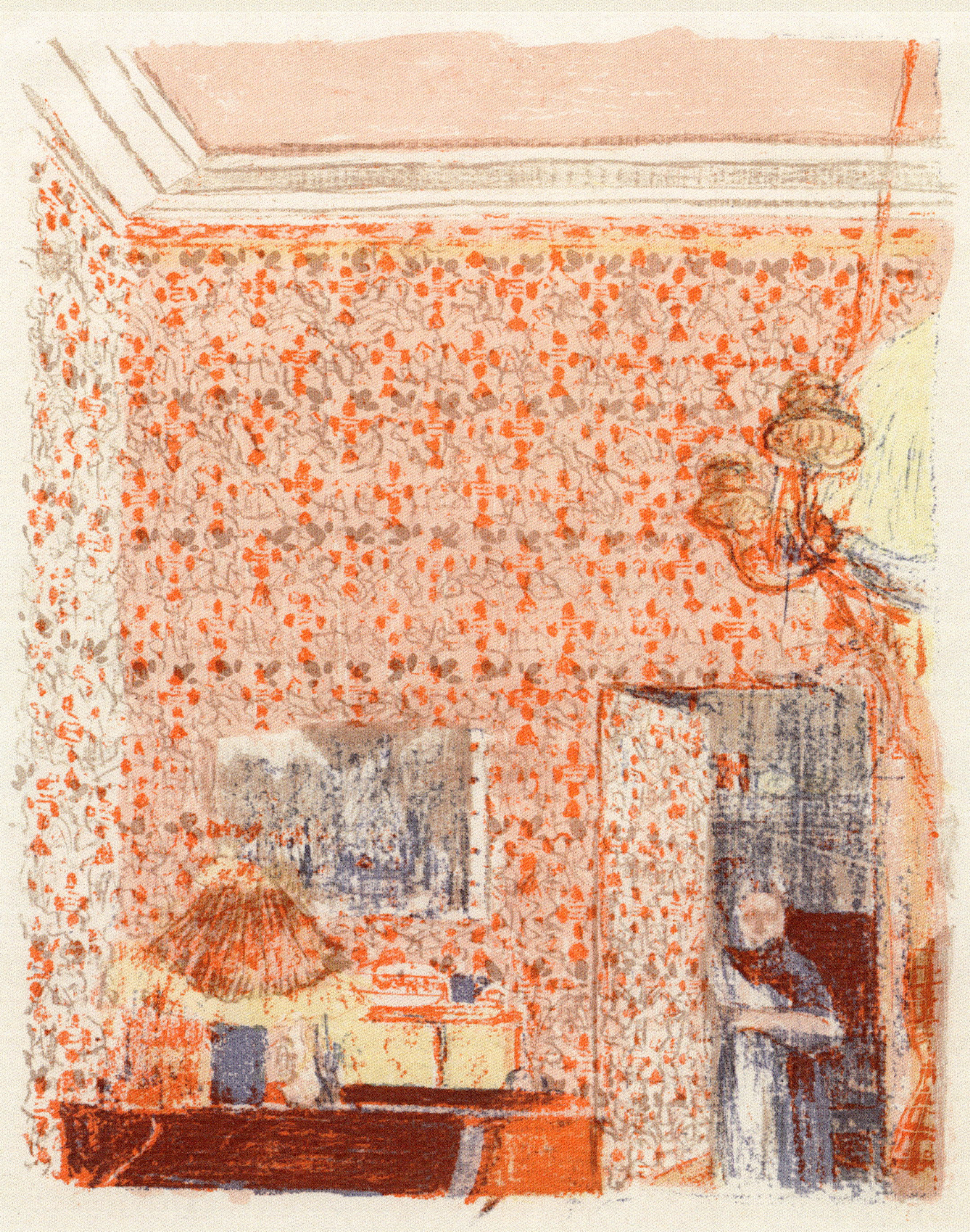

6.
Intérieur aux tentures roses II
*Interior with Pink Wallpaper II*

346 x 282 mm

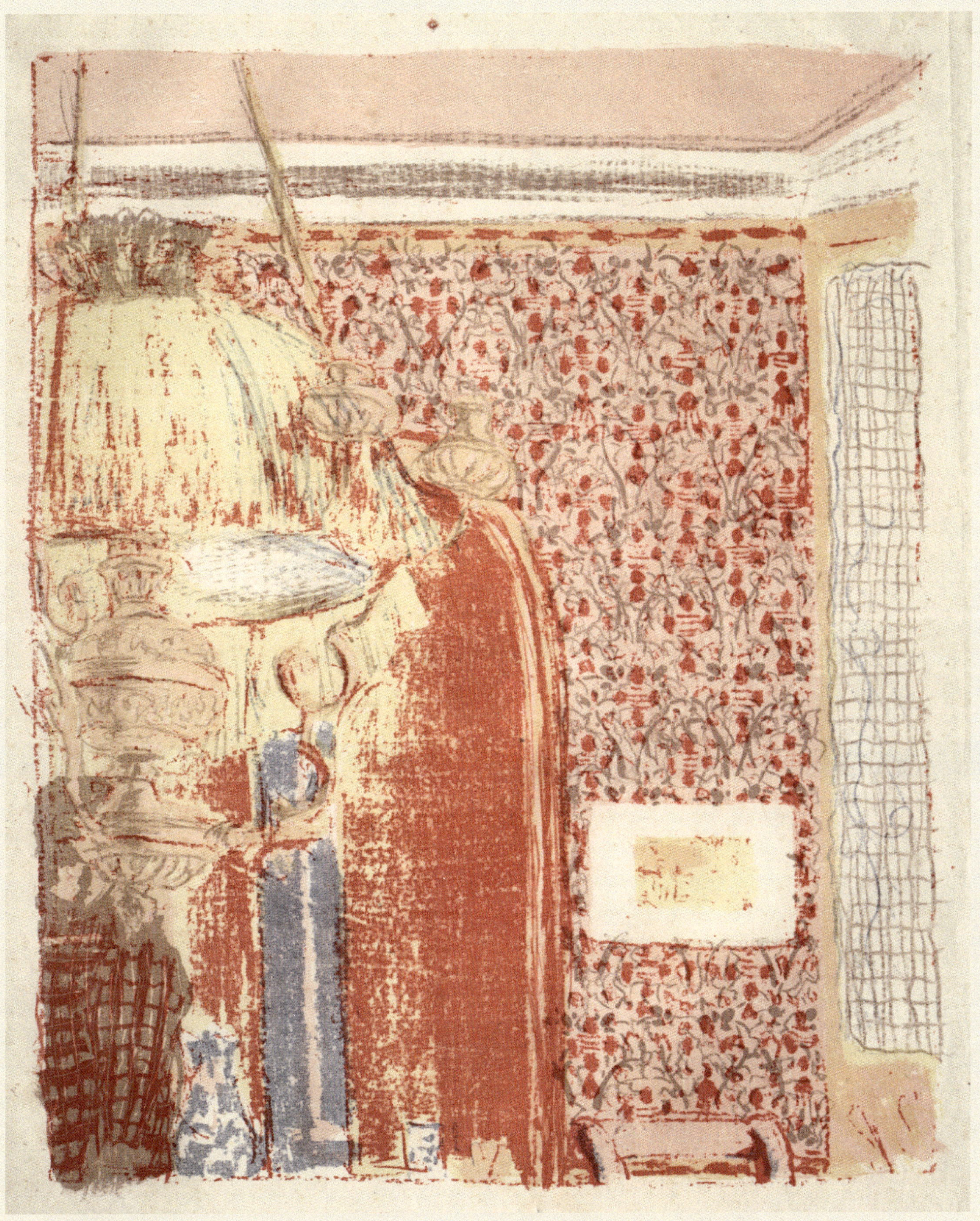

7.
Intérieur aux tentures roses III
*Interior with Pink Wallpaper III*

342 x 273 mm

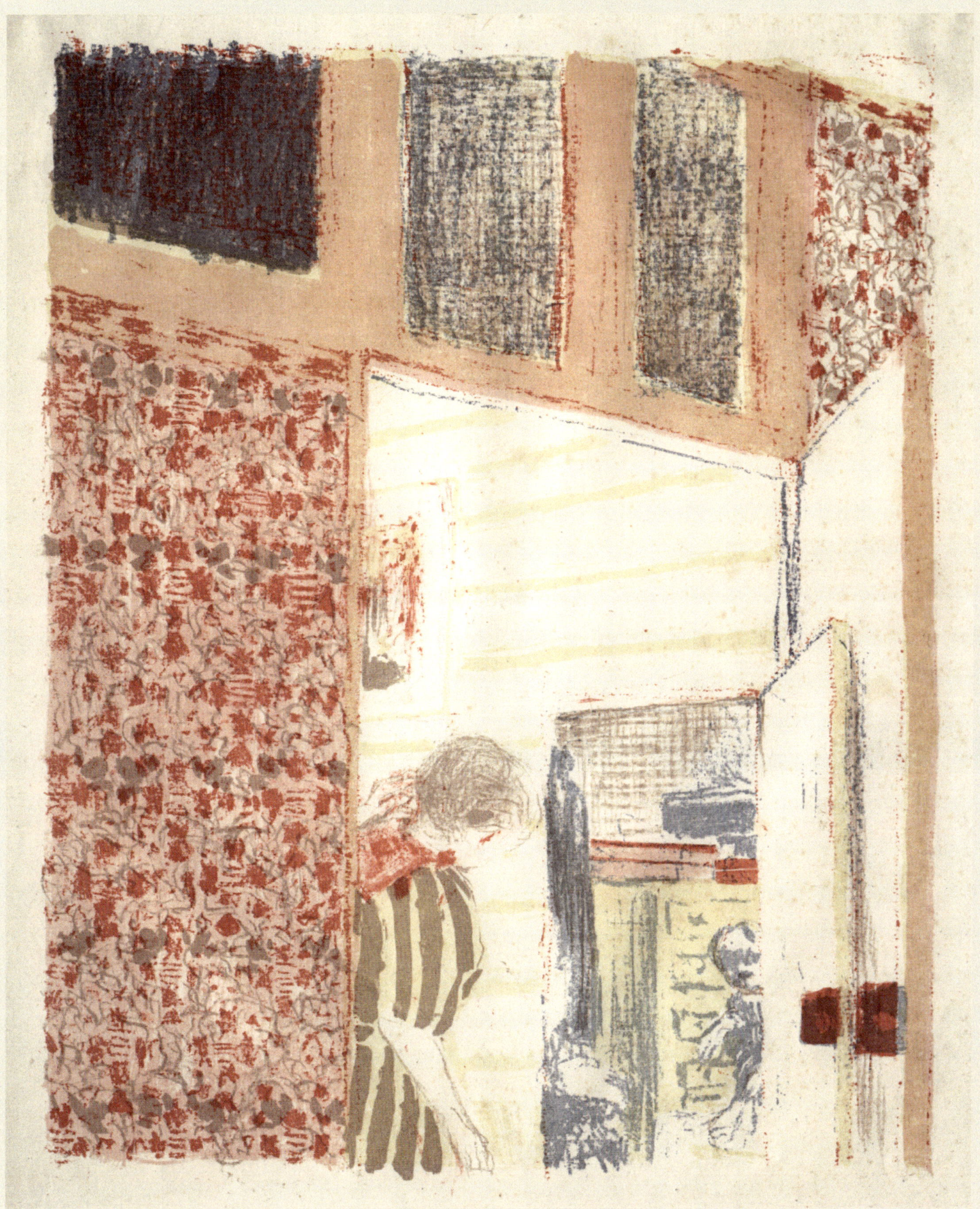

8.
L'Âtre
*The Hearth*

343 x 277 mm

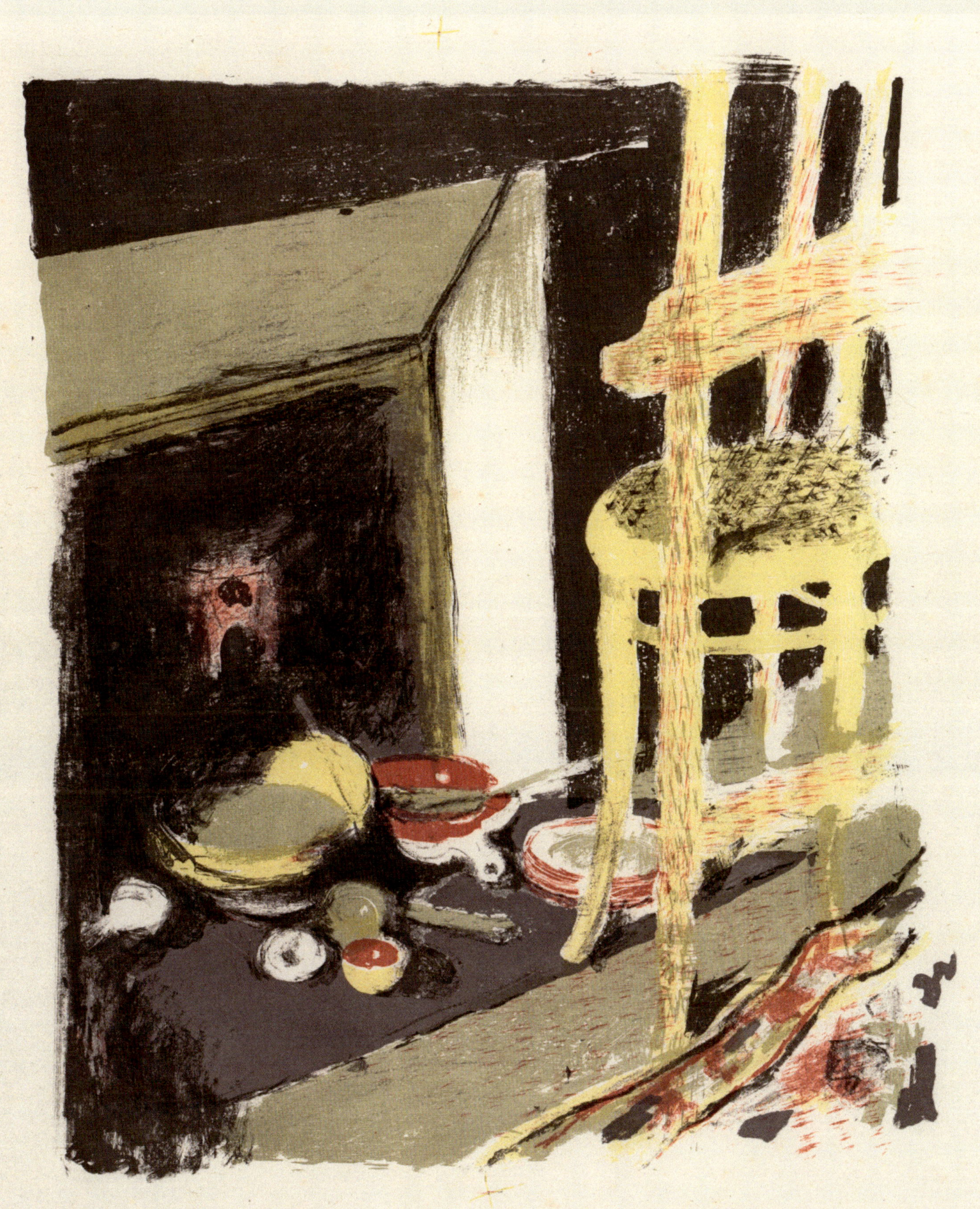

9.
Sur le pont de l'Europe
*On the Pont de l'Europe*

343 x 277 mm

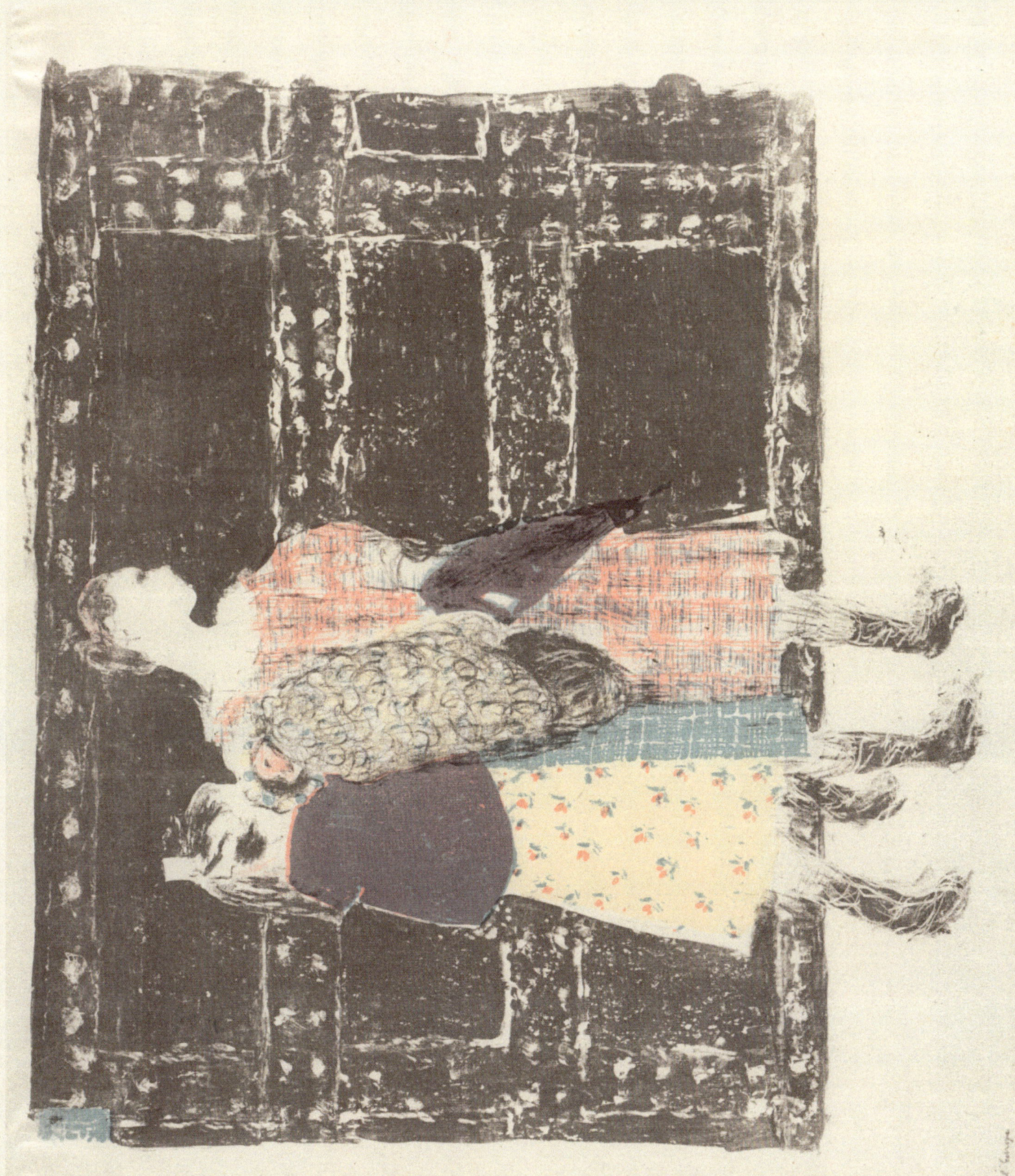

10.
La Pâtisserie
*The Pastry Shop*

351 x 275 mm

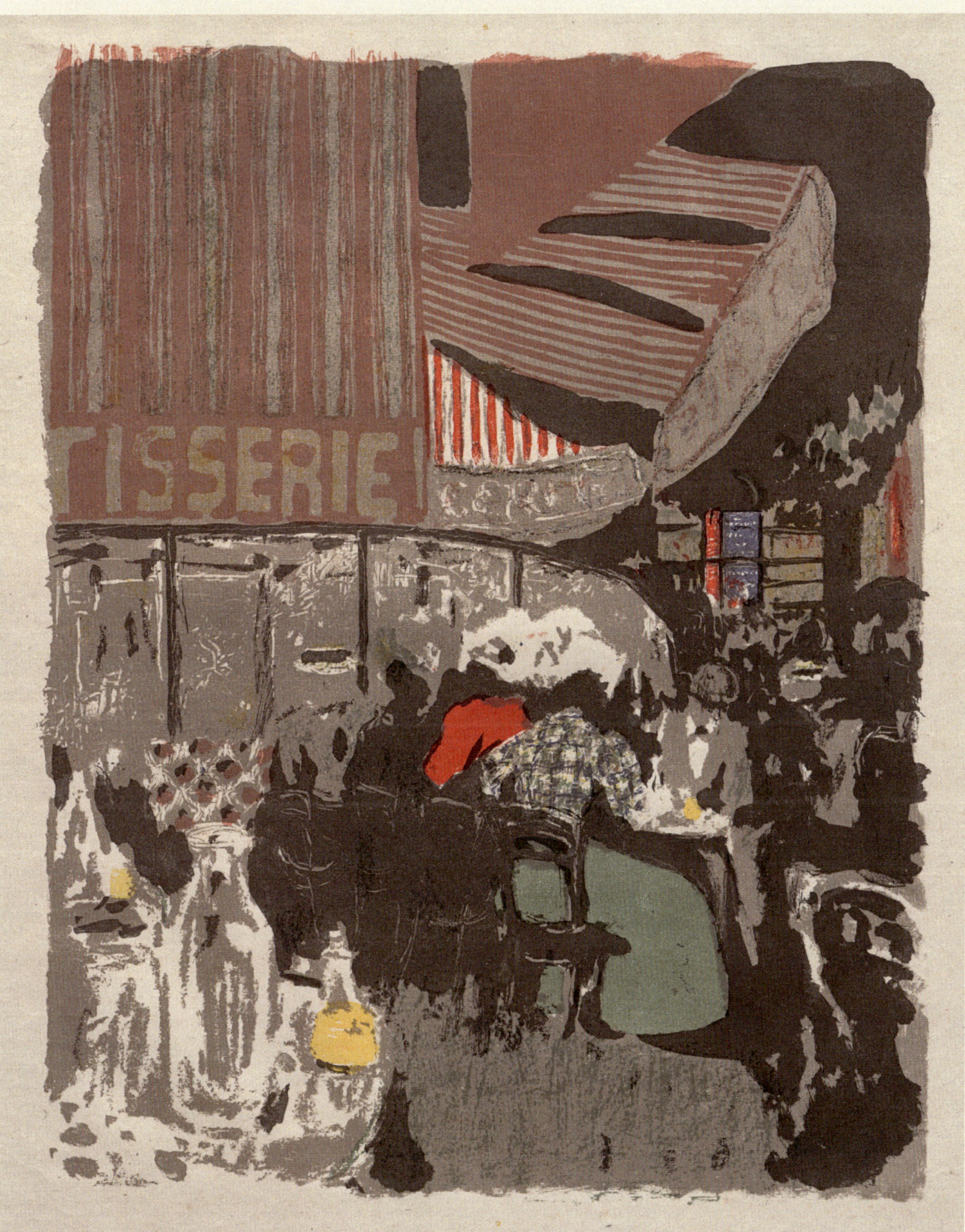
TISSERIE

11.

La Cuisinière (la mère de l'artiste)
*The Cook (the artist's mother)*

350 x 277 mm

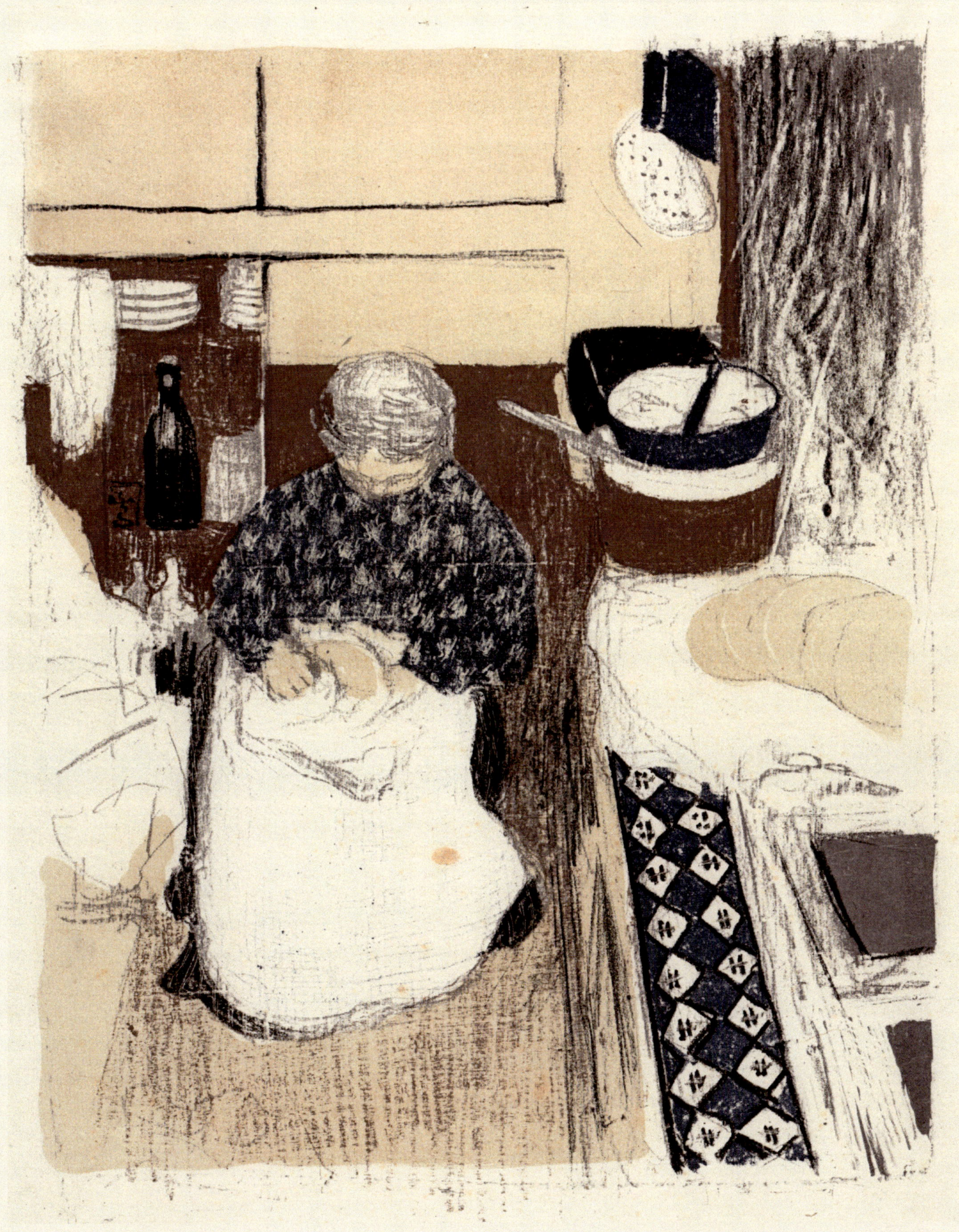

12.

Les deux belles-sœurs
*The Two Sisters-in-Law*

368 x 294 mm

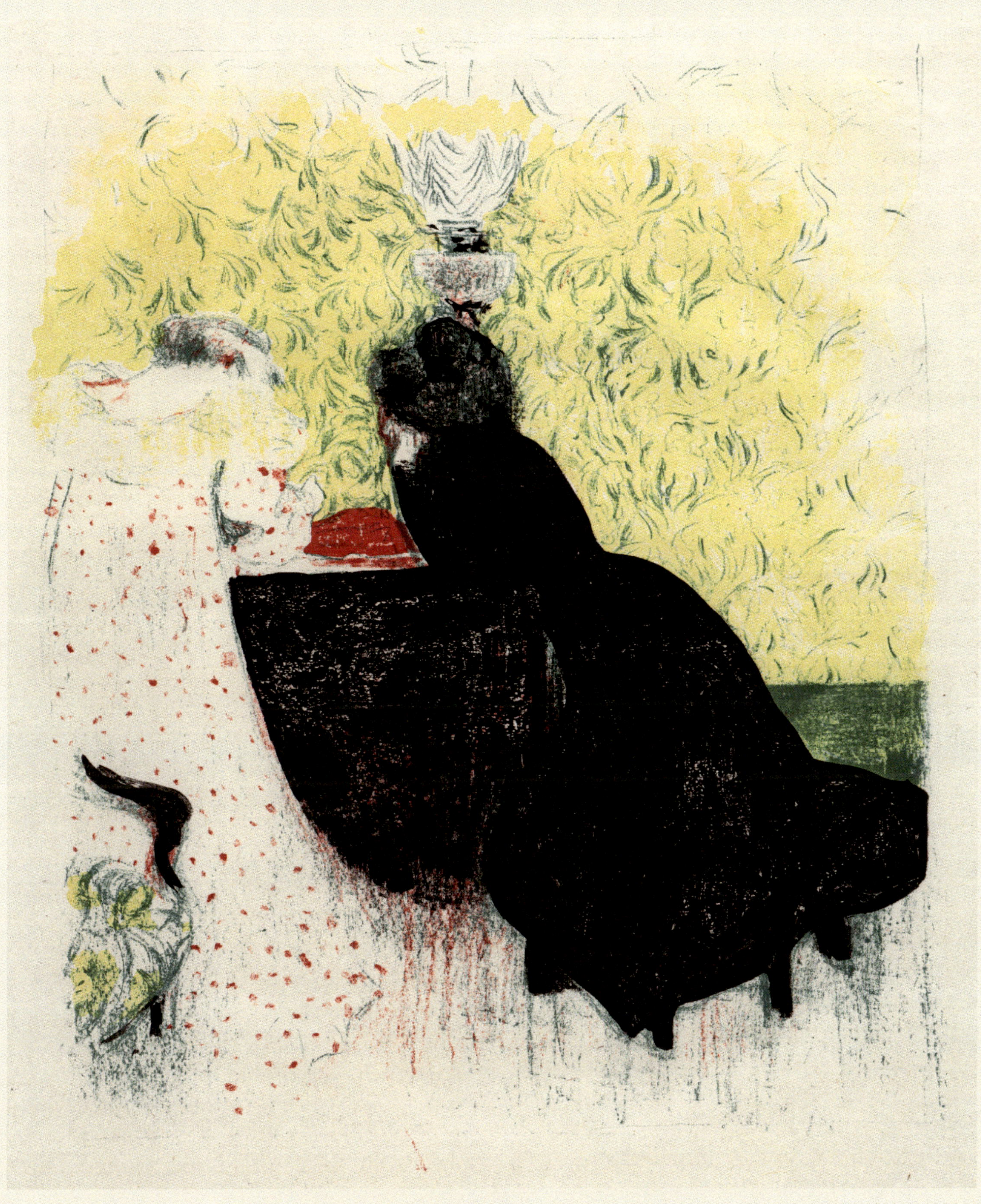

PAYSAGES ET INTÉRIEURS/
LANDSCAPES AND INTERIORS
Suite de 12 planches et une couverture,
imprimée par Auguste Clot. Éditée à
Paris par Ambroise Vollard en 1899,
et tirée à 100 exemplaires./
*Suite of 12 plates and a cover, printed
by Auguste Clot. Published in Paris by
Ambroise Vollard in 1899, in an edition
of 100 copies.*

Cette édition/*This edition*
© Pallas Athene (Publishers) Ltd,
London, 2026

Pallas Athene (Publishers) Ltd,
2 Birch Close, London N19 5XD

**www.pallasathene.co.uk**

ISBN 978 1 84368 299 8 (édition française)
ISBN 978 1 84368 298 1 (English edition)

Imprimé en Angleterre par Blissetts/
*Printed in England by Blissetts*

3

# PAYSAGES
# ET INTÉRIEURS

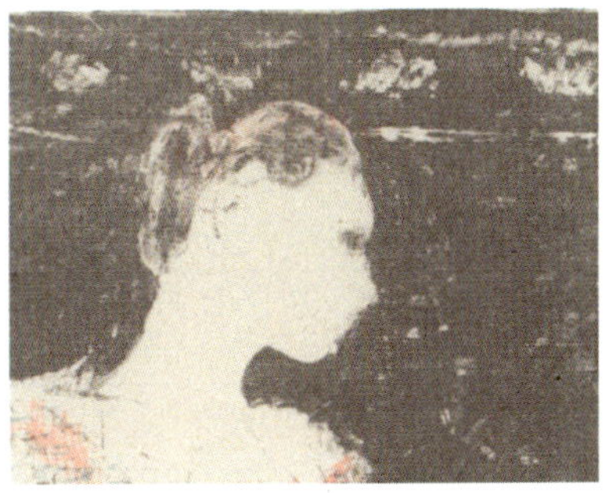

# LANDSCAPES AND
# INTERIORS

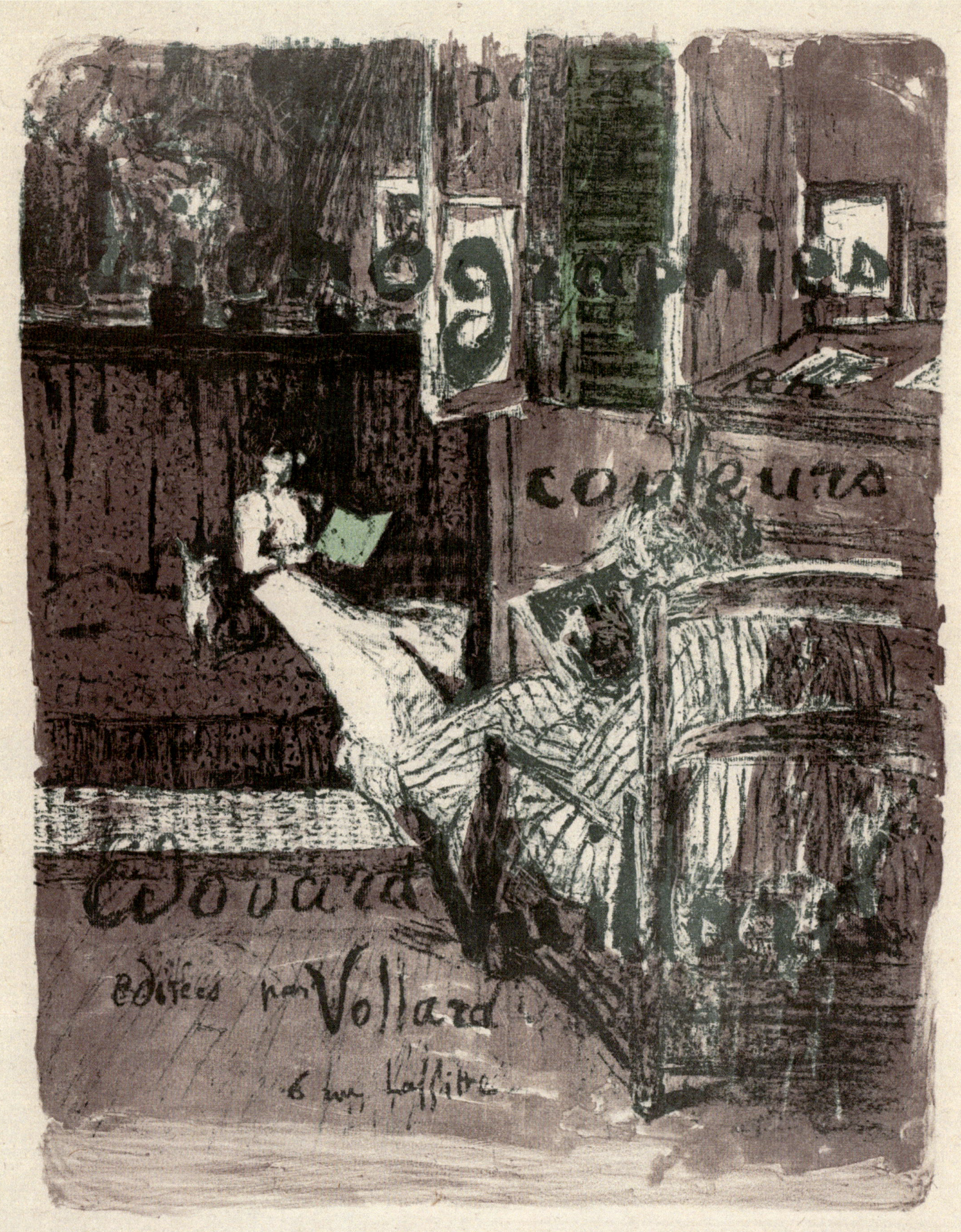

Douze
lithographies
en
couleurs
Bonnard
Editées par Vollard
6 rue Laffitte

# Paysages et intérieurs

# *Landscapes and Interiors*

## Édouard Vuillard

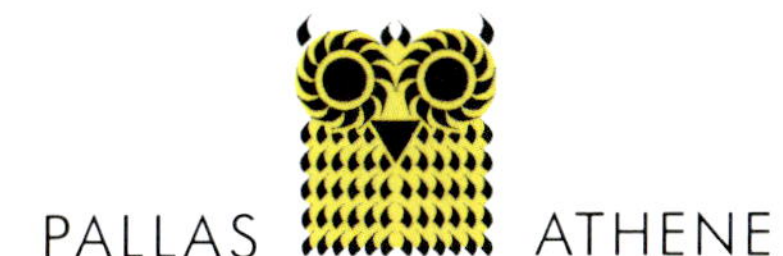

1.

La partie de dames
*The Game of Checkers*

330 x 257 mm

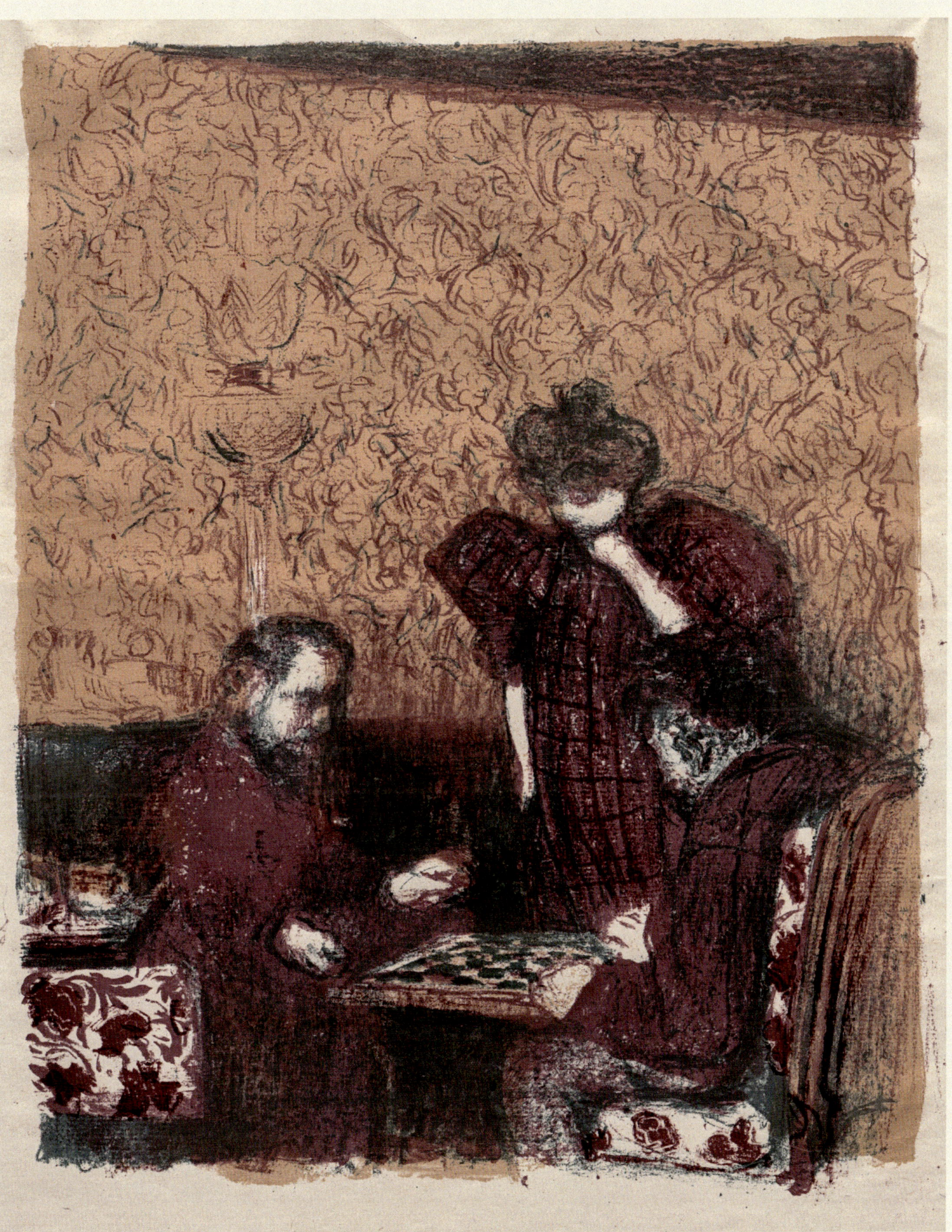

2.
L'Avenue
*The Avenue*

311 x 414 mm

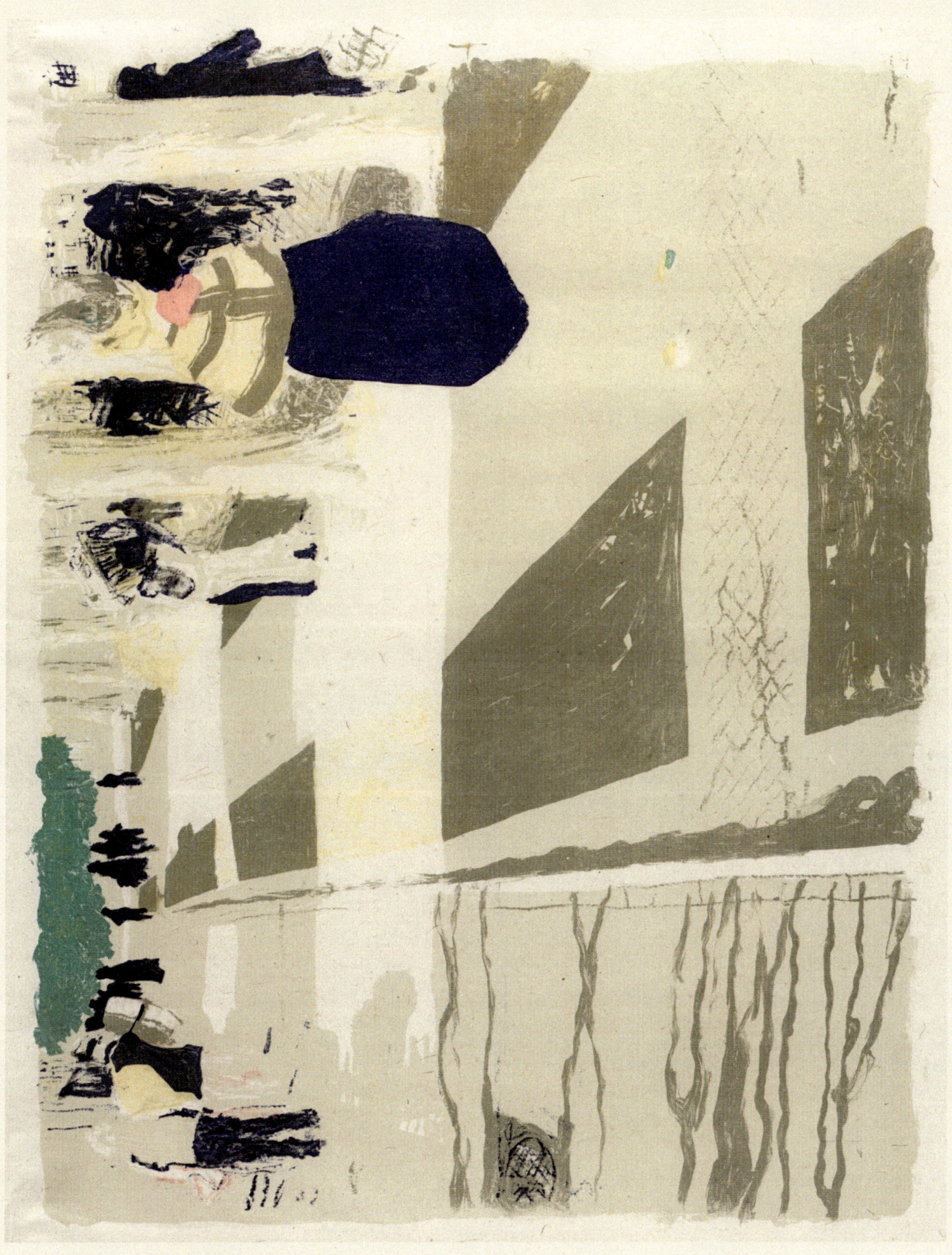

3.
À travers champs
*Across the Fields*

260 x 345 mm

4.
Intérieur à la suspension
*Interior with Ceiling Lamp*

356 x 282 mm

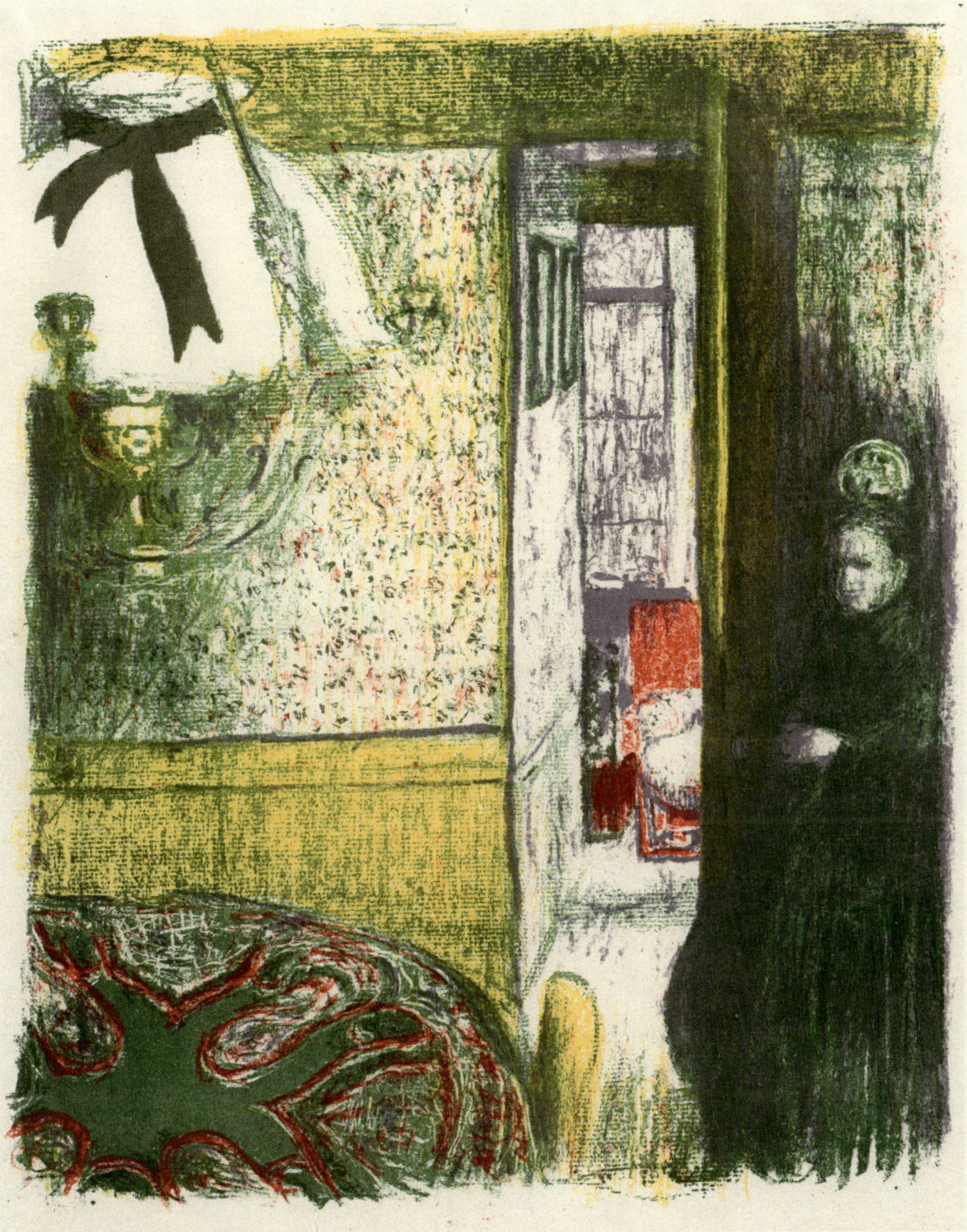

5.
Intérieur aux tentures roses I
*Interior with Pink Wallpaper I*

354 x 278 mm

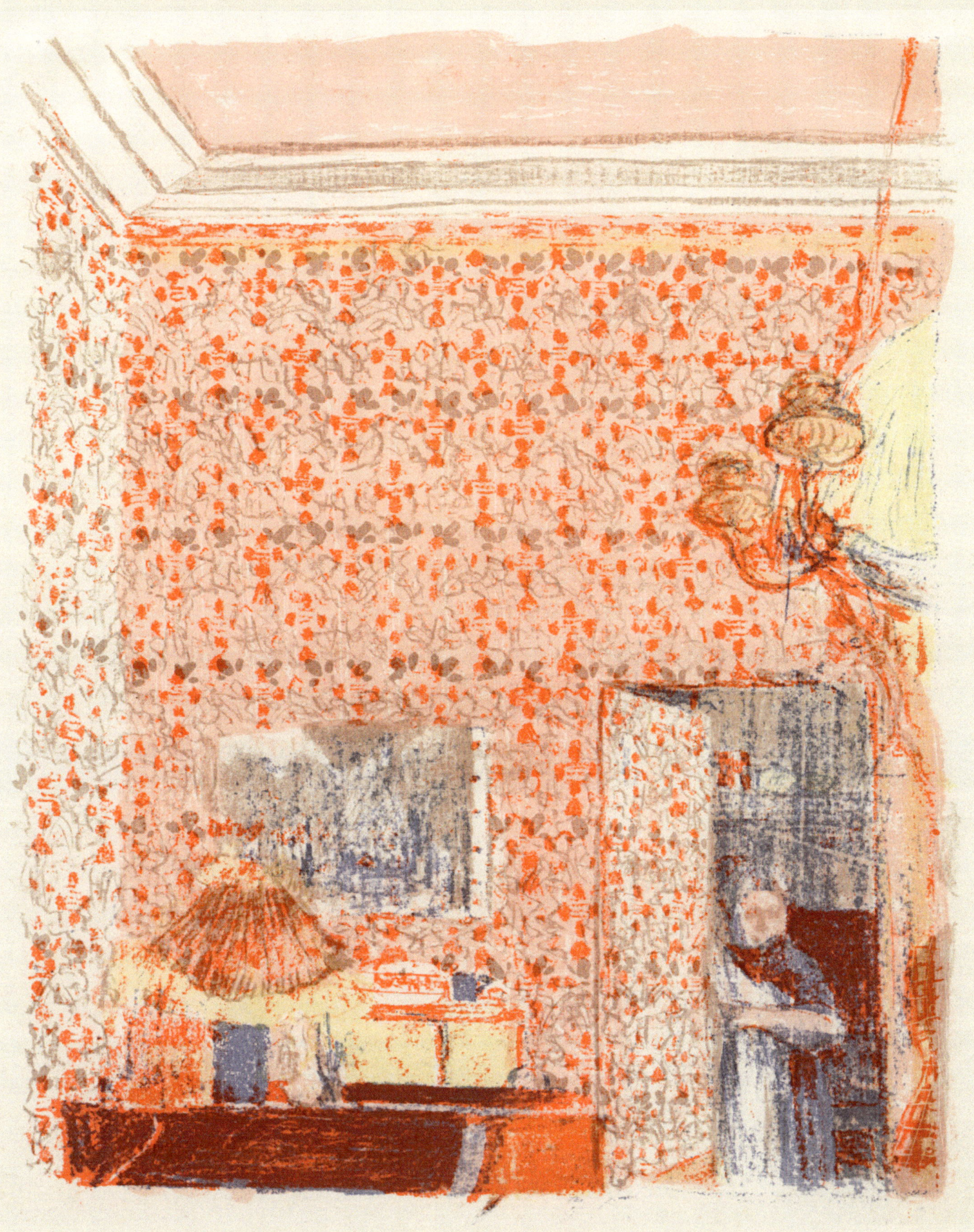

6.
Intérieur aux tentures roses II
*Interior with Pink Wallpaper II*

346 x 282 mm

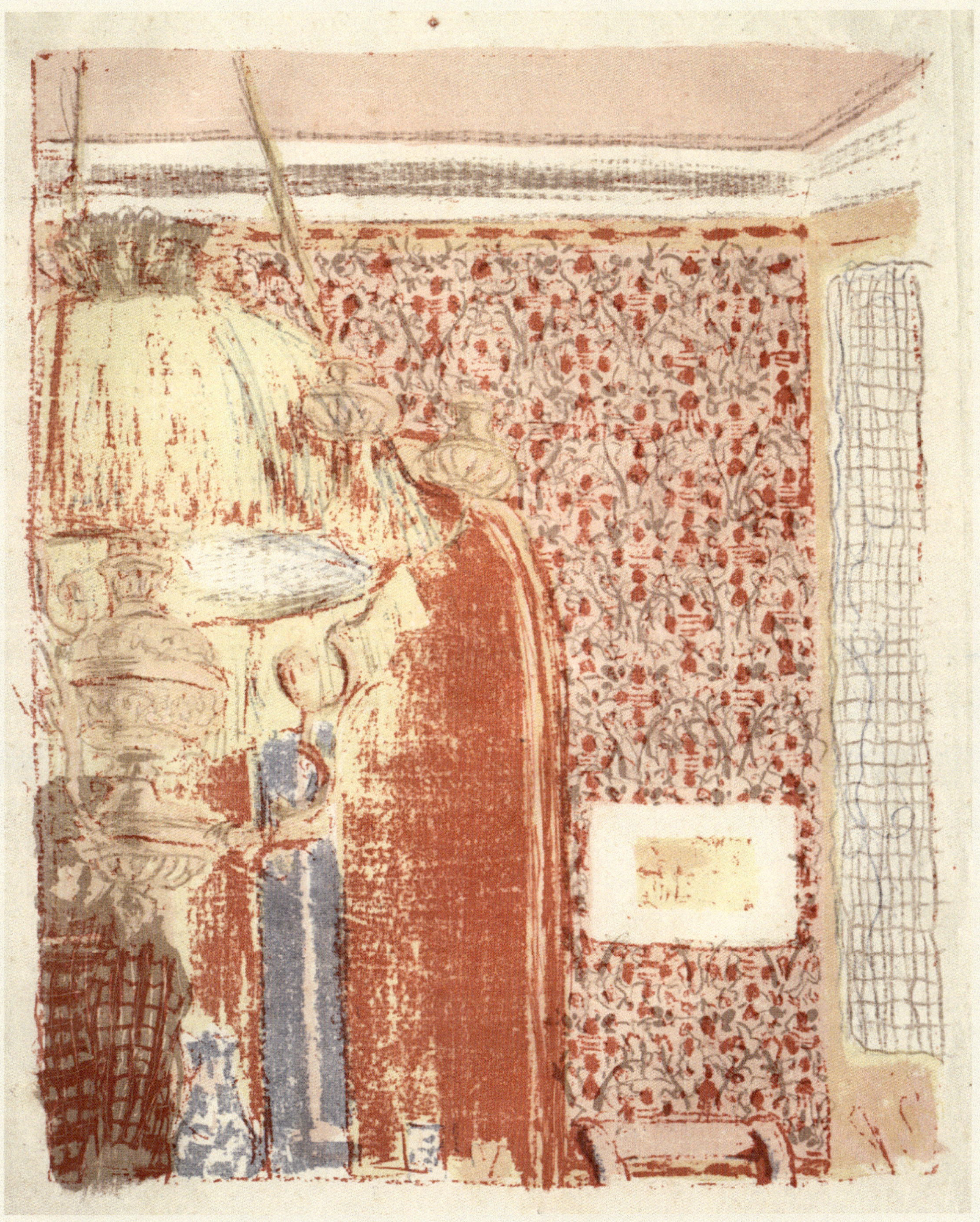

7.
Intérieur aux tentures roses III
*Interior with Pink Wallpaper III*

342 x 273 mm

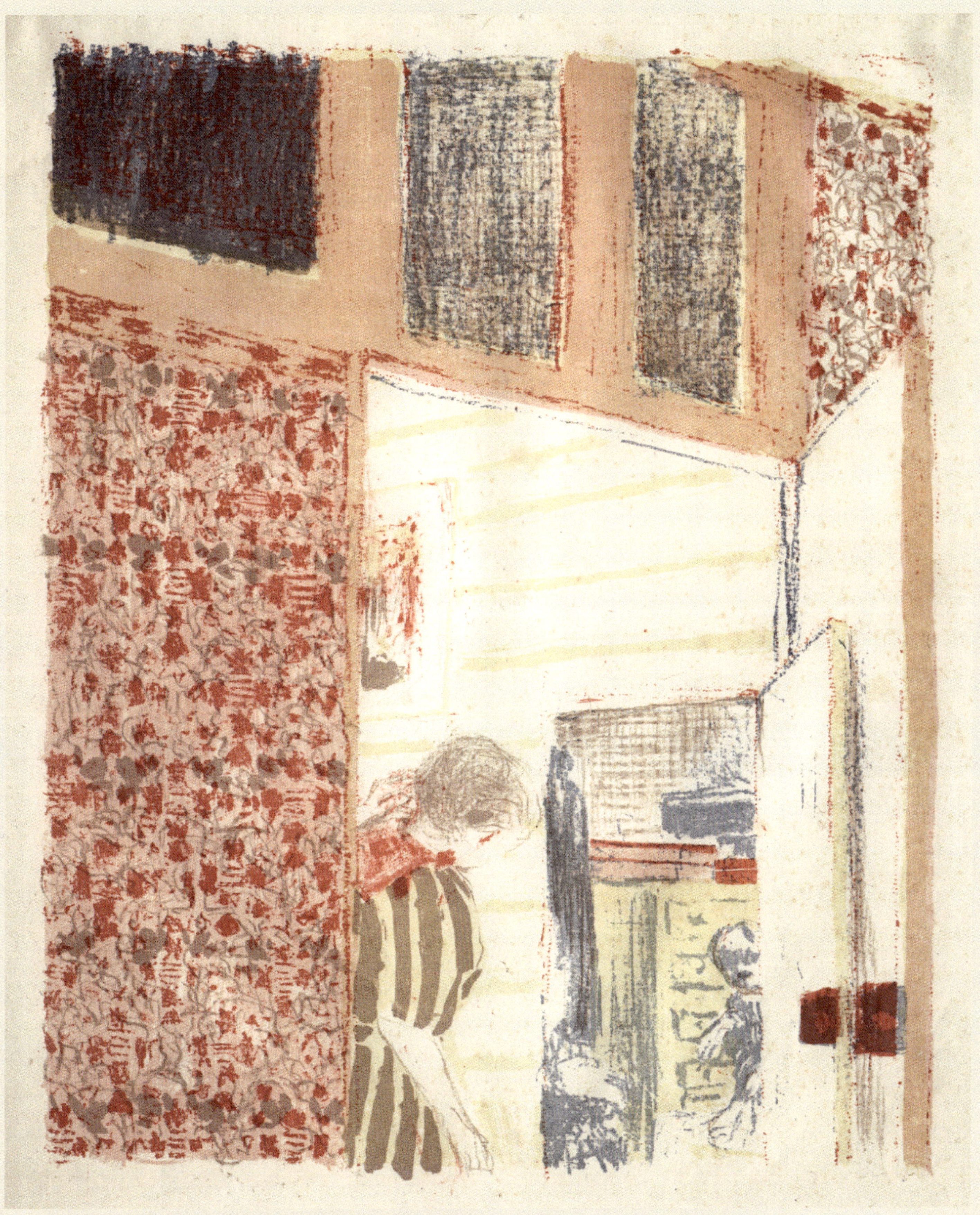

8.

L'Âtre

*The Hearth*

343 x 277 mm

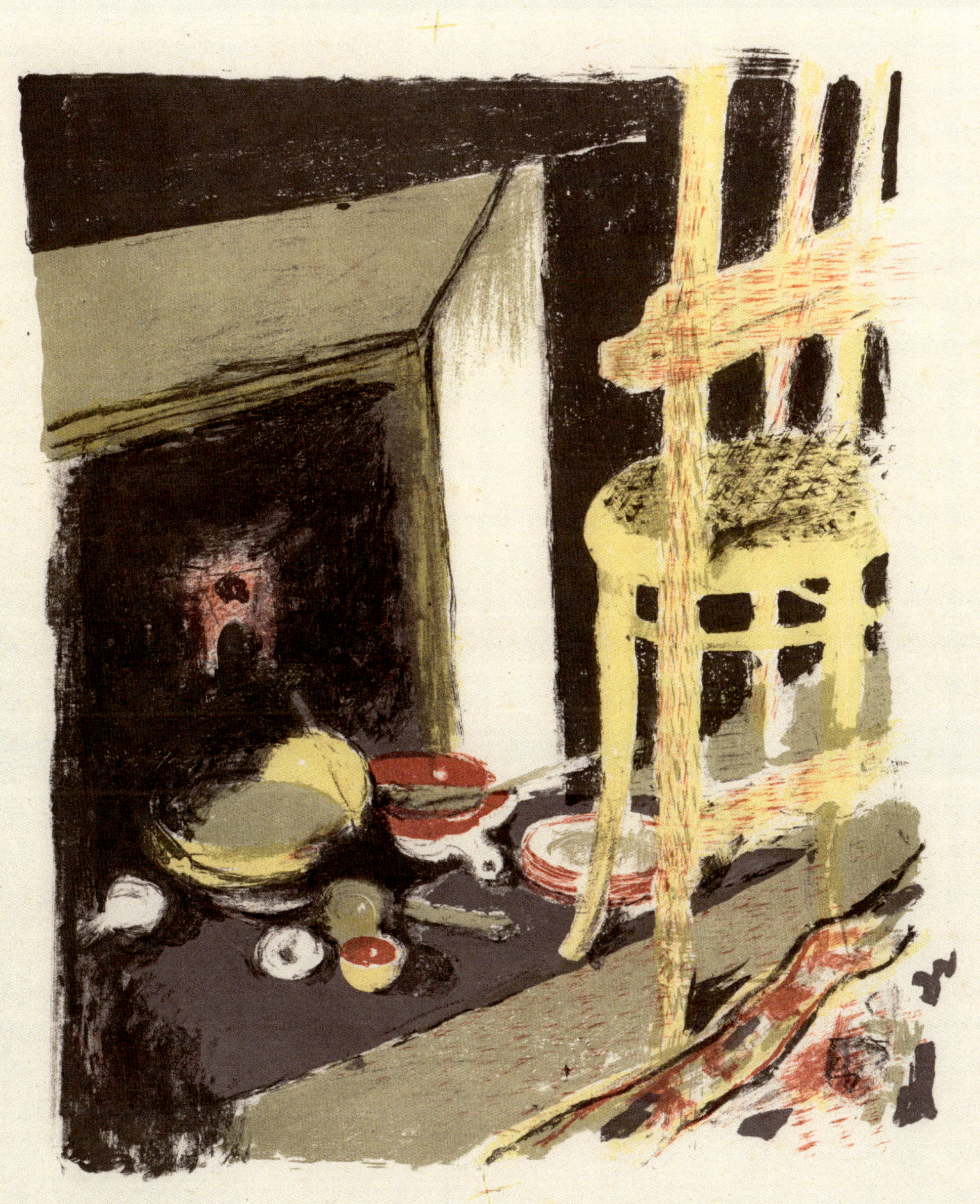

9.
Sur le pont de l'Europe
*On the Pont de l'Europe*

343 x 277 mm

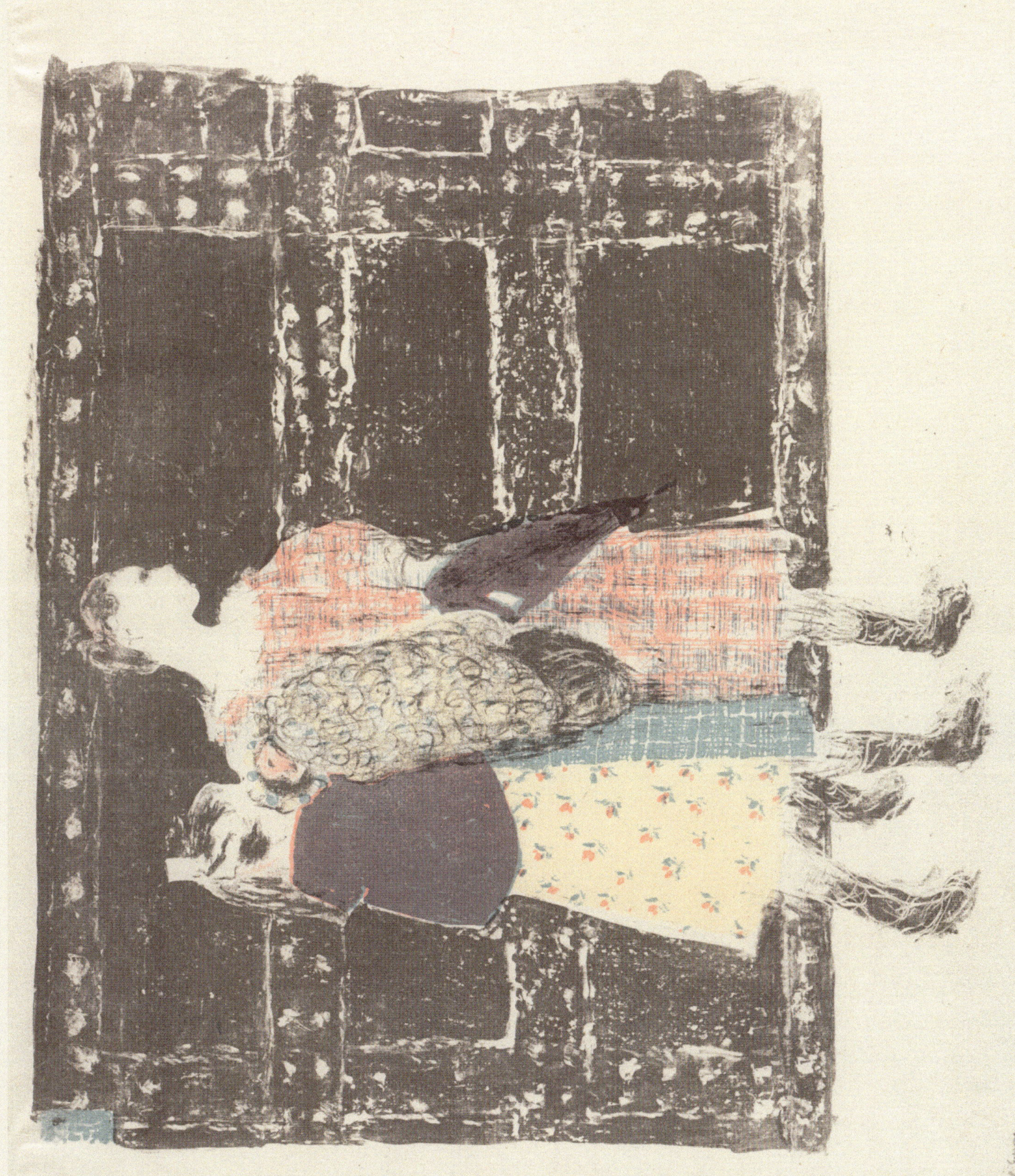

10.
La Pâtisserie
*The Pastry Shop*

351 x 275 mm

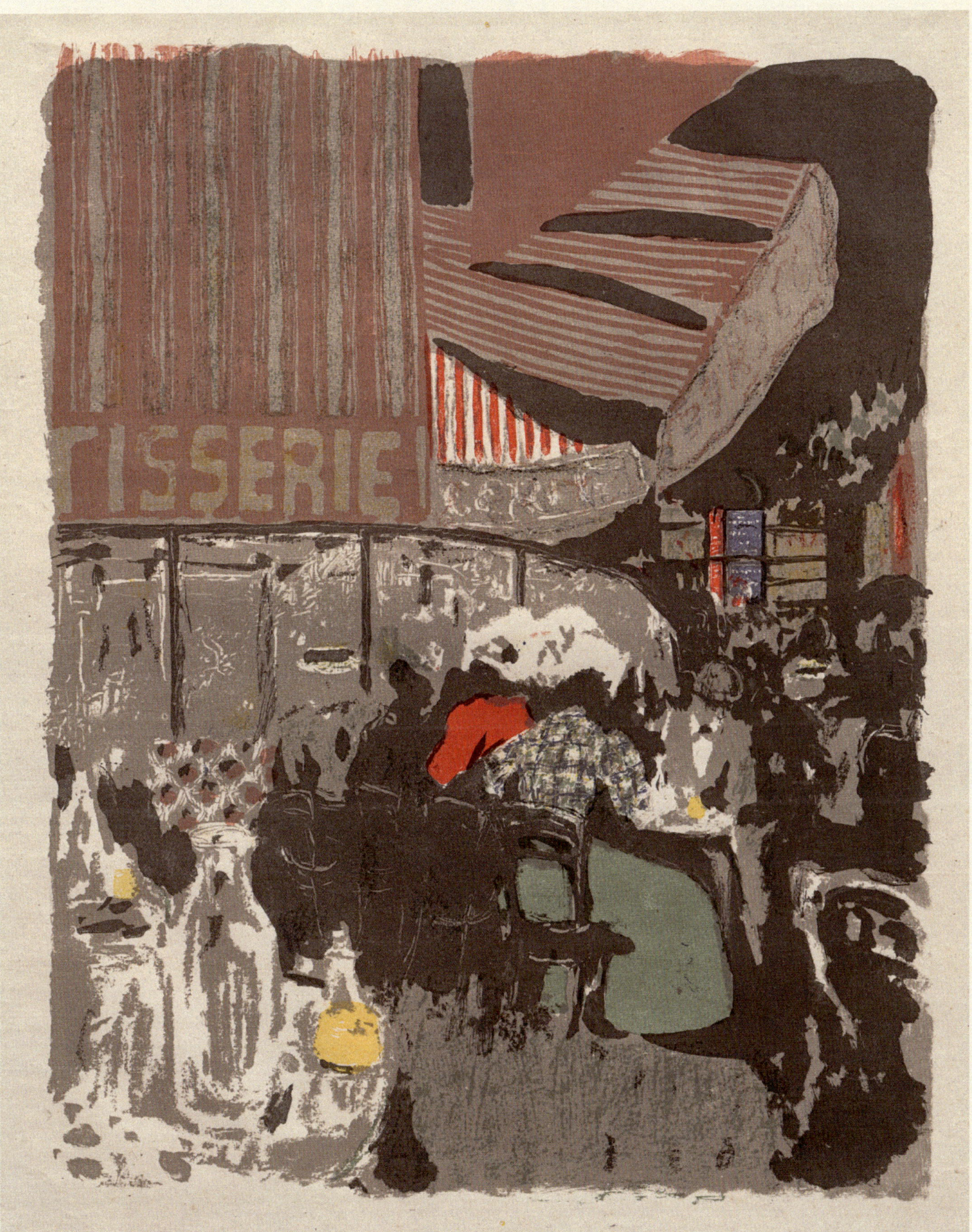
TISSERIE

11.

II.

La Cuisinière (la mère de l'artiste)
*The Cook (the artist's mother)*

350 x 277 mm

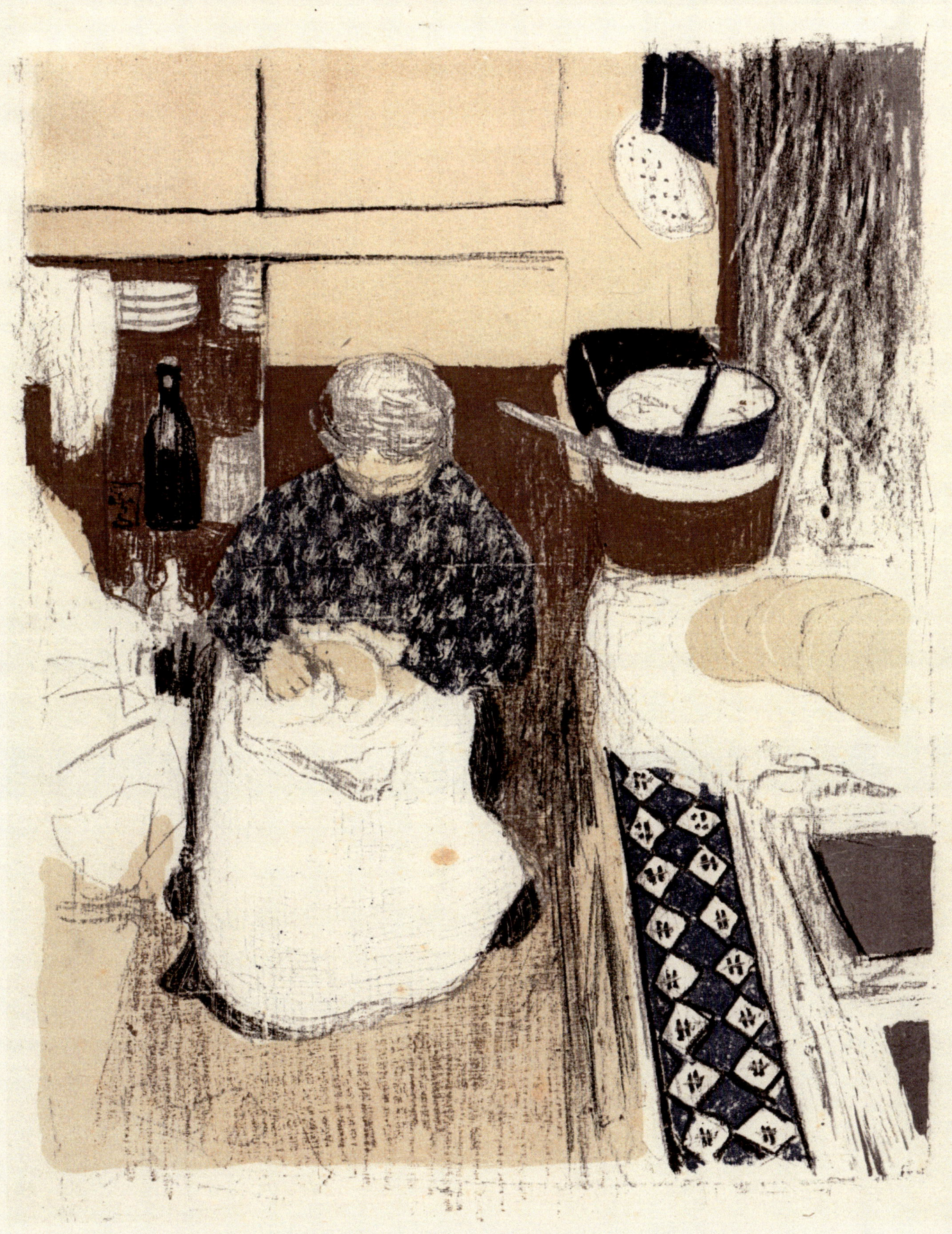

12.
Les deux belles-sœurs
*The Two Sisters-in-Law*

368 x 294 mm

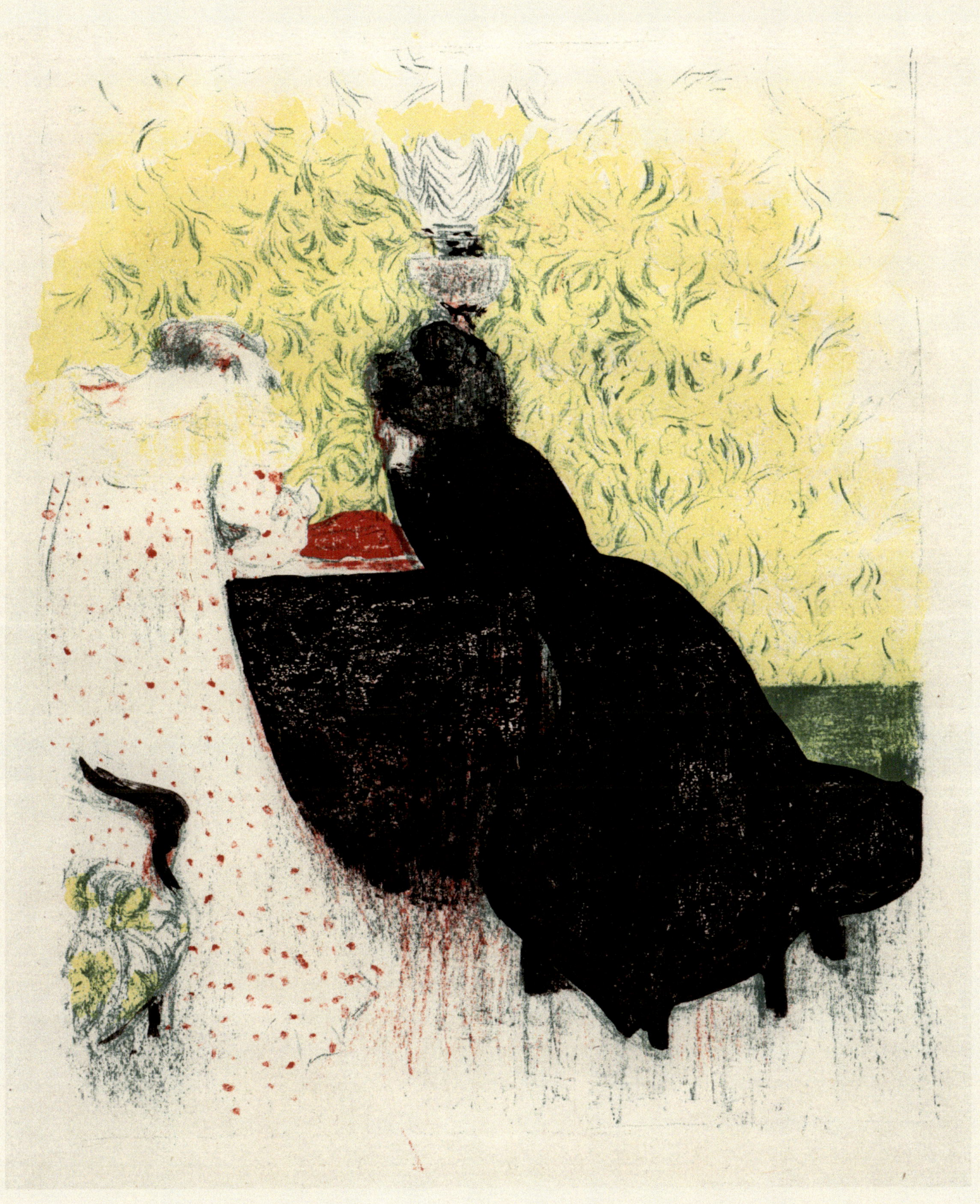

PAYSAGES ET INTÉRIEURS/
LANDSCAPES AND INTERIORS
Suite de 12 planches et une couverture,
imprimée par Auguste Clot. Éditée à
Paris par Ambroise Vollard en 1899,
et tirée à 100 exemplaires./
*Suite of 12 plates and a cover, printed*
*by Auguste Clot. Published in Paris by*
*Ambroise Vollard in 1899, in an edition*
*of 100 copies.*

Cette édition/*This edition*
© Pallas Athene (Publishers) Ltd,
London, 2026

Pallas Athene (Publishers) Ltd,
2 Birch Close, London N19 5XD

**www.pallasathene.co.uk**

ISBN 978 1 84368 299 8 (édition française)
ISBN 978 1 84368 298 1 (English edition)

Imprimé en Angleterre par Blissetts/
*Printed in England by Blissetts*

3